The Measurement of Affect, Mood, and Emotion

The role of affective constructs in human behavior in general, and health behavior in particular, is recapturing the attention of researchers. Affect, mood, and emotion are again considered powerful motives behind dietary choices, physical activity participation, cigarette smoking, alcohol over-consumption, and drug abuse. However, researchers entering the fray must confront a vast and confusing theoretical and technical literature. The enormity of this challenge is reflected in numerous problems plaguing recent studies, from selecting measures without offering a rationale, to interchanging terms that are routinely misconstrued. *The Measurement of Affect, Mood, and Emotion* cuts through the jargon, clarifies controversies, and proposes a sound three-tiered system for selecting measures that can rectify past mistakes and accelerate future progress. Panteleimon Ekkekakis offers an accessible and comprehensive guidebook of great value to academic researchers and postgraduate students in the fields of psychology, behavioral and preventive medicine, behavioral nutrition, exercise science, and public health.

PANTELEIMON EKKEKAKIS is an associate professor in the Department of Kinesiology at Iowa State University.

D1158681

The Measurement of Affect, Mood, and Emotion

A Guide for Health-Behavioral Research

Panteleimon Ekkekakis

Iowa State University

CAMBRIDGE
UNIVERSITY PRESS

CAMBRIDGE UNIVERSITY PRESS
Cambridge, New York, Melbourne, Madrid, Cape Town,
Singapore, São Paulo, Delhi, Mexico City

Cambridge University Press
The Edinburgh Building, Cambridge CB2 8RU, UK

Published in the United States of America by Cambridge University Press,
New York

www.cambridge.org
Information on this title: www.cambridge.org/9781107648203

© Panteleimon Ekkekakis 2013

First published 2013

Printed and bound in the United Kingdom by the MPG Books Group

A catalogue record for this publication is available from the British Library

Library of Congress Cataloguing in Publication data
Ekkekakis, Panteleimon, 1968-
  The measurement of affect, mood, and emotion : a guide for
  health-behavioral research / Panteleimon Ekkekakis.
    p. cm.
  Includes bibliographical references and index.
  ISBN 978-1-107-01100-7 (hardback) – ISBN 978-1-107-64820-3 (pbk.)
  1. Affect (Psychology) 2. Emotions. 3. Emotions–Health aspects.
  I. Title.
  [DNLM: 1. Affect. 2. Behavioral Research. 3. Health Behavior.
  BF 511]
  BF511.E37 2013
  152.4028'7–dc23   2012033205

ISBN 978-1-107-01100-7 Hardback
ISBN 978-1-107-64820-3 Paperback

To the sources of all affect, mood, and emotion in my life, my wife and my son

Contents

Figures

Foreword

Emotions, moods, passions, feelings, and other affectively charged states are now recognized as essential in the human condition. With the fading of behaviorism and then cognitivism a generation ago, emotions and the rest won their rightful status within the human sciences as a legitimate topic. It's fair to ask how the field of affective science is doing.

Panteleimon Ekkekakis provides a frank, sobering, and unfortunately accurate answer: the basic building blocks of science – clearly defined concepts and valid tools to measure them – are missing from much of the research. Ekkekakis focuses on health research, but his diagnosis applies as well to any branch of human science, including education, social welfare, and psychology in general. Fortunately, he also provides a much needed practical remedy.

Progress in affective science has been slow – as if our party won the election but then failed to form a new government. The explanation for the slow progress may be that science is not simply the accumulation of facts. Creation of a new science is not a transition from a blank slate to a scientific paradigm, but from one paradigm to another. The initial pre-scientific paradigm is the set of everyday, lay folk concepts and assumptions. We inherit concepts from angst to zeal with the preconceptions that accompany them. Astronomy, physics, and biology all show how difficult this transition is and how qualitatively different the initial folk concepts typically are from later scientific ones.

The affective domain is heterogeneous. The everyday concept of emotion is too heterogeneous, for it includes object-directed states (such as loving someone) and object-free or free-floating ones (such as malaise or anxiety) and includes long-term states (such as loving someone) and short-term ones (such as startle). To assess an emotional episode, one must therefore consider its object and its temporal dimension; simply checking a word on a list hardly suffices.

The affective domain lacks a superordinate term. For that reason, I used the cumbersome phrase "emotions, moods, passions, feelings, and other affectively charged states." "Affect" is now sometimes used as the superordinate, but its boundaries are vague. I especially want to distinguish affect used as a superordinate from Core Affect. Core Affect is an ingredient in most (not all) emotions, moods, and so forth, but not a superordinate – much as flour is an ingredient in most (but not all) baked goods, but would not do as a substitute for the term "baked good."

The book you hold in your hands is a powerful plea for a qualitative shift in the way research is conducted. It is a wise, thoughtful, and much needed guidebook for the transition from a prescientific to a scientific paradigm. If researchers read this book, they will be convinced, they will change their behavior, and their research will advance. I'm often asked to recommend a measure for emotion or mood, and I never have a simple answer. Now I do: read Ekkekakis.

James A. Russell
Boston College

Prologue

Simple can be harder than complex. You have to work hard to get your thinking clean to make it simple.
— Steve Jobs, in an interview to *Business Week*, May 25, 1998

My goal was to write the guidebook I wish I had available to me when I was starting out as a junior researcher 25 years ago. While still an undergraduate student, I became interested in learning more about the affective changes that occur when people participate in physical activity. At that time, I had some elementary background in psychology but had not taken even a single course on emotional or affective phenomena for the simple reason that such courses did not exist back then, at least at the universities I attended. My knowledge about emotion was limited to the highly abridged summaries of the classic theories of William James and Walter Cannon contained in introductory textbooks.

Lacking background and guidance, I made every mistake imaginable. I used measures without knowing much about them and certainly without having a good grasp of their theoretical underpinnings or their relative strengths and limitations. I selected one measure over another on the basis of such profoundly naive criteria as their brevity or popularity. I measured one variable (e.g., emotion) but discussed my results as if I had measured another (e.g., mood). I measured only a small part of a domain of content (e.g., only a few discrete mood states) but my ignorance led me to generalize to the entire domain (e.g., the global domain of mood). I based my conclusions on measures that were deeply flawed although even a rudimentary psychometric analysis would have alerted me to this fact. I was in way over my head and, for many years, I did not even realize it because, frankly, I was just using the measures that "everyone" (or so it seemed) was using in the published literature, including researchers with decades of experience, great academic credentials, and worldwide name recognition. I was just emulating what I perceived as common arguments and common practices. So what could I possibly be doing wrong?

My perspective started to change when I entered graduate school. One upside to my youthful naïveté was that it allowed me to take a plunge into deep waters, a course of action I might have avoided if I had any realistic idea about the enormity of the gaps in my knowledge or the magnitude of the challenge I faced. And so my journey into the world of affect, mood, and emotion research began. I started studying about affective phenomena, taking courses from brilliant teachers, communicating with recognized leaders in the field, and, more than anything else, reading voraciously. Now, with the benefit of hindsight and 25 years of working exclusively on affective phenomena, I can recognize (and feel deeply embarrassed about) my own past mistakes. At the same time, based on what I see as a manuscript reviewer and editor on a daily basis, I have become increasingly concerned about what I perceive as signs of a storm gathering over this research area. My growing concern provided the impetus for this book. Let me explain.

First the good news

After decades of modeling humans as data processors engaged in a perpetual cycle of information gathering, cognitive analysis and appraisal, weighing pros and cons, and rational decision making, psychologists and other behavioral scientists are, once again, willing to consider the possibility that affective constructs, such as core affect, mood, and emotion, influence human behavior. This has been a long and arduous process. In the 1950s, as B. F. Skinner (1953) was characterizing "emotions" (his quotation marks) as "excellent examples of the fictional causes to which we commonly attribute behavior" (p. 160), Paul Young (1959) was trying to convince his peers that "any theory of behavior which ignores the concept of affectivity will be found inadequate as an explanation of the total facts" (p. 106). In the 1960s, during the transition from behaviorism to cognitivism, Silvan Tomkins (1962) attempted to resurrect psychological hedonism by conceptualizing affect as "the primary motivational system in human beings" (p. 108). However, these voices were simply too few and too isolated to generate momentum and shift the paradigm. As Kuhn (1962/1996) warned, ideas that go against the dominant paradigm of an era are usually ignored, marginalized, or suppressed. At least the cognitive theories of emotion by Magda Arnold, Stanley Schachter, and Jerome Singer and Richard Lazarus, as well as the exciting cross-cultural research by Paul Ekman on facial emotional expression, kept interest in the topic of emotion alive.

Then, thankfully, came a stream of "outsiders" so brilliant and creative that scientists and the general public alike had to take notice.

Nobel laureate in economics Herbert Simon, after raising questions about the true limits of human rationality, called attention to the role of emotion in judgment and decision making. Michel Cabanac in applied physiology proposed that pleasure serves as the "common currency" by which organisms, including humans, decide on appropriate courses of action in the presence of competing priorities. Antonio Damasio in neurology reignited the conversation on the deeply disruptive effects that damage to emotion-related areas of the brain have on behavioral decision making. Joseph LeDoux in basic neuroscience ruffled a few cognitivist feathers by arguing for a possible precognitive mode of eliciting emotional responses to frightening stimuli. By operating mainly outside psychology proper, and therefore the narrow confines of the cognitivist paradigm, these influential thinkers got scientists across a broad spectrum of disciplines talking about affective phenomena and their role in behavior once again.

Within the core of psychology, the debate between Robert Zajonc and Richard Lazarus that started in the early 1980s probably convinced more than a few skeptics that the area of emotion research represented an enormous pool of fascinating questions, surprising phenomena, and intriguing mysteries central to understanding human behavior. Although it would be hard to identify a single pivotal event, study, research line, or inspirational figure as the main instigator of this trend, during the 1990s and 2000s, interest in affect, mood, and emotion among psychologists rose perhaps to the highest level since the James–Cannon debates of the early twentieth century. A psychologist, Daniel Kahneman, won the Nobel Prize (in economics) in part for reminding behavioral researchers of the timeless insight encapsulated in the words of English philosopher Jeremy Bentham, the central figure of the school of utilitarianism: "nature has placed mankind under the governance of two sovereign masters, pain and pleasure; it is for them alone to point out what we ought to do, as well as to determine what we shall do" (from the opening lines of his 1789 *An Introduction to the Principles of Morals and Legislation*). Kahneman, Paul Slovic, and others initiated research on a mechanism, named the "affect heuristic," according to which pleasure guides judgments and decisions, assigns priorities to different goals, and ultimately serves as a powerful motive in human behavior. Writing in the *American Psychologist* after receiving the Nobel Prize, Kahneman (2003) described the affect heuristic as "probably the most important development in the study of judgment heuristics in the past few decades" (p. 710). Jaak Panksepp in animal research and Richard Davidson in human research led the evolution of the new field of affective neuroscience into one of the most vibrant and prolific domains of modern psychological research. John Cacioppo and Gary Berntson put affective phenomena at the center of the budding interdisciplinary field of social neuroscience. James Gross and Kevin Ochsner pioneered the field of emotion regulation. And in a series of captivating debates that served as the foundation for most of the chapters of this book, James Russell, Lisa Feldman Barrett, and David Watson shed greatly needed light on several crucial conceptual issues long enveloped in a thick cloud of confusion and controversy.

Today, as psychology is slowly regaining a more balanced perspective after the cognitivist fascination that characterized the past few decades, interest in affective phenomena is rising rapidly. New dedicated journals, such as *Emotion* and *Emotion Review*, were created to accommodate the growing number of article submissions. Importantly, interest in affective phenomena is now also growing in a broad range of research fields investigating the driving forces behind human health behaviors. Why do humans overeat, smoke cigarettes, abuse drugs and alcohol, or avoid exercise? Until recently, the standard answers pointed to cognitive processes: because they lack education, because they have low outcome expectations, because perceived benefits do not outweigh perceived risks, because of low self-efficacy. As acknowledged by Ajzen and Fishbein (2005), "much of the research [stemming from cognitive theories of motivation and behavior] has devoted little attention to the role of emotion in the prediction of intentions and actions" (p. 203). Today, however, as the limitations of cognitivist explanations are becoming apparent to an increasing number of investigators, the role of affective and hedonic processes is attracting attention. Extensive literatures have now emerged on the links between affect, mood, and emotion with eating behaviors, obesity, drug abuse, smoking cigarettes, drinking alcohol, and exercising. Most studies in these areas were conducted within the last decade and the rate of publication continues to increase. In sum, it is clear we are now in the midst of a paradigmatic transition; affective processes are regaining their rightful place among the major motives driving human behavioral decisions. A new, more refined, more sophisticated version of psychological hedonism is emerging.

Now the not-so-good news

The nature of academe is changing dramatically. It is fair to say that, at most major academic institutions, professors are allocating their time in a substantially different manner compared to their mentors just a generation ago. They devote more work hours to applying for funding, networking, preparing budgets, hiring and firing personnel (e.g., postdoctoral researchers, information technology professionals, study coordinators), and managing the logistics of multimillion-dollar grants. Success in these activities has become the main criterion by which applicants for faculty positions are selected, promotion and tenure decisions are made, awards are given, salaries are adjusted, startup and retention packages are offered, and the overall quality of scholarship is evaluated.

Since time is a precious and finite commodity, and institutional pressures to generate funds are constantly rising, something "has to give." Usually, that something is the time to study, reflect, and broaden and deepen one's conceptual knowledge and understanding. Who has time to educate oneself about a new area outside of one's own narrowly demarcated line of research? Who has time to delve into a century-old literature, retrace the evolution of ideas through time, carefully scrutinize methods, critically analyze assumptions, or contemplate arcane theoretical arguments? In my work as editor and reviewer for journals and granting agencies, I see that, increasingly, academics resort to choosing ideas, measures, and methods on the basis of much more superficial criteria. What is the latest trend? What is mentioned more frequently in the current literature or talked about at conferences? What are the established authority figures in the field doing these days?

Psychological measures, in particular, seem to be picked "off the shelf" and treated as "plug-and-play" devices. For many time-pressed investigators, the process of selecting a measure for a particular variable (e.g., "affect" or "mood") has been reduced to running a computer search for that keyword and selecting the measure that seems to pop up more frequently than others. Evidently there is no longer the expectation that the investigator will have a thorough, deep understanding of the developmental history, the conceptual bases, the intricate psychometric details, or the strengths and limitations of the measure.

One of my biggest pet peeves is the phrase "to measure variable X, we used measure Y because it has been used extensively in previous studies." I am not sure when or why this type of "justification" came to be viewed as adequate in the research literature. I do know, however, that researchers should not allow it to become the norm. Measurement is too important, too central to the research enterprise to be treated with such laxity and superficiality. Measurement is perhaps one of the most delicate and challenging elements of the research process because it represents the intersection of theory, method, analysis, and interpretation. As such, it requires more conceptual sophistication and technical expertise than most other components of research methodology. Unfortunately, as I read manuscripts and research proposals, I am all too often reminded of this excerpt by Kerlinger (1979) I once read:

Measurement can be the Achilles' heel of behavioral research. Too often investigations are carefully planned and executed with too little attention paid to the measurement of the variables of the research ... All fields of human effort have their shares of mythology and nonsense. Measurement is unfortunately particularly burdened with both. Negative attitudes toward psychological measurement are part of the cause. But ignorance and misunderstanding are probably a greater part. (pp. 141–142)

Mythology, nonsense, negative attitudes toward psychological measurement, ignorance, and misunderstanding; Kerlinger said it all. And his words, unfortunately, ring as true today as they did more than three decades ago.

The goal of this book

This guidebook is about the measurement of a specific category of variables within a specific research domain; it is about the study of affective phenomena as they relate to health behaviors. Why the focus on health-behavioral research? One part of the answer is that, as I mentioned earlier, interest in affective phenomena within health-behavioral research is rising at an astonishing pace. The other part of the answer is that, at least within the English-speaking world (United States, Canada, United Kingdom, Australia) and much of Europe, research on health behaviors is among the most heavily funded areas of behavioral and biomedical research. Health behaviors pertain mainly to prevention and, as such, represent a much more cost-efficient option than treatment. In addition, a person engaging in health behaviors typically reports more satisfaction with life and better perceived quality of life than someone receiving treatment for a chronic disease. Given these economic and humanitarian reasons, it is logical that funding agencies, governmental and private alike, are interested in exploring the potential of health behaviors for reducing the personal and societal burden of chronic disease.

Therefore, in the domain of health behaviors one sees the ominous intersection of the two trends I described in this prologue. On one hand, investigators with very diverse educational backgrounds and research foci are becoming interested in affective phenomena. On the other hand, most of these investigators operate under extreme pressure within an increasingly competitive environment for a limited pot of research funds. Hence the problem. Oftentimes, no matter how noble the intentions and how deep the desire of the investigator to do top-notch innovative research, when the quantitative performance expectations are as high as they are these days, corners must be cut. Researchers simply do not have the time to scrutinize their measurement options, so they rely on indirect sources of evidence to establish their quality.

- I want to measure "affect" and this questionnaire says that it is a measure of "affect."
- This was published in a decent journal, so it must have undergone rigorous peer review; if the experts who looked at it thought it was fine, it must be fine.
- Everybody seems to be using it, so it must be good.
- This questionnaire was developed by famous professor X, who claims it is valid and reliable.

At least in my eyes, it seems the problems Kerlinger identified in the 1970s are even more exacerbated, more dramatic, in research dealing with affective phenomena than most research areas. As Kerlinger said, "ignorance and misunderstanding" are perhaps the main contributors to problematic measurement practices. The theoretical and empirical literatures on affect, mood, and emotion are notorious for being extraordinarily convoluted and confusing, so "ignorance and misunderstanding" tend to be quite prevalent phenomena in this area. Of course, I realize that most researchers would passionately argue that their area of research is the most complex, the most challenging, the one with the most delicate conceptual distinctions. Nevertheless, for reasons that will become apparent in this book, I maintain that the domain of affect, mood, and emotion research, when examined with a sense of perspective, is *even* more perplexing than most other areas of psychological investigation.

In this guidebook, my highly ambitious goal is to help bring some order to the chaos. It is important to warn readers up front that, while selecting a measure of affect, mood, or emotion, they will never be able to use a "cookbook" approach (i.e., a fully standardized, truly algorithmic step-by-step protocol) as has now become the norm, for example, in fields like endocrinology, immunology, or molecular biology. Nevertheless, I am proposing a workable three-step method, which, if properly implemented, should help reduce arbitrary decisions and, in the process, lower the risk that the research enterprise might be led astray by unfortunate measurement choices.

The guidebook is intentionally short because it is meant to be read cover to cover, even when taking into account the enormous pressures of contemporary academic life. I have also tried to strike a balance between avoiding the use of baffling jargon (a key contributor to the very problem I am trying to address) and not oversimplifying inherently complex and "fuzzy" concepts. Finding the right balance is, of course, a difficult task and, although I hope to have succeeded in some cases, I am afraid that I have probably failed in others.

I am sure that experts in affective psychology will find the descriptions of some issues underdeveloped or unrefined, perhaps too rudimentary or overly abridged. I am also certain that some experts will object that I am presenting some issues that they might consider open or still unsettled in a more definitive tone than is warranted by the empirical evidence. And, naturally, in cases in which I take sides in ongoing debates (as I often do), there will be those who believe I am wrong. To all these colleagues, I offer my sincere apologies, as I openly acknowledge my limitations. My hope in providing this guidebook to the scientific community is to initiate a move in the right direction – or at least a conversation. If I am lucky, things will snowball from there!

1 Documenting the breadth and depth of the problem

> Measurement issues are very frequently ignored, or treated cavalierly, almost mindlessly, in research reports. Measures seem to be used because they are "there," because someone else has used them, because nothing "better" is available. One cannot help but be amazed at the naive faith invested in what are at best crude measures by researchers who exhibit healthy skepticism, care, and sophistication with respect to other aspects of their studies. (Pedhazur & Pedhazur Schmelkin, 1991, p. 28)

A growing number of behavioral scientists across a broad range of disciplines now recognize the central role of affect, mood, and emotion in human behavior in general, and in health behavior in particular (see Figure 1.1). For example, reference to these constructs is made at an increasing rate in the literatures on eating behavior and food choices (e.g., Lutter & Nestler, 2009; Macht, 2008; Moore & O'Donohue, 2008; Stroebe, Papies, & Aarts, 2008), the causes of the obesity epidemic (e.g., Kishi & Elmquist, 2005; Rolls, 2007), the addictive effects of drugs of abuse (e.g., Baker, Piper, McCarthy, Majeskie, & Fiore, 2004; Bechara, 2005; Koob, 2008; Robinson & Berridge, 2008), the initiation and cessation of cigarette smoking (e.g., Carmody, Vieten, & Astin, 2007; Schleicher, Harris, Catley, & Nazir, 2009), the antecedents and consequences of drinking alcohol (e.g., Gilman, Ramchandani, Davis, Bjork, & Hommer, 2008; King, de Wit, McNamara, & Cao, 2011; McKinney, 2010; McKinney & Coyle, 2006), the effects of sleep and the predictors of sleep disruptions (e.g., McCrae, McNamara, Rowe, Dzierzewski, Dirk, Marsiske, & Craggs, 2008; Walker, 2009), and the effects of exercise and the reasons behind physical inactivity (Ekkekakis, Parfitt, & Petruzzello, 2011; Rhodes, Fiala, & Conner, 2009; Williams, 2008). In these diverse literatures, affect, mood, and emotion are treated as independent variables (e.g., predicting the health behavior), as dependent variables (e.g., studies on the effects of the health behavior on depression), or as mediators and moderators of various behavioral interventions for a wide range of outcomes.

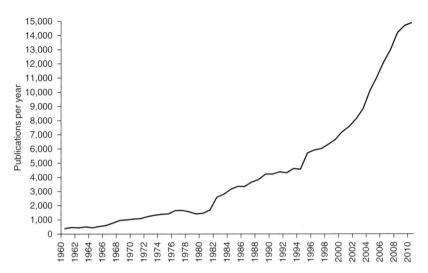

Figure 1.1. The number of entries in the PsycINFO™ database over the past 50 years (1960–2010) that include the keywords "affective," "mood★," or "emotion★." The number of entries has increased from almost zero to nearly 15,000 per year.

It is, of course, unrealistic to dissect all issues specific to the various research areas of health-behavioral research in which affect, mood, and emotion have now become focal topics. Nevertheless, the measurement problems identified, the conclusions drawn, and the recommendations issued are relevant to a very wide swath of behavioral research, including health psychology, behavioral medicine, preventive medicine, applied gerontology, and many others.

By all indications, the range of research areas in which the relevance of affective constructs is being explored is constantly expanding. This means that many new investigators, with limited or no prior experience in affect, mood, or emotion theory and research, will probably enter the fray in the coming years. Under growing pressure to seek funding and publish, they will need a rapid introduction to the theories surrounding these constructs and the measurement options available. Unfortunately, if the "newcomers" attempt to shorten their period of induction to this field by simply replicating some of the views and practices now prevalent in this literature, the prognosis for the future growth and productivity of this research does not seem promising.

The purpose of this introductory chapter is to document some of the specific problems that plague the assessment of affect, mood, and emotion in many areas of behavioral research dealing with human health.

Hopefully, by shedding light on some of the pitfalls and fallacies that are now so widespread in the literature, this chapter will act as a stimulus for researchers to approach the measurement of affect, mood, and emotion from a different, more critical perspective.

Newcomers, beware: brace yourselves 'cause this ain't gonna be easy!

Let us consider an imaginary, yet realistic, scenario. Let us assume that you are a behavioral scientist (perhaps with a background in clinical, social, health, or exercise psychology) working with an interdisciplinary group of investigators. You find yourself a few days before the deadline for a grant application to a major funding agency. The topic of your application deals with the effects of a physical activity intervention on alcohol dependence. After reading your draft, an experienced colleague suggests that you incorporate a measure of self-efficacy as a possible mediator of the effects of physical activity. You promptly identify some key references on self-efficacy from the recognized authority on this topic (Bandura, 1977, 1997, 2001) and then construct a self-efficacy instrument by carefully following the step-by-step instructions in the aptly titled "Guide for constructing self-efficacy scales," which was developed by the same authoritative figure (Bandura, 2006). The reviewers of the grant application confirm that your choice of measure is consistent with literature-wide conventions, express no concerns, and your application is funded.

This scenario could have followed a very similar course if the colleague had suggested any number of other social-cognitive constructs that have become the mainstays of behavioral interventions in recent decades, such as attitudes, social norms, behavioral intentions, goal orientations, or behavioral regulations. Each of these constructs is typically linked to one authoritative source, is embedded within one well-known and well-defined theoretical framework, and is operationally defined by one measure that has emerged as the de facto literature-wide standard.

Now let us suppose that the wise colleague suggested incorporating a measure of "affect." If your psychological training was like most others' (except until recently), then you probably never took a course exclusively devoted to affect, mood, or emotion. At best, you might have taken a course on "motivation and emotion," with ideas such as "drive" or "reinforcement" that seem outdated and irrelevant to your research. You are also fairly certain that the "affect" to which your colleague was referring does not resemble anything in your clinical psychology course or your copy of the *Diagnostic and Statistical Manual of Mental Disorders*.

The tens of thousands of references that come up after the first exploratory database searches also do not appear helpful, as they seem to refer
to a hodgepodge of different things. No single author emerges as a central figure, no conceptual model seems to be cited more frequently than
others, and no single measure appears to have risen to the status of de
facto standard. Nervousness creeps in as you begin to realize that this
is an area unlike most others. It is vast, it is diverse, and, as becomes
apparent after reading a few articles, it is immersed in confusion and
controversy. So what can you possibly do given the time constraints?
Can you really navigate the maze of this literature, cut through the
jargon, and articulate an intelligent argument for selecting a particular
measure?

The honest, albeit intensely unpopular, answer is that you cannot.
The harsh reality is that the study of affect, mood, and emotion will
challenge a researcher more than most other topics due to the sheer
amount and complexity of information that one needs to master before
being ready to make a meaningful contribution. This is clearly not
an area of a singular authority figure, a singular theory, or a singular
measure. Consequently, researchers accustomed to "off the shelf" or
"plug-and-play" measurement solutions will quickly be overwhelmed,
fall easy victim to uninformed advice, and, perhaps more important,
reproduce more misinformation into an already confusing literature.
On the other hand, the dedicated and patient scholar entering this field
will discover a truly fascinating wealth of ideas and an area of study that
has intrigued humanity since the days of Aristotle.

The aim of this book is to serve as a rudimentary guide to the measurement of affect, mood, and emotion for researchers working in the
broad field of health behavior. Given the challenges inherent in this
task, the objective is not to provide an all-encompassing reference but
rather a springboard for more focused study. To accomplish this goal,
the book follows a systematic approach, from examining key theoretical issues to reviewing specific measures. In the process, an effort is
made to highlight the most influential conceptual and psychometric
works in this field. Most important, the analysis is critical, identifying unanswered questions, issues of concern, and unsettled points of
debate, in addition to points of convergence and consensus.

How bad is the situation, really?

The first step toward positive reform is realizing that the current situation deviates from an optimal standard. Presumably, all researchers

want to do the best work possible and improve their chances of produc-ing meaningful and valid results. In most research areas, this is ensured mainly by (a) the quality of training provided at the undergraduate and postgraduate levels, (b) to some extent, the relatively manageable size and straightforward nature of most topical literatures, and (c) the sys-tem of peer review. Put differently, research generally functions well because researchers are adequately trained in their particular area of study, the areas themselves have a reasonable size and relatively few controversial aspects, and, if something goes awry, a knowledgeable and alert peer reviewer will probably catch it before it goes to print.

Unfortunately, most of these safeguards seem absent in areas of health-behavioral research dealing with affect, mood, and emotion. First, at most institutions, formal courses devoted to emotional and affective phenomena are a very recent development. Furthermore, it must be recognized that both undergraduate and postgraduate curric-ula in most areas of psychology reflect the current zeitgeist. This means that graduates are considered adequately trained if they have learned the theories in line with the current paradigm, which is still heavily influenced by cognitivism. If the contents of textbooks in health psych-ology or health promotion, for example, are any indication, students must be well versed in such topics as social-cognitive theory, the theory of planned behavior, or the transtheoretical model. On the other hand, how many students or recent graduates of health behavior programs are aware of the landmark theories that have defined the fields of affect, mood, and emotion research over the last century?

Second, the theoretical and empirical literature on affect, mood, and emotion is extremely convoluted, reflecting more controversy than con-sensus. Although many researchers will find this diversity of ideas fas-cinating, for the majority it will probably act as a deterrent. Especially considering the lack of a previous classroom-based or textbook-guided introduction to this field, the time and effort required to gain a firm understanding of this literature will probably seem prohibitive.

Third, judging from the quality of measurement choices in many published articles, the effectiveness of the peer review process appears limited. This is due to the fact that most reviewers are typically no more educated about the conceptualization and assessment of affect, mood, and emotion than most authors.

The unfortunate outcome of this breakdown of the system is that misguided practices and erroneous claims have seeped into the pub-lished literature. Once this started happening, the problems were exac-erbated. The culprit is the well-known tendency to reproduce practices and claims that have appeared in the secondary literature instead of undertaking the incomparably more demanding task of plunging into the huge and unwelcoming primary literature to perform one's own independent and critical analysis of the issues. Obviously, the longer this trend continues unabated, the worse the situation will get.

With this as background, it is probably fair to say that the measurement of affect, mood, and emotion in the field of research dealing with health behaviors is presently, by and large, far from optimal. Certainly, the persistent rift between theory and application will always result in a "phase delay" before conceptual advances trickle down to the measurement practices followed in any field of applied research. However, arguably, in this field, there is yet to be clear evidence of a trickle-down effect. Instead, there seems to be a disconnect from theoretical and psychometric advances in affective psychology. So a lot needs to be done to get things moving in the right direction.

As a referee of a measurement-related manuscript once wrote as part of a five-line review culminating in the recommendation to "reject unconditionally," measurement issues are "arcane" and "of interest to only a few." Evidently, mysterious forces operating over the past few years have made it acceptable for researchers to select measures without taking the time to study and understand them. Scrutinizing measurement issues seems to have become something that is looked upon by some as a banality.

Other investigators, perhaps the majority, may still recognize the importance of measurement issues but, discouraged by the size and complexity of the literature, seek shortcuts. Graduate students often ask their advisors or other researchers to resolve their conundrums for them: "Which measure should I use for my thesis or dissertation?" This is sometimes followed by "Should I use X, I've been told it's good" or "I was thinking of using Y because of reason Z" (but, alas, "reason Z" usually represents a false or irrelevant premise). Similarly, grant proposals and manuscripts submitted for review to scientific journals frequently contain glaring mistakes on the theory and measurement of affective constructs. In some cases, these mistakes echo false statements that have appeared in the secondary literature. In other cases, the mistakes are peculiar, often remarkably creative, misconstruals of conceptual positions, presumably the result of the authors' cursory or uncritical inspection of the primary sources.

At this point, it seems that research investigating the role of affect, mood, and emotion in health behaviors is at a critical juncture. As these constructs become focal topics in research agendas, researchers must decide what standards they consider acceptable. Requiring all authors to become thoroughly familiar with the conceptual basis and psycho-metric properties of each measure of affect, mood, or emotion before they use it would be highly desirable, but this standard seems idealistic and unattainable at this point. On the other hand, it is fairly clear that, if the threshold of acceptability is continuously lowered, the overall quality of the research will suffer. Improving the quality, persuasive-ness, and overall impact of a line of research is not just about designing larger clinical trials, following meticulous randomization procedures, or blinding the outcome assessors to group allocation. It is also about selecting constructs and measures of those constructs that can stand up to the strictest standards of theoretical and psychometric scrutiny and about articulating and documenting the rationale behind these selections.

The head-in-the-sand approach: choosing a measure without providing a rationale

By far the most frequently encountered problem is pretending there is no decision-making process involved in choosing a measure. In such cases, reference to the issue of measurement is made for the first time in the Methods section, where the instruments simply appear "out of the blue," unaccompanied by a rationale to support their selection (often as a laundry list). When this approach is applied to a topic characterized by such diversity of constructs, theories, and measurement options, one can easily appreciate its fundamental inadequacy. The omitted infor-mation is of paramount importance to readers trying to evaluate the reasoning behind crucial methodological decisions.

The following excerpt from a published article is both typical, in that it is very similar to text used in hundreds of other published articles, and somewhat atypical, in that it was published in one of the most pres-tigious and highly selective journals in the field of health-behavioral research, as evidenced by its top-tier impact factor and extremely high rejection rate for submitted manuscripts:

Measures of mood. We included two measures of mood, one a domain general and well-established scale and the second a newer, exercise-specific measure. The Profile of Mood States (POMS; McNair, Lorr, & Droppleman, 1971) uses bipolar adjective scales to assess mood. Four POMS dimensions (vigor, tension, depression, elation) were utilized in this research. The POMS is a domain general measure but has been widely utilized in exercise research ... The Physical Activity Affect Scale (PAAS; Lox, Jackson, Tuholski, Wasley, & Treasure, 2000) assesses exercise-induced feeling states of positive affect, negative affect, tranquility, and physical fatigue. The PAAS was developed in response to concerns about the lack of exercise-specificity of measures like the POMS and shows adequate internal consistency and discriminant validity among the factors.

This excerpt exemplifies several practices that have become common-place in this literature. Perhaps the most striking element is that conceptual considerations are conspicuously absent. Nothing is mentioned about the theoretical basis upon which these measures were built or why these particular theoretical frameworks were deemed most appropriate for this study. In lieu of a conceptual rationale, reference is made to other, more superficial features: (a) one measure is older and more extensively used while the other is newer and (b) one was developed for use in a variety of contexts whereas the other was developed for use specifically in the context of exercise. However, closer analysis reveals that several important pieces of information are missing.

First, why was "mood" selected as the most appropriate construct to target in this study? According to an undergraduate textbook on emotion theory and research, "the term 'mood' refers to a state that typically lasts for hours, days, or weeks, sometimes as a low-intensity background" and, furthermore, "moods are often objectless, free-floating" (Oatley, Keltner, & Jenkins, 2006, p. 30). Given this definition, the relevance of mood to a study aimed at investigating the immediate response to a brief session of physical activity among participants without a mood disorder is not entirely obvious, so readers would benefit from an explanation.

Second, although the Profile of Mood States and the Physical Activity Affect Scale are both listed as measures of "mood," one is labeled a measure of "affect." As will be explained in the next chapter, "mood" and "affect" are not synonymous terms. So readers might want to know why it was deemed necessary in the context of this study to assess both constructs and, secondarily, why it was deemed conceptually justified, given their differences, to subsume both measures under the rubric "measures of mood."

Third, there is considerable ambiguity regarding the use of the Profile of Mood States, ultimately making it impossible for readers to decipher which items were presented to respondents. There are two versions of the Profile of Mood States, an older unipolar version (McNair et al., 1971), and a newer bipolar one (Lorr, McNair, & Heuchert, 2003). Which one was used in this study is not clear because the reference given is for the unipolar version of 1971, yet the authors noted that the version they employed "uses bipolar adjective scales to assess mood." Moreover, it seems reasonable to suggest that, since the researchers had to choose between two conceptual alternatives (or indeed opposites), namely unipolar states versus bipolar dimensions, readers would benefit from knowing the considerations upon which this important decision was based.

To complicate matters, in this case, the authors appear to have used only some of the "poles" of the six factors of the bipolar Profile of Mood States. The bipolar Profile of Mood States consists of the following six scales: (a) Composed-Anxious, (b) Agreeable-Hostile, (c) Elated-Depressed, (d) Confident-Unsure, (e) Energetic-Tired, and (f) Clearheaded-Confused (see Figure 1.2). Each scale consists of 12 items, half of which represent one pole and half the other. By choosing to measure only "vigor, tension, depression, elation," the authors in effect limited the universe of content the instrument was intended to assess but provided no explanation for the reasoning behind or the necessity of this decision. Furthermore, there are no scales named "vigor" or "tension" in the bipolar Profile of Mood States (only in the older, unipolar version). It is possible, though uncertain, that these labels refer to the "Energetic" and "Anxious" poles of the Energetic-Tired and Composed-Anxious factors, respectively. More important, despite noting that the version of the Profile of Mood States that was used consists of "bipolar adjective scales," the authors apparently only scored unipolar half-scales. One pair (Elated and Depressed) is theorized to form a single bipolar factor but was scored as two separate unipolar scales. The other two (Vigor, Tension) represent single poles, each possibly extracted from a different bipolar factor. Once again, it appears that, since the instrument was scored and interpreted in a manner different from the way its developers intended, readers should have been informed of the rationale behind these changes.

Fourth, the selection of the Physical Activity Affect Scale appears to have been based on its presumed "exercise specificity." To readers willing to place this claim under appropriate scrutiny, this warrants an explanation. One may wonder, for example, why some items are characterized as more "exercise specific" than others. For example, why are *alert*, *vigorous*, or *lively* (items from the Energetic pole of the bipolar Profile of Mood States) less exercise specific than *enthusiastic*, *energetic*, or *upbeat* (items from the Positive Affect scale of the Physical Activity Affect Scale)? Why are *miserable* and *discouraged* (items from the Negative Affect scale of the Physical Activity Affect Scale) more exercise specific than *dejected* and *discouraged* (items from the Depressed half-scale of the bipolar Profile of Mood States)? While the focus was placed on the (debatable) issue of exercise specificity, it is interesting to point out that

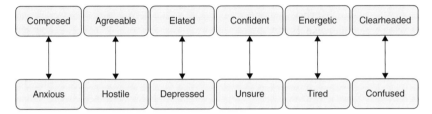

Figure 1.2. The factors of the older, unipolar Profile of Mood States (top row) and the newer, bipolar version of the Profile of Mood States (bottom row).

the conceptual features of the Physical Activity Affect Scale (e.g., the theorized nature, polarity, and relations among the factors) were not mentioned as a consideration that led to its selection.

Readers also frequently encounter studies with similar aims employing measures vastly different from a conceptual standpoint but are given no explanation that could justify these differences. Having no explanation for the different measurement decisions, readers are often left confused and frustrated. For example, commenting on studies investigating the relationship between sleep and affect by using different measures, such as a list of items previously used by Lorr, Daston, and Smith (1967) or the University of Wales Institute of Science and Technology Mood Adjective Checklist (Matthews, Jones, & Chamberlain, 1990), McCrae et al. (2008) noted that this complicates "the interpretation and con-textualization of these findings" (p. 43). However, they then proceeded to use yet another measure, the Positive and Negative Affect Schedule (Watson, Clark, & Tellegen, 1988), without providing any explanation or justification for this decision.

Similarly, authors often use combinations of measures without explaining why the use of multiple measures was necessary or how the multiple measures complement each other. For example, one study was designed to examine the effects of two forms of exercise (stationary cycling and martial arts) on "mood" in a sample of individuals with recurrent major depressive disorder (Bodin & Martinsen, 2004). In the Methods section, the authors listed two measures, both reportedly used to assess the target construct of "mood": the Positive and Negative Affect Schedule (Watson, Clark, & Tellegen, 1988) and the state-anxiety portion of the State-Trait Anxiety Inventory (Spielberger, Gorsuch, & Lushene, 1970).

Another study examined the effects of a bout of exercise (treadmill walking) on "mood and well-being" in a sample of individuals with major depressive disorder (Bartholomew, Morrison, & Ciccolo, 2005). In the Methods section, the authors listed two measures: the Subjective Exercise Experiences Scale (McAuley & Courneya, 1994) and the Profile of Mood States (McNair et al., 1971). In neither study did the authors present a rationale substantiating their choice of measures. However, clearly this would have been very useful information to readers trying to understand why two investigations targeting the same dependent variable within the same population used two different combinations of measures. As will become clear in subsequent chapters, the conceptual bases of these four measures are fundamentally different. Since the outcome of the decision-making process was so different, the basic considerations taken into account and the algorithm that led to the final decision would have been truly illuminating and would have helped readers evaluate the studies in a more meaningful manner.

In reality, when the decision-making process that led to the selection of a measure is not articulated, the likely reason is that no formal decision-making process was followed and, instead, the measure was selected on the basis of an "alternative" or "shortcut" method. A shortcut method often amounts to nothing more than using a measure perceived as popular or a measure a colleague happened to recommend. To paraphrase Paul Meehl's (1999) famous aphorism about the way psychologists often choose theories, researchers often choose measures like "a willful child contemplating the offerings in a candy store, 'That one looks good,' 'I'll take two of those,' 'I hate chocolate,' and the like" (p. 165). Pushing researchers to explain their choice of measure often results in statements such as "I don't know, that's what I've always used" or "I like it because it's short" or "my doctoral advisor told me to use it and I've been using it ever since." To point out the obvious, this approach cannot guarantee that researchers will choose the optimal measurement option for their investigations.

The dreadful but all too common "this measure was used because it has been used before"

Another common problem (arguably a variant of the previous problem) is the reliance on precedence as a basis for making decisions about measurement. In some cases, this problem manifests itself as the selection of a measure because it is the measure of choice of researchers perceived as experts in this area. In other cases, researchers simply choose to adopt a measure they see as commonly used.

For example, in a study investigating the hypothesis that smoking provides relief from negative affect, four different measures were used on the basis of their "frequency of use in acute mood induction studies" (Perkins, Karelitz, Conklin, Sayette, & Giedgowd, 2010, p. 708). It has now become commonplace to see this type of argument as the sole reason offered for selecting popular measures such as the Profile of Mood States, the State-Trait Anxiety Inventory, or the Positive and Negative Affect Schedule (see Figure 1.3). Wide popularity is portrayed as a justification so compelling that it obliterates the need for a more concrete rationale. Thus, authors who select the Profile of Mood States, for example, do so on the basis of claims that this measure "has been used extensively to assess the acute effects of exercise on mood" (Hoffman & Hoffman, 2008, p. 359), or "has been widely utilized in exercise research" (Bryan, Hutchison, Seals, & Allen, 2007, p. 33), or is "one of the most frequently used mood measures in sport and exercise psychology" (Johansson, Hassmén, & Jouper, 2008, p. 201), or is "historically the most frequently used measure in exercise and mood state studies" (Hansen, Stevens, & Coast, 2001, p. 269). Similarly, authors who select the State-Trait Anxiety Inventory do so on the basis of the argument that it is the "most widely used measure of anxiety in exercise research" (Knapen et al., 2009, p. 757), the "most widely used anxiety measure in exercise studies" (Youngstedt, 2010, p. 254), it has been "employed in nearly 50% of studies on exercise and anxiety" (Motl, O'Connor, & Dishman, 2004, p. 98), or is "the most often employed measure of state anxiety in the exercise literature" (Bartholomew & Linder, 1998, p. 208). Authors who prefer the Positive and Negative Affect Schedule claim that "this measure is one of the most commonly used ways of assessing state affect" (LePage & Crowther, 2010, p. 126), it "has been used extensively" (Puente & Anshel, 2010, p. 41), or "has successfully been used to indicate affect in conjunction with exercise" (Miller, Bartholomew, & Springer, 2005, p. 266).

The phrase "this measure was used because it has been used before" (and all variations thereof, including "this measure was used to maintain consistency with previous studies" or "this measure was used to enable comparisons with previous studies") is indeed so common in the literature that it is rarely, if ever, identified by reviewers, editors, or

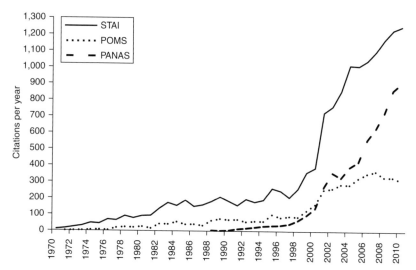

Figure 1.3. The number of entries in the PsycINFO™ database citing the State-Trait Anxiety Inventory (STAI; Spielberger, 1983; Spielberger et al., 1970), the Profile of Mood States (POMS; McNair et al. 1971), and the Positive and Negative Affect Schedule (PANAS; Watson, Clark, & Tellegen, 1988).

readers as problematic. Although the phrase may seem to provide some sort of justification, it cannot withstand close scrutiny for the simple reason that previous uses of the measure (no matter how numerous) might have also lacked a substantive rationale or might have been based on a faulty rationale. In essence, this phrase, more often than not, represents a thinly veiled admission that, once again, no specific conceptual or psychometric reasons for the selection of the particular measure can be articulated.

"They're all the same": interchanging terms referring to substantively different constructs

Imagine for a moment that you are reviewing a manuscript in which the authors show complete disregard for the distinctions between "efficacy expectations" and "outcome expectations," interchanging these terms freely as if they described the same construct. Alternatively, you can use any other pair of terms referring to concepts you know to be different (e.g., "self-esteem" and "self-concept"). There is little doubt that most of us would interpret such an error as evidence of an unacceptably deficient conceptual foundation and, in most cases, we would recommend the outright rejection of the manuscript. Now let us take an even more extreme scenario. Imagine reviewing a manuscript in which the authors identified a variable as "achievement goals" in the title, used a measure of "perceived competence" to assess this variable, and then interpreted their findings as referring to "self-esteem." This would obviously confuse any reader. It seems reasonable to assume that most diligent reviewers would issue a strong rebuke to the authors for this gross mistake.

Unfortunately, similar mistakes are very common in studies dealing with affect, mood, and emotion. These three terms are used indiscriminately and inconsistently on a regular basis. To make matters worse, the lack of respect for the crucial distinctions between these constructs often manifests itself in the use of an instrument specifically designed to measure one construct to assess and draw conclusions about another.

For example, a recent meta-analysis on the effects of exercise on anxiety was introduced with the sentence: "anxiety, an unpleasant *mood* characterized by thoughts of worry, is an adaptive response to perceived threats that can develop into a maladaptive anxiety disorder if it becomes severe and chronic" (Herring, O'Connor, & Dishman, 2010, p. 321, italics added). Is anxiety a *mood*? According to the American Psychiatric Association (2000), anxiety disorders and mood disorders are distinct and thus form separate diagnostic categories. Similarly, in psychology, although there can be such a thing as an "anxious mood," anxiety itself is consistently characterized as an *emotion*, not a mood, by leading theorists (Lazarus, 1991a; Spielberger & Reheiser, 2004). Nevertheless, this difference (mood versus emotion) is very commonly ignored as if it were insignificant.

In one aforementioned study (Bodin & Martinsen, 2004), for example, careful readers might have noticed that a measure developed to assess the *emotional* state of state anxiety, namely the state-anxiety portion of the State-Trait Anxiety Inventory (Spielberger et al., 1970), was reportedly used to assess "mood." Based on the analysis of data from the State-Trait Anxiety Inventory, the authors concluded that "changes in *mood* were not dependent on whether the first exercise was stationary bike use or martial arts" (p. 630, italics added). If this statement is scrutinized, it becomes apparent that results referring to the precisely defined and demarcated *emotional* state of anxiety were used as the basis for drawing conclusions about a content domain that is not only conceptually quite different but also very broad in scope, namely the global domain of *mood*.

To use another example, in a study investigating the effects of moderate and vigorous exercise in abstaining cigarette smokers (Everson, Daly, & Ussher, 2008), the authors referred to an earlier call to incorporate assessments of mood disturbances in smoking cessation trials "because they adversely affect quality of life and may in some cases help to lead smokers to resume smoking" (Shiffman, West, & Gilbert, 2004, p. 602). Shiffman et al. (2004) recommended the study of specific mood states as restlessness, depressed mood, and irritability because each has been linked to cigarette withdrawal. Agreeing that "*mood state* can be instrumental in facilitating smoking lapses during a cessation attempt," Everson et al. (2008) stated that "therefore, in the present study, *exercise-induced affect* was measured using self-ratings on the Subjective Exercise Experience Scale" (p. 28, italics added). Readers might again notice an inconsistency. A "mood state" is not the same thing as "exercise-induced affect." By "mood disturbances," Shiffman et al. (2004) referred to specific states presumed linked to nicotine withdrawal (i.e., restlessness, depressed mood, and irritability). By "exercise-induced affect" and "subjective exercise experiences," McAuley and Courneya (1994), the developers of the Subjective Exercise Experience Scale, referred to "subjective experiences that are unique to the exercise domain" (p. 165). Although many readers might not identify this as irregular during the first reading, it is not really different from the "extreme" scenario discussed in the opening paragraph of this section. A measure of *affective* states presumed to be "unique to the exercise domain" was used as a basis for drawing inferences about *mood* states presumed to be characteristic of nicotine withdrawal.

Once a reader "tunes in" to the problem of the inappropriate interchange of terms and constructs, he or she might be shocked by how widespread this problem is. One might be even more shocked after realizing how desensitized many of us have become to a problem that, when evaluated under an appropriately critical light, seems entirely unacceptable. As a test, readers may want to spot the problem here: "Researchers have reported consistently that mood states, such as state anxiety, are improved after an acute bout of physical activity" (Smith, O'Connor, Crabbe, & Dishman, 2002, p. 1158); or here: "Single episodes of aerobic exercise have been associated with mood improvements, the most commonly studied of which has been reductions in state anxiety" (Focht & Koltyn, 1999, p. 456). Similarly, examine the following conclusions, drawn from studies in which the only dependent variable was the specific emotion of state anxiety: "mood improvements associated with resistance exercise are optimized by moderate intensity exercise" (O'Connor, Bryant, Veltri, & Gebhardt, 1993, p. 520); or "maximal exercise testing can be associated with negative mood shifts" (O'Connor, Petruzzello, Kubitz, & Robinson, 1995, p. 101).

Measures as sacrosanct legacies: sticking with a measure no matter what

There seems to be an astonishing commitment to measures for which there is compelling evidence of their inappropriateness on either theoretical or psychometric grounds. Critiques of measures are rare. Measures (which should, in theory, undergo periodic evaluations and revisions) are often treated as if they were sacrosanct artifacts not to be questioned or altered in any way. For example, responding to a wave of papers critical of using the state-anxiety portion of the State-Trait Anxiety Inventory in conjunction with bouts of physical activity, O'Connor, Raglin, and Martinsen (2000) urged researchers to continue using this questionnaire based on the argument that it has been used in a "large body of research" (p. 138).

To some extent, a defensive attitude toward and a downplaying of criticisms is to be expected. The reason is that, when the conceptual bases or the psychometric properties of a measure that has already been used in several studies are shown to be problematic, this automatically renders the findings of these previous studies suspect. In the eyes of many researchers, this seems like backtracking, rather than progressing, along the knowledge development process. Ideally, this process should be cumulative, not cyclical.

On the other hand, since conceptual models are bound to evolve and more sophisticated psychometric techniques are bound to emerge over time, expecting a measure to remain invariant without being scrutinized or questioned is unrealistic and, frankly, myopic. As Schutz (1993) emphasized, "it is my view that no test is sacred – just because an instrument … has been around for years and used in dozens of published studies does not necessarily mean it is a valid and reliable instrument. In other fields, even the most venerable of tests are constantly being reevaluated and questioned" (p. 128). The American Psychological Association Task Force on Statistical Inference, despite acknowledging that "researchers are reluctant to change" measures found to be problematic, urges editors and reviewers to "pay special attention to the psychometric properties of the instruments used" and to "encourage revisions (even if not by the scale's author) to prevent the accumulation of results based on relatively invalid or unreliable measures" (Wilkinson, 1999, p. 596).

It seems reasonable to suggest that, if a measure has received criticism, especially if the criticism has come from multiple, independent sources and has concentrated on the same key attributes, any researcher who chooses this measure should offer concrete arguments defending this choice. It does not seem appropriate to either ignore the criticism altogether or attempt to circumvent it by arguing that the past popularity of the measure can somehow serve to counterbalance or neutralize its flaws.

Internal consistency as the summary index of psychometric merit

In substantiating the selection of the State-Trait Anxiety Inventory in their study, Mackay and Neill (2010) wrote that this questionnaire "was used due to its brevity and reliability in measuring state anxiety" (p. 240) and supported this statement by citing high coefficients of internal consistency. Citing Cronbach's (1951) alpha coefficient of internal consistency to justify the selection of self-report measures has become very common. On the surface, since internal consistency is an important psychometric property for a multi-item measure, this may seem a positive development. The problem is that this is often the only concrete piece of information given in support of a chosen measure. In that sense, although this easy-to-compute coefficient may give a semblance of psychometric sophistication, in actuality, it only provides a tiny fraction of the information needed for a meaningful evaluation of the measure and its role within the context of a given investigation. According to Gill (1997):

Psychometric analyses [stop] with alpha coefficients of internal consistency and never consider the more important validity issues ... Of course, we cannot assess validity if we do not know what we are trying to measure, and we return to the bottom-line message: Conceptual clarity is the first step. If we know what we want to measure, we can consider validity of purported measures. Otherwise, inventories might include interrelated items yielding a score, but we have no justification for interpreting the score. (pp. 44–45)

It is important to remember what the alpha coefficient reflects. It is a joint index of (a) the average intercorrelation between the items of a scale and (b) the number of items comprising the scale. As numerous insightful analyses have highlighted, this coefficient does not provide a good indication of the lower bound of the reliability of a scale and it is certainly not an indication of unidimensionality among a set of items (Cortina, 1993; Cronbach & Shavelson, 2004; Green, Lissitz, & Mulaik, 1977; Osburn, 2000; Schmitt, 1996; Shevlin, Miles, Davies, & Walker, 2000; Sijtsma, 2009).

Moreover, even if we were to assume that the alpha coefficient offered a good indication of reliability, it should be clear that reliability is not a property of the test itself but rather a property of the scores on the test (i.e., a particular data set), obtained within a particular sample under a particular set of conditions. According to the American Psychological Association Task Force on Statistical Inference, "it is important to remember that a test is not reliable or unreliable. Reliability is a property of the scores on a test for a particular population of examinees" (Wilkinson, 1999, p. 596). Therefore, citing indices of reliability of any kind from other samples (such as the development sample of a questionnaire) is of minimal usefulness (Thompson & Vacha-Haase, 2000).

In sum, the alpha coefficient is not the most crucial, most meaningful, or most informative psychometric datum one can report. As Gill correctly pointed out, under no circumstances should the reporting of alpha be regarded as providing sufficient justification for the selection of a measure. The considerably more complex issues of theoretical appropriateness and validity should never be overlooked.

Armed with easy to use software but no theory: confirmatory factor analysis misapplied

Occasionally, besides alpha, some authors make reference to results of confirmatory factor analyses in support of their selection of a measure. This is often done in lieu of providing other validity-related information. For example, the use of the Exercise-induced Feeling Inventory (Gauvin & Rejeski, 1993) in a study examining the relation between postexercise feelings and the "flow" state was justified because structural equation modeling showed that "the a priori four-factor model had a good fit to the data and alpha coefficients were satisfactory for all subscales" (Karageorghis, Vlachopoulos, & Terry, 2000, p. 237). Similarly, in a study investigating the role of the exercise setting, the use of attentional focus techniques, and gender on "affect," the Exercise-induced Feeling Inventory was selected because "factor analysis has supported the validity of the four-factor model (the fit index exceeded 0.90) and Cronbach alphas have often exceeded 0.80" (LaCaille, Masters, & Heath, 2004, p. 467). Of course, a goodness-of-fit index in the 0.90s may seem impressive but, in actuality, it may be uninformative or even misleading unless the model fitted to the data was meaningful and specified in a manner consistent with theoretical postulates.

The problem with many confirmatory factor analyses that appear in the domain of health-behavioral research (e.g., Sonnentag, Binnewies, & Mojza, 2008), including the many conducted in the domain of physical activity (Carpenter, Tompkins, Schmiege, Nilsson, & Bryan, 2010; Crocker, 1997; Driver, 2006; Gauvin & Rejeski, 1993; Lox et al., 2000; Lox & Rudolph, 1994; Markland, Emberton, & Tallon, 1997; McAuley & Courneya, 1994; Vlachopoulos, Biddle, & Fox, 1996), is that they are only concerned with whether the items load on the postulated factors. As important as this information is, it does not suffice to declare the structure of a measure as valid and, consequently, quoting a goodness-of-fit index is meaningless in the absence of a critical appraisal of (a) the theoretical model of which the measure is supposed to be a valid representation and (b) whether the postulates of the theory were correctly modeled in the confirmatory factor analysis.

To illustrate point (a), it should be clear that, if a content domain comprises, for example, three factors but the item pool of a questionnaire and the factor model tested with the confirmatory factor analysis reflect only two of these, the analysis might show "good fit" even though the measurement instrument would not offer a valid representation of the content domain (in this example, it would underrepresent the content domain, leaving out one factor). To use a more specific example, for reasons that will be summarized when this instrument is reviewed in more detail, in the theoretical model that formed the basis of the Positive and Negative Affect Schedule (Watson, Clark, & Tellegen, 1988), all low-activation states were discarded as non-affective, a position that has been widely criticized (see Figure 1.4). Consequently, the Positive and Negative Affect Schedule only includes items denoting high activation and excludes items or scales that tap either pleasant (e.g., calmness, serenity) or unpleasant (e.g., tiredness, fatigue) low-activation states (Watson & Clark, 1997, p. 276). After conducting a confirmatory factor analysis and finding a goodness-of-fit index of 0.95, Crocker (1997) declared that his data provided "factor validation evidence for the use of [the Positive and Negative Affect Schedule] in sporting contexts with youth populations" (p. 96). Others agreed, noting, for example, that "recent research has confirmed the factor structure of this schedule among young athletes (Crocker, 1997)" (Terry, Lane, Lane, & Keohane, 1999, p. 868). While it is true that the 20 items included in the Positive and Negative Affect Schedule loaded on the two hypothesized latent factors (Positive Affect and Negative Affect), whether the Positive and Negative Affect Schedule can be regarded a valid measure of the domain of "affect" or "mood" depends on whether

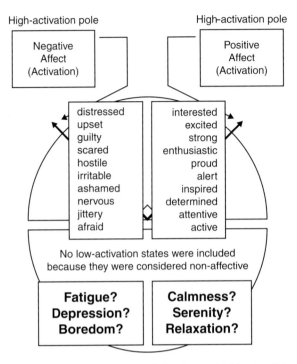

Figure 1.4. In the context of the theoretical basis of the Positive and Negative Affect Schedule, "positive affect" does not mean pleasure and "negative affect" does not mean displeasure. As the item composition of the two scales shows, all the items of the Positive Affect scale combine pleasure with high activation, whereas all the items of the Negative Affect scale combine displeasure with high activation. Because low-activation states are considered by Watson and Clark as non-affective, the scales of the Positive and Negative Affect Schedule "include no terms assessing fatigue and serenity" (Watson & Clark, 1997, p. 276).

one accepts the crucial theoretical position that states such as fatigue and calmness do not belong in these domains.

Another relevant example pertains to the problem of "fission" or taking a homogeneous set of items and considering them as indicators of two latent factors. If no constraint is placed on the intercorrelation between the two latent factors to guarantee some degree of discriminant validity, not only will the model fit the data well but, as a general rule, the fit may even be better than if all items had been modeled as indicators of a single factor. This is because, everything else being equal, adding more parameters (drawing a less parsimonious model) usually improves some indices of fit. According to Brown (2006):

If too many factors have been specified in the [confirmatory factor-analytic] model, this is likely to be detected by correlations between factors that approximate ±1.0, and so the latent dimensions have poor discriminant validity. In applied research, a factor correlation that equals or exceeds .85 is often used as the cutoff criterion for problematic discriminant validity ... When factors overlap to this degree, it may be possible to combine factors to acquire a more parsimonious solution. The goal of such respecification is not to improve the overall fit of the model (e.g., a model with fewer factors entails a smaller number of freely estimated parameters), but ideally the fit of the more parsimonious solution will be similar to the initial model, assuming that overall fit of the initial model was satisfactory, except for the excessive correlation between two factors. (p. 166)

Consider again the example of the Exercise-induced Feeling Inventory (Gauvin & Rejeski, 1993), which, among others, includes a "Positive Engagement" factor and a "Revitalization" factor, both of which consist of items that reflect a state of pleasant high activation (e.g., *enthusiastic* and *upbeat* in the Positive Engagement factor and *energetic* and *refreshed* in the Revitalization factor). In the original confirmatory factor analysis, the two latent factors were correlated 0.86 (Gauvin & Rejeski, 1993, p. 413). In a subsequent confirmatory factor analysis, the two factors were correlated 0.98 (Lox et al., 2000, p. 89). Nevertheless, users of this questionnaire were satisfied that "factor analysis has supported the validity of the four-factor model (the fit index exceeded 0.90)" (LaCaille et al., 2004, p. 467) and that "the structure of the [Exercise-induced Feeling Inventory] has been supported by confirmatory factor analysis" (Blanchard, Rodgers, & Gauvin, 2004, p. 123). Although the indices of fit were high, the four-factor model being tested made little sense from a conceptual and a psychometric standpoint given the clear lack of discriminant validity of two of the factors.

Now let us turn to problem (b), namely whether the models tested in confirmatory factor analyses are faithful representations of the theoretical models upon which the measures were based. It should be clear that, unless this is done correctly, the results of a confirmatory factor analysis cannot be deemed as providing evidence of construct validity. Besides the number of latent factors that are theorized to define a domain of content, an equally critical issue pertains to the theorized relation between the factors. For example, in some cases, the theory may postulate that the factors are orthogonal (uncorrelated), in other cases that they are oblique (correlated), and in a few cases, such as the affect circumplex, the theory may posit a very unique and highly specific pattern of intercorrelations (Cudeck, 1986; Wiggins, Steiger, & Gaelick, 1981). These intercorrelations are integral and defining attributes of the theoretical models.

One of the benefits of using structural equation modeling to perform confirmatory factor analysis is that researchers can specify the correlation postulated by the theory in the model being tested. Thus, "strong theories [can] exploit the effects of being able to fix and/or constrain parameter estimates" (Nunnally & Bernstein, 1994, p. 577). For example, if a theory posits that two factors are orthogonal, a researcher can constrain the correlation between the postulated latent factors to zero. According to John and Benet-Martinez (2000), "rather than letting [structural equation modeling] estimate the correlation (or covariation) between the latent factors as a free parameter, we can fix it at a value that would allow us to make strong inferences about the independence of the two constructs" (p. 361). Although measures subjected to confirmatory factor analysis in health-behavioral research are often presented as stemming directly from a strong theoretical basis, such constrains are not always imposed.

For example, the Positive and Negative Affect Schedule (Watson, Clark, & Tellegen, 1988) was based on the fundamental theoretical premise that the dimensions of Positive Affect (PA) and Negative Affect (PA) are "independent, uncorrelated dimensions" (Watson & Tellegen, 1985, p. 221). Consistent with this position, Watson, Clark, and Tellegen (1988) took specific steps to ensure that the PA and NA scales would be uncorrelated, excluding all items that had a secondary loading of |.25| or higher and employing a Varimax rotation of the two factors in their initial exploratory factor analysis. As a result, they indeed found that "the correlation between the NA and PA scales is invariably low, ranging from -.12 to -.23; thus, the two scales share approximately 1% to 5% of their variance" (Watson, Clark, & Tellegen, 1988, p. 1065). It is important to understand that this is not an obscure or minor conceptual feature of the Positive and Negative Affect Schedule but rather perhaps its most central and most widely touted characteristic. Watson and coworkers gave clear instructions to future factor analysts, stating that the PA and NA dimensions "can be meaningfully represented as orthogonal dimensions in factor analytic studies of affect" (Watson, Clark, & Tellegen, 1988, p. 1063). Furthermore, because the PA/NA model "is based on an orthogonal rotation (in which the factors are constrained to be uncorrelated), this conceptualization posits that variations in positive and negative mood are largely independent of one another" (Watson & Clark, 1997, p. 270).

Naturally, most subsequent confirmatory factor analyses of the Positive and Negative Affect Schedule that were informed by this theoretical framework tested models in which the PA–NA correlation was constrained to zero. For example, Lonigan, Hooe, David, and Kistner (1999) tested the "two-factor orthogonal model" by "constraining [the PA-NA] correlation to 0" (p. 378). Terracciano, McCrae, and Costa (2003) tested the "two-factor orthogonal model (with the correlation between PA and NA fixed to zero)" (p. 137). Crawford and Henry (2004) tested a model in which "these two factors were constrained to be orthogonal, reflecting the original hypothesis (Watson & Clark, 1997)" (p. 251). Tuccitto, Giacobbi, and Leite (2010) tested the "original orthogonal two-factor structure of the [Positive and Negative Affect Schedule] proposed by Watson, Clark, and Tellegen (1988)" (p. 132). On the other hand, in a confirmatory factor analysis of the Positive and Negative Affect Schedule conducted with youth sport participants, although it was stated that "model specifications were based on the two uncorrelated factor hypothesized configuration proposed by Watson, Clark, and Tellegen (1988)" (Crocker, 1997, p. 93), there was no indication that a constraint was actually placed on the PA–NA correlation. The correlation was left as a free parameter to be estimated (and was found to be low at -.17, p. 94). Although it was concluded that "the hypothesized two-factor structure ... seems to have acceptable fit with the data" (pp. 95–96), it is unclear whether "the hypothesized two-factor structure" was properly specified, since the most central element of the theory does not appear to have been incorporated in the model.

This problem also extends to the confirmatory factor analyses of other measures based on similar structural postulates. For example, in developing the Physical Activity Affect Scale, Lox et al. (2000) claimed that the factor structure of this four-factor instrument fits the circumplex model of affect proposed by Russell (1980). As explained in more detail in Chapter 3, according to the circumplex model, the domain of affect is defined by two orthogonal and bipolar dimensions, namely valence (pleasure-displeasure) and activation. These two dimensions divide the affective space into four quadrants. Specifically, according to Lox et al. (2000):

The factor structure of the [Physical Activity Affect Scale] is ... well supported, theoretically, by the four quadrants of the circumplex model of affect proposed by Russell (1980). Specifically, positive affect items [enthusiastic, energetic, upbeat] would be expected to fall within the positive-high activation quadrant, negative affect items [crummy, miserable, discouraged] are predicted to fall within the negative-high activation quadrant, fatigue items [fatigued, tired, worn out] should be contained within the negative-low activation quadrant, and tranquility items [calm, peaceful, relaxed] are hypothesized to fall within the positive-low activation quadrant. (p. 92)

This theoretical postulate, according to which the four factors of the Physical Activity Affect Scale are hypothesized to represent the four quadrants of a circle (see Figure 1.5), entails a specific pattern of intercorrelations between the latent factors (Steiger, 1979, 1980;

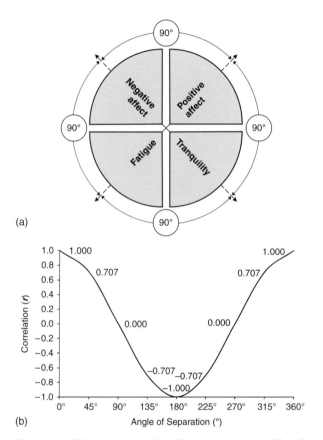

Figure 1.5. The structure of the Physical Activity Affect Scale was postulated to be consistent with the circumplex model of affect (panel a). However, the circumplex model makes specific predictions about the intercorrelations among factors theorized to represent the four quadrants of circumplex space (panel b). For example, scales theorized to represent adjacent quadrants should have intercorrelations approaching zero, whereas scales theorized to represent diametrically opposite quadrants should have intercorrelations approaching −1.00. To substantiate the claim that the structure of the Physical Activity Affect Scale conforms to the circumplex, this theorized pattern of intercorrelations should be modeled in confirmatory factor analyses based on structural equation modeling (panel c).

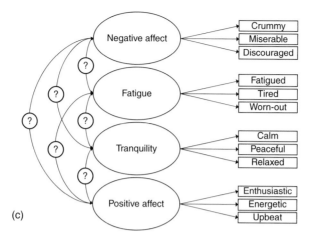

(c)

Figure 1.5. (*cont.*)

Wiggins et al., 1981). Specifically, factors theorized to reflect two adjacent quadrants should be more or less orthogonal (separated by 90°, correlated 0.00), whereas factors theorized to reflect two diametrically opposite quadrants should have a more or less reciprocal relationship (separated by 180°, correlated −1.00). Because of the highly specific pattern of correlations that must be demonstrated to establish a circumplex structure, analyses are typically based on specialized models and statistical procedures (e.g., Acton & Revelle, 2002; Browne, 1992; Cudeck, 1986; Fabrigar, Visser, & Browne, 1997; Gurtman & Pincus, 2000, 2003; Tracey, 2000). One such procedure (circular stochastic process model with a Fourier series correlation function) has been applied, for example, to test the circumplex structure of the Activation Deactivation Adjective Check List (Ekkekakis, Hall, & Petruzzello, 2005). Even if these specialized procedures are not used, however, constrained confirmatory factor analysis can also be used in some cases, by fixing factor correlations to hypothesized values (e.g., see Perrinjaquet, Furrer, Usunier, Cestre, & Valette-Florence, 2007; Schwartz & Boehnke, 2004; Yik & Russell, 2003). It should again be clear that, unless a specific pattern of factor correlations is modeled and tested, any claims linking the structure of a measure to the circumplex model would be unsubstantiated.

Despite claims that the structure of the Physical Activity Affect Scale is consistent with the circumplex, none of the confirmatory factor analyses of the Physical Activity Affect Scale (Carpenter et al., 2010; Driver, 2006; Lox et al., 2000) tested models with appropriate constraints on the factor correlations. These correlations were again left as free parameters to be estimated and none have yielded evidence that supports the claim of circumplex structure. Specifically, as noted earlier, factors theorized to reflect adjacent quadrants should be approximately orthogonal (with a correlation close to zero). Instead, across four samples, the Positive Affect-Negative Affect correlation was −.35, −.46, −.33, −.41; the Negative Affect-Fatigue correlation was .18, .59, .59, .41; the Fatigue-Tranquility correlation was −.28, −.18, −.08, −.08; and the Tranquility-Positive Affect correlation was .39, .58, .47, .47 (for the samples from Lox et al., 2000; Driver 2006; and the two samples from Carpenter et al., 2010, respectively). On the other hand, the correlations between factors theorized to reflect diametrically opposite quadrants should approximate −1.00 (especially considering that latent factors are estimated as free of measurement error and, therefore, their intercorrelations are essentially corrected for the attenuating effect of unreliability). Instead, across the same four samples, the correlation between Positive Affect and Fatigue was −.25, −.27, −.32, and −.32, and that between Negative Affect and Tranquility was −.16, −.40, −.18, and −.10. With the possible exception of the Fatigue-Tranquility correlation, which approached the hypothesized value in some cases, these data contradict the claims for a link of the Physical Activity Affect Scale to a circumplex structure.

Nevertheless, the researchers who performed the confirmatory factor analyses unanimously concluded that, despite the lack of constraints, the tested models provided evidence for a circumplex structure. According to Driver (2006), "the [Physical Activity Affect Scale] is an encompassing measurement tool, based on Russell's circumplex model" (p. 2) and this is "supported by the correlations between the latent variables" (p. 11). According to Carpenter et al. (2010), the "multi-dimensional structure [of the Physical Activity Affect Scale] is based on models of valence and arousal, and its subscales have been shown to correspond with existing theory (i.e., Russell's circumplex)" (p. 3). Users of the Physical Activity Affect Scale have also accepted these claims. For example, according to Loughead, Patterson, and Carron (2008), "the [Physical Activity Affect Scale] is an exercise-specific measure based on Russell's (1980) circumplex model of affect" (p. 57). Specifically commenting on confirmatory factor-analytic results, these authors concluded that the "overall fit of the model was good" (p. 58). According to Kwan and Bryan (2010a), "the [Physical Activity Affect Scale] is theoretically supported by the circumplex model of affect (Russell, 1980)" (p. 119) and, according to the same authors, "it has been shown that the [Physical Activity Affect Scale] subscales satisfactorily map onto the four quadrants of the circumplex model of affect" (Kwan & Bryan, 2010b, p. 73).

The examples listed here (and many others) illustrate that references to the numerical results of confirmatory factor analyses (i.e., goodness-of-fit indices) as a means of substantiating the selection of a measure are also fundamentally inadequate. With or without post hoc modifications, most confirmatory factor-analytic studies that enter the literature contain evidence that the models being tested should not be rejected on the basis of goodness-of-fit indices. Echoing these "acceptable" or "satisfactory" indices or claims of "good fit" is easy but generally uninformative and, in many cases, misleading. The difficulty lies in critically evaluating the confirmatory factor analysis, which in turn means being able to appraise (a) the meaningfulness of the theoretical model that supposedly formed the basis of the measure and (b) whether the theory was accurately modeled in the confirmatory factor analysis.

Domain specificity as panacea

In several areas of health-behavioral research, investigators have speculated that particular types of affective states precipitate a certain behavior (e.g., people overeat when bored, smoke when depressed, anxious, or irritable) or that a certain behavior results in particular types of affective states (e.g., overeating results in feelings of guilt, smoking transiently alleviates the negative affect associated with temporary smoking abstinence). This speculation has prompted the development of domain-specific measures of affect, mood, and emotion. The promise of "specificity" appears to give such measures a significant boost and many of them tend to be widely adopted within their respective fields of research. In the field of physical activity research, for example, during the 1990s, several measures reportedly specifically engineered to be relevant and responsive to exercise were published, including the Exercise-induced Feeling Inventory (Gauvin & Rejeski, 1993), the Subjective Exercise Experiences Scale (McAuley & Courneya, 1994), and the Physical Activity Affect Scale (Lox et al., 2000). These were hailed as a sign of progress (Gauvin & Russell, 1993; Gill, 1997) and characterized as "auspicious beginnings to a solution" (McAuley & Rudolph, 1995, p. 90).

An important point, however, is often overlooked. In some cases, domain-specific measures were based on preexisting theory, usually adopted from other areas of psychology. They were made domain specific by the rather innocuous and uncontroversial process of adding domain-specific referents to item stems (e.g., "I feel anxious" becomes "When I haven't smoked in a while, I feel anxious"). In other cases, domain-specific measures contain only a sample of distinct states from a broader, global domain, such as affect or mood, believed relevant to the particular domain or behavior of interest (e.g., in smoking, the focus might be placed on restlessness, depressed mood, and irritability). Finally, in other cases, including research investigating affective changes that occur following bouts of physical activity, investigators have made claims that the resultant states are *unique* (i.e., do not occur under other circumstances). For example, the aim of the Subjective Exercise Experiences Scale was to "assess subjective experiences that are *unique* to the exercise domain" (McAuley & Courneya, 1994, p. 165, italics added), while the Exercise-induced Feeling Inventory was based on the assumption that "the stimulus properties of physical activity are capable of producing several distinct feelings states" (Gauvin & Rejeski, 1993, p. 404). These positions imply that those measures were developed to tap a new and unexplored domain of content, a vastly more challenging and complicated undertaking than writing items with domain-specific references. In other words, these were not meant to be exercise-specific measures of "feelings" or "subjective experiences" but rather measures of "exercise-specific feelings" or "exercise-specific subjective experiences," a very different idea. The uniqueness and novelty of the intended domain of content entailed the need to explore this terra incognita for the first time in order to discover its exact nature, its limits, and its structure.

Unfortunately, preexisting theory from affective psychology has not been used as a guide in the development of most domain-specific measures. In the domain of exercise, for example, although several attempts were made to retrofit the circumplex model (e.g., Lox et al., 2000; Rejeski, Reboussin, Dunn, King, & Sallis, 1999), the absence of theory during the developmental stages produced several problems, which have been detailed elsewhere (Ekkekakis & Petruzzello, 2001a, 2001b, 2004).

One of the most troubling issues is that of domain underrepresentation; can the states assessed by these measures be considered fully representative of the phenomenology of exercise? Can researchers assume that by using these measures they can fully capture the "subjective experiences that are unique to the exercise domain" or the "distinct feelings states" that emanate from the "stimulus properties of physical activity"? A critical analysis of the methods followed in the development of these measures leads to a negative answer. The main reason is that the empirical derivation of the content and structure of the measures was based exclusively on the experiences of young, healthy, and physically active respondents. It seems reasonable to suggest that the experience of physical activity will differ considerably between a healthy and active 20-year-old versus an inactive or physically limited 65-year-old. Nevertheless, these measures have been used with diverse populations, very different from those on which their development was based, such as sedentary middle-aged adults (Gauvin, Rejeski, Norris, & Lutes, 1997), sedentary older adults (McAuley, Blissmer, Katula, & Duncan, 2000), obese older adults with knee osteoarthritis (Focht, Gauvin, & Rejeski, 2004), and adults with brain injuries (Driver, 2006).

A related problem stems from the fact that, in many cases, authors have attempted to support their selection of domain-specific measures by arguing that they are "sensitive to change." For example, Gauvin and Rejeski (2001) emphasized that the "sensitivity to change criterion was central to the development of the [Exercise-induced Feeling Inventory]" (p. 74). Subsequent adopters of this measure have widely echoed this argument, stating that the Exercise-induced Feeling Inventory is "sensitive to the stimulus properties of exercise" (Cramp & Bray, 2010, p. 345) or that this measure "was selected ... based on its established sensitivity to change with acute exercise" (Focht, 2009, p. 614). Likewise, the Subjective Exercise Experiences Scale was chosen in several studies because it "has been found to be sensitive to exercise interventions" (Blanchard, Rodgers, Spence, & Courneya, 2001, p. 32) and it "appears ... sensitive to the exercise stimulus" (Jerome, Marquez, McAuley, Canaklisova, Snook, & Vickers, 2002, p. 152).

Sensitivity to change is not a separate psychometric property. If the quantity being measured changes but the measure fails to reflect the change, then the measure is not "insensitive to change" but rather unreliable, invalid, or both. Once reliability and validity are properly established, the measure will inevitably reflect whether the targeted variable does or does not change and, if it does, to what extent. So a reference to "sensitivity" as a justification for selecting a measure adds confusion but not much meaningful information.

This issue has even more troubling ramifications, however. For example, there is a historically deep-rooted tendency for proponents of physical activity in the domain of mental health to occasionally cross the thin red line that separates scientific impartiality from advocacy (see Ekkekakis & Backhouse, 2009; Salmon, 2001 on this issue). Because of this negative precedent, researchers should exercise caution in how they approach the concept of "sensitivity to change." Potentially hidden behind this seemingly innocuous phrase is the fact that a certain measure may tend to show what we "know in our heart" to be true, namely that "exercise makes people feel better." As one example, the original version of the Profile of Mood States has been portrayed as preferable over the newer bipolar version because the bipolar Profile of Mood States (POMS) seems to be "a less sensitive measure of mood state than the unipolar POMS" (Terry & Lane, 2000, p. 97). This conclusion was based on the results of one exercise study in which "significant mood enhancements emerged for participants profiled using the original POMS, whereas no mood changes were evident for the POMS-Bi group" (Terry, 1995, p. 315). Writing about this phenomenon, Kuhn (1962/1996) warned that, as a paradigm solidifies its position and begins to dictate an "orthodox" point of view, proponents of the paradigm tend to prefer or to develop measurement instruments more likely to detect the sort of outcomes the paradigm predicts.

One way that a measure can yield results consistent with the predictions of the current paradigm is by construct underrepresentation. Simply put, a measure cannot show that physical activity elicits negative states if it does not tap any negative states (Backhouse, Ekkekakis, Biddle, Foskett, & Williams, 2007). It is interesting, for example, that the Exercise-induced Feeling Inventory, "designed to assess feelings associated with the stimulus properties of acute bouts of physical activity" (Gauvin & Rejeski, 1993, p. 406), does not tap any unequivocally unpleasant states (with the possible exception of fatigue). Commenting on this issue, the developers of the Exercise-induced Feeling Inventory stated that their "interest in developing the [Exercise-induced Feeling Inventory] was to provide a measure that would be beneficial for research that has more of a public health focus" (Gauvin & Rejeski, 2001, p. 79). In other words, it seems that implicit in the development of the Exercise-induced Feeling Inventory was the a priori assumption that physical activity in the context of public health cannot induce, for example, tension, pain, embarrassment, disappointment, or boredom; these "feelings" cannot be associated with the "stimulus properties of acute bouts of physical activity." Practitioners working in the field of public health should consider whether this assumption is really true.

Another way to ensure that the predictions of the paradigm are confirmed (i.e., that "exercise makes people feel better") is to accentuate any positive effects. For example, in the development of the Exercise-induced Feeling Inventory, the experts who screened the items were asked to select those that reflected feelings that "(a) occurred during exercise; (b) occurred following exercise; (c) occurred both during and following exercise" (Gauvin & Rejeski, 1993, p. 407). In other words, by design, items were not selected to be relevant to "before exercise" baseline conditions, even though the questionnaire was intended for use under such conditions as well. Half of the items of the Exercise-induced Feeling Inventory are past participles that seem to presuppose a prior eliciting stimulus or to set up a comparison to a prior state (e.g., *refreshed, revived*). Nevertheless, as one might expect, in all subsequent studies in which the Exercise-induced Feeling Inventory was employed, this measure was also administered *before* exercise while the respondents were resting passively. Since exercise-induced changes are evaluated against such sedentary baseline conditions but the items were specifically selected a priori to be relevant only during or after exercise (not while resting), how meaningful or unbiased would any such comparison be?

In sum, the notion of domain specificity entails several conceptual challenges and complications that may not be immediately apparent. The fact that a measure is domain specific should not be automatically seen by researchers as a de facto guarantee that it is a conceptually and psychometrically appropriate option. As in every other case, all aspects of the measure must be placed under a critical light and closely scrutinized.

Conclusion

The measurement of affect, mood, and emotion is an exceptionally challenging undertaking in any context. Research linking these constructs to various health behaviors is certainly no exception. As this survey of common problems indicates, the current situation deviates considerably from an optimal standard to which researchers typically aspire. The problems are diverse and widespread enough to suggest a generalized, or systemic, dysfunction.

In most cases, measures are presented without a supporting rationale. However, it should be clear that the decision-making process that led to the selection of a measure could contain crucial information that might be invaluable to readers. In cases in which some type of rationale is offered (e.g., alpha coefficients of internal consistency, goodness-of-fit statistics from a confirmatory factor analysis, or claims of "sensitivity to change"), there are signs that these statements are often made uncritically and without a deeper or more thorough contemplation of the underlying issues. In some of the most disconcerting cases, researchers measure one construct but draw conclusions about another.

It should also be noted that a deliberate decision was made to limit the coverage of the present chapter to conceptual and psychometric problems and not address a long list of other issues (e.g., inadvertently using measures with different items or number of items compared to the originals, using non-validated abbreviations or modifications of measures, using a different response scale than the original, or modifying copyrighted instruments without permission). Although these issues are serious and this database is voluminous, the problems are of a different nature from those targeted here. Nevertheless, these may also be symptoms of a generalized tendency to treat the measurement of affect, mood, and emotion in a haphazard manner uncharacteristic of rigorous research. Overall, it seems fair to conclude that there is a serious crisis, one that must be remedied before the full potential of this line of inquiry can be realized. The subsequent chapters of this book have been developed with this ambitious goal in mind.

2 Untangling the terminological Gordian knot

The introductory chapter presented evidence that the conceptualization and measurement of affect, mood, and emotion within the field of health-behavioral research is presently not optimal. Among the problems identified, the most prevalent is the tendency to employ measures without presenting a supporting rationale. There are indications that this widespread phenomenon may reflect a serious underlying problem, namely that measures are often selected without following a systematic and well-grounded decision-making process.

Primary among the problems surveyed in the first chapter is the fact that the important distinctions between the constructs of affect, mood, and emotion are commonly ignored and the terms are used interchangeably. Thus, the aim of the present chapter is to codify the major differences between the constructs of affect, mood, and emotion. The main challenge inherent in this task is that these distinctions are neither clear-cut nor universally agreed upon. So, in attempting this tentative codification, one looks for the "lowest common denominator," namely any detectable signs of consensus in the contemporary theoretical literature on this topic. Even with this challenge, drawing some lines of demarcation remains of paramount importance. For researchers contemplating the selection of a measure, forming a crystalized decision about which construct they want to study should be considered the essential first step, a sine qua non.

The differences between affect, emotion, and mood

Almost two decades ago, reflecting a view commonly held at the time, a review on the effects of physical activity on mental health began with the phrase "this chapter ... views affect and mood as being synonymous with emotion" (Boutcher, 1993, p. 800). A few years later, a research article opened with the sentence: "The quest to understand the psychology of *emotion* has generated persistent investigation of the construct of *mood*" (Terry et al., 1999, p. 861, italics added).

Still today, it would not be surprising to encounter an article freely interchanging the terms *affect*, *mood*, and *emotion*. For example, as noted in Chapter 1, state anxiety, conceptualized and defined by Spielberger (1972a) as an *emotional* state, is so commonly labeled a *mood* (e.g., Bartholomew & Linder, 1998; Berger & Motl, 2000; Raglin, Turner, & Eksten, 1993) that, as readers, most of us have probably become desensitized to this problem. Yet, if one attempts to find a reason to justify or rationalize this common practice, one would be hard-pressed to locate anything convincing. State anxiety is defined as "the *emotional* reaction or response that is evoked when a person perceives a particular situation as personally dangerous or frightening" (Spielberger, Lushene, & McAdoo, 1977, p. 242, emphasis added). The manual of the State-Trait Anxiety Inventory (Spielberger, 1983) does not include even a single occurrence of the term *mood*. Furthermore, researchers with a clinical background are well aware that anxiety disorders and mood disorders are classified in separate categories, with distinct symptomatology and diagnostic criteria, in the *Diagnostic and Statistical Manual* of the American Psychiatric Association (2000) and the *International Classification of Diseases* (World Health Organization, 2008). Finally, because anxiety and mood disorders are often comorbid conditions, researchers have undertaken large-scale efforts to ensure that they can be properly differentiated from a measurement perspective (e.g., Clark & Watson, 1991).

Despite the many signs pointing to important distinctions between emotion and mood, it seems that chronic exposure to imprecise terminology and blurred conceptual distinctions has caused many of us to start glossing over mistakes that, under normal conditions, we would have criticized as unacceptable. As scientists, most of us can presumably agree that, in research, the indiscriminate and imprecise use of terms does nothing but engender confusion and controversy.

Before delving into the definitions, it is important to underscore two points. First, health-behavioral research is not alone in facing the problem of inconsistent terminology. The problem certainly did not originate in this field. It stems from the emulation of practices that were (and, in some cases, still are) common in other fields. For example, the mislabeling of the state-anxiety portion of the State-Trait Anxiety Inventory as a measure of "mood" is also found in other literatures. In the article describing the development of the Positive and Negative Affect Schedule, for example, Watson, Clark, and Tellegen (1988) claimed that the state-anxiety portion of the State-Trait Anxiety Inventory "has repeatedly demonstrated its usefulness as a sensitive measure of unpleasant mood states" (p. 1068).

Besides the many other domains of applied and clinical psychology, where similar confusion did and still does reign supreme, the truth is that the first signs of a consensus did not start to emerge even within affective psychology until the early 2000s. According to Morris (1992), several recognized leaders in the field were among the authors who did not distinguish between the constructs of affect, mood, and emotion. Some might have distinguished between two of these constructs but not between all three (e.g., emotion from mood but not mood from affect). For example, Watson and Clark (1994a) drew some distinctions between emotion and mood, but, with regard to mood and affect, they made statements such as "we can broadly define a *mood* as a transient episode of feeling or *affect*" or "waking consciousness is experienced as a continuous stream of *affect*, such that people are always experiencing some type of *mood*" (p. 90, italics added).

To illustrate the recency of the developments on this issue, notice the difference between the following positions, published only a few years apart. As recently as 2003, Watson and Vaidya (2003) considered the construct of *mood* indistinguishable from *affect*. This was also reflected in the fact that the Positive and Negative Affect Schedule, despite being labeled a measure of *affect*, was characterized by Watson, Clark, and Tellegen (1988) as "a reliable, valid, and efficient means for measuring ... two important dimensions of *mood*" (p. 1069, italics added). Mood was conceptualized as the "subjective" or "experiential" or "feeling" component of all related states, including emotions: "the concept of *mood* subsumes all subjective feeling states, not simply those experiences that accompany classical, prototypical emotions such as fear and anger" (Watson, Clark, & Carey, 1988, p. 351). In that sense, Watson (2002) has also stated that the two dimensions he considers the basic dimensions of "mood" (i.e., positive affect and negative affect) also "constitute the basic dimensions of *emotional experience*" (p. 107, italics added).

However, Watson seems to have revised his position and apparently adopted the same terminological system outlined here. Thus, according to Gray and Watson (2007), compared to emotion and mood, "affect is a broader, more inclusive psychological construct that refers to mental states involving evaluative feelings, that is, states in which a person feels good or bad or likes or dislikes what is happening" (p. 171). Furthermore, regarding the differences between mood and emotion, Gray and Watson (2007) emphasized that, although these constructs are closely related, "they also reflect a number of fundamental differences, including duration, frequency, intensity, and pattern of activation" (p. 171). Importantly, Gray and Watson (2007) advised that "these differences should be considered carefully by the researcher before choosing a specific assessment technique" (p. 171).

The important point here is not to condemn past research in which the terms *affect, mood,* and *emotion* were used interchangeably or inconsistently but rather to underscore that the potential pitfalls associated with undifferentiated terminology are now more widely recognized. As a result, a quasi-consensual system has emerged and its adoption is being recommended as a way to "bring some degree of order to the conceptual and definitional chaos that characterizes this area of research" (Buck, 1990, p. 330). Importantly, although the system of definitions and distinctions presented here is not universally accepted, it has started to make its way into psychology textbooks (e.g., see Fox, 2008, pp. 23–30; Oatley et al., 2006, pp. 29–30), an observation that is consistent with the characterization of this system as slowly but steadily approaching the status of consensus.

Second, it is crucial to clarify that definitions are ultimately mere conventions. As such, they reflect the prevailing intellectual or theoretical trends (the zeitgeist) within a particular field during a particular historical period. They are rarely universally agreed upon and they do not remain invariant over time. According to Scherer (2005):

Definitions cannot be proven. They need to be consensually considered as useful by a research community in order to guide research, make research comparable across laboratories and disciplines, and allow some degree of cumulativeness, and they are quite central for the development of instruments and measurement operations – as well as for the communication of results and the discussion between scientists. (p. 724)

At present, the prevailing theoretical perspective in the field of emotion research is cognitive, emphasizing the central role of appraisal processes. However, it should be clear that not all researchers currently working in this vast area subscribe to the cognitive paradigm. Many (e.g., most scholars in biological psychology) would probably not agree with the definitions presented here.

Recognizing the pitfalls of imprecise and inconsistent terminology

In the early 1990s, Batson, Shaw, and Oleson (1992) noted that, within psychology, "most often, the terms *affect, mood,* and *emotion* are used interchangeably, without any attempt at conceptual differentiation" (p. 295). Today, progress is being made in drawing at least some lines of demarcation (Alpert & Rosen, 1990; Batson et al., 1992; Beedie, Terry, & Lane, 2005; Russell, 2003, 2005; Russell & Feldman Barrett, 1999).

Thanks to considerable convergence among these views, a workable classification scheme has started to emerge and is being adopted by an increasing number of researchers working in this area.

The need to draw distinctions between the different constructs that comprise the global affective domain became evident in general psychology especially during the 1990s and 2000s. The main impetus for initiating an effort to draw such distinctions was the realization that clarifying semantic issues could help resolve substantive debates that had consumed considerable intellectual energy. According to Scherer (2005), "without consensual conceptualization and operationalization of exactly what phenomenon is to be studied, progress in theory and research is difficult to achieve and fruitless debates are likely to proliferate" (p. 695).

Let us examine one debate, which, although far from being "fruitless," did help to underscore the importance of precise and consensual definitions. From the prevailing cognitive perspective, *emotion* depends on cognition. According to Lazarus' (1991b) highly influential theory, cognition is considered "both a necessary and sufficient condition" for emotion: "*Sufficient* means that thoughts are capable of producing emotions; *necessary* means that emotions cannot occur without some kind of thought" (p. 353). However, this strong claim has been questioned by others who believe that *affective responses* can be generated without an antecedent cognitive appraisal (notice the change in terms, from *emotion* to *affect*).

In a widely cited article, Zajonc (1980) argued that "the fact that cognitions can produce feelings – as in listening to a joke, for example, where affect comes at the end with a punch line or as a result of postdecision dissonance – need not imply that cognitions are necessary components of affect" (p. 154). In support of this view, Kunst-Wilson and Zajonc (1980) presented data showing that participants could form preferences for meaningless visual stimuli (Chinese ideograms viewed by American participants) that were superimposed upon images of happy or angry faces at a speed faster than the threshold for conscious awareness (i.e., before the participants could consciously recognize what they had seen). Interestingly, in his 1980 article, Zajonc referred consistently to *affect*, not emotion, and carefully pointed out that "the class of feelings considered here is that involved in the general quality of behavior that underlies the approach–avoidance distinction," whereas "emotions such as surprise, anger, guilt, or shame … are ignored" (p. 152).

Nevertheless, this crucial point was evidently missed by Lazarus (1982), who opened his rebuttal by characterizing Zajonc's (1980) article as a "challenge to the assumption that cognition occurs prior to *emotion*" (p. 1019, italics added). Importantly, the states Lazarus considered *emotions* and, therefore, valid objects of his cognitive theory were precisely those Zajonc had specified as falling outside the scope of his argument (i.e., anger, anxiety, guilt, sadness, envy, disgust, happiness, pride, love, relief). This type of miscommunication exemplifies the pitfalls associated with the indiscriminate use of the terms *emotion*, *mood*, and *affect*. Other authors detected that the disagreement largely revolved around semantics and started proposing tentative rules for differentiating between the multitude of relevant constructs (Leventhal & Scherer, 1987).

Unfortunately, despite several important steps in the right direction, problems arising from the absence of a universally agreed upon terminological system continue to plague the exchange of ideas in affective psychology. For example, in a response to critiques of their article on the motivational properties of anger, Carver and Harmon-Jones (2009a) wrote with palpable exasperation:

It may be time for all of us to be more pointed about the fact that [mood and affect] are not the same. If we fail to recognize that the structure of mood is a topic that differs in important ways from the bases of specific affects, we will continue to expend our energies in what may amount to talking past one another. (p. 217)

What is core affect?

In an article creatively subtitled "Dissecting the elephant" (to indicate the vastness of this content domain), Russell and Feldman Barrett (1999) defined "core affect" as "the most elementary consciously accessible affective feelings (and their neurophysiological counterparts) that need not be directed at anything" (p. 806). Similarly, according to an updated version of this definition, "core affect is defined as a neurophysiological state consciously accessible as a simple primitive nonreflective feeling most evident in mood and emotion but always available to consciousness" (Russell & Feldman Barrett, 2009, p. 104). Russell (2003) emphasizes that "as consciously experienced, core affect is mental but not cognitive or reflective" (p. 148) and this noncognitive and nonreflective character is its most crucial defining attribute. Examples of core affect include pleasure, displeasure, tension, calmness, energy, and tiredness. A person experiences core affect constantly, although the nature and intensity of affect varies over time. Bodily movements, for example, such as "dancing or jogging" can induce changes in core affect (Russell, 2005).

This meaning of affect can probably be traced to Scherer (1984), who proposed that the term *affective states* be used as a broad "umbrella" rubric. Specifically, he wrote:

Apart from the lack of theory, we have a serious terminological problem: Which generic term are we to use for states of the organism that have both organic and psychological components, only some of which we will want to call emotions? I suggest the term "affective states" as such a generic term. The original meaning of the Latin root *"afficere"* seems perfectly suitable to denote the various types of states to be subsumed under such a term: (1) to bring somebody into a bodily or organic state, condition or disposition, (2) to bring somebody into a mental or psychological mood, to excite or stimulate or to move or touch, (3) to attack, weaken or exhaust someone. (p. 298)

Many authors have since followed Scherer's suggestion. Batson et al. (1992) wrote that "of affect, mood, and emotion, affect is the most general" (p. 298). Similarly, Gross (1998) noted: "Following Scherer (1984), I use affect as the superordinate category for valenced states, including emotions such as anger and sadness, emotion episodes such as a barroom brawl and delivering bad news to a close friend, moods such as depression and euphoria, dispositional states such as liking and hating, and traits such as cheerfulness and irascibility" (p. 273). Likewise, echoing these views, Fredrickson (2001) noted that "affect, a more general concept, refers to consciously accessible feelings. Although affect is present within emotions (as the component of subjective experience), it is also present within many other affective phenomena, including physical sensations, attitudes, moods, and even affective traits" (p. 218).

Thus, core affect can occur in "pure" or isolate form, but it is also a component of emotions and moods (defined next). In other words, core affect is "experienced embedded with other elements of consciousness as one interacts with the world" (Russell, 2005, p. 29; see Figure 2.1). Russell and Feldman Barrett (1999) offered the following example:

Consider the word *happy*. On receiving a gift, Sally feels happy, smiles, and hugs the person who gave her the gift. Another time, Sally feels happy for no known reason. The first case would be a prototypical emotional episode, the second not. Both involve core affect. (p. 806)

Russell (2003) clarified this point further: "*pride* can be thought of as feeling good about oneself. The 'feeling good' is core affect and the 'about oneself' is an additional (cognitive) component" (p. 148), which, as explained next, qualifies *pride* as an *emotion*. In a nutshell, "core affect is part of, not the whole of, moods and emotions" (Russell & Feldman Barrett, 2009, p. 104).

In their analysis, Batson et al. (1992) incorporated an insightful evolutionary dimension, noting that affect is "phylogenetically and

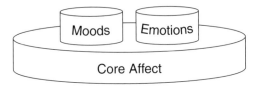

Figure 2.1. Core affect is a broader concept than mood and emotion. It provides the experiential substrate upon which the rich tapestry of moods and emotions is woven.

ontogenetically the most primitive" and, as such, it is "present in the yelp of a dog and in the coo or cry of an infant" (p. 298). So what function did core affect evolve to serve within an evolutionary context? According to Batson et al. (1992), "affect seems to reveal preference; it informs the organism experiencing it about those states of affairs that it values more than others" (p. 298). Specifically, "change from a less valued to a more valued state is accompanied by positive affect; change from a more valued to a less valued state is accompanied by negative affect" and "the intensity of the affect reveals the magnitude of the value preference" (p. 298). Given this function, "basic affect seems crucial to the very existence of motivation" (pp. 308–309), since "without it, we would probably have no inclination to move toward or away from anything" (p. 309). The view that pleasant affect signals utility and, therefore, approach toward a stimulus, whereas unpleasant affect signals danger and, therefore, avoidance of a stimulus is widely held among the many authors who espouse an evolutionary functionalist perspective (e.g., Cabanac, 1979; Panksepp, 1998, 2005).

What is emotion?

In an earlier attempt to resolve the "terminological confusion" (p. 345), Kleinginna and Kleinginna (1981) retrieved and categorized no fewer than 92 definitions of the concept of emotion. From this analysis, they arrived at the following synthetic definition:

Emotion is a complex set of interactions among subjective and objective factors, mediated by neural-hormonal systems, which can (a) give rise to affective experiences such as feelings of arousal, pleasure/displeasure; (b) generate cognitive processes such as emotionally relevant perceptual effects, appraisals, labeling processes; (c) activate widespread physiological adjustments to the arousing conditions; and (d) lead to behavior that is often, but not always, expressive, goal-directed, and adaptive. (p. 355)

Most contemporary definitions also reflect the notion that the construct of emotion comprises multiple interconnected and coordinated components (i.e., feeling, appraisal, physiology, expression, action). According to Scherer (2005, pp. 697–698) and Frijda and Scherer (2009, p. 143), emotions involve a coordinated response of the following five major systems: (a) the information-processing cognitive (appraisal) component, (b) the neurophysiological component (bodily changes), (c) the executive component, which prepares and directs responsive actions, (d) the expressive component, which communicates the emotion via vocal and facial expressions, and (e) an experiential component, which monitors the internal state of the organism and its interaction with the environment and generates subjective feelings (i.e., "emotional experiences"). Scherer (2005) theorized that "all subsystems underlying emotion components function independently much of the time and that the special nature of emotion as a hypothetical construct consists of the coordination and synchronization of all of these systems during an emotion episode, driven by appraisal" (pp. 698–699). Thus, Scherer (2005) defined emotion as "an episode of interrelated, synchronized changes in the states of all or most of the five organismic subsystems in response to the evaluation of an external or internal stimulus event as relevant to major concerns of the organism" (p. 697). On the basis of this definition, Frijda and Scherer (2009) argued that emotions (a) are focused on specific events, (b) involve a process of cognitive appraisal as a defining feature, (c) affect most or all bodily subsystems, which may become, to some extent, synchronized, (d) are subject to rapid changes due to the continuous unfolding of events and reappraisals, and (e) have a strong impact on behavior due to their inherent linkage to specific action tendencies consonant with each emotion.

Along similar lines, according to Russell and Feldman Barrett (1999), a "prototypical emotional episode" can be defined as a "complex set of interrelated subevents concerned with a specific object" (p. 806), such as a person, an event, or a thing; past, present, or future; real or imagined. The cooccurring components that compose a prototypical emotional episode include: (a) core affect (as defined earlier), (b) overt behavior congruent with the emotion (e.g., a smile or a facial expression of fear), (c) attention directed toward the eliciting stimulus, (d) cognitive appraisal of the meaning and possible implications of the stimulus, (e) attribution of the genesis of the episode to the stimulus, (f) the experience of the particular emotion, and (g) neural (peripheral and central) and endocrine changes consistent with the particular emotion.

Given the fact that emotions entail such a large-scale and engross-
ing mobilization of organismic resources, their intensity tends to be
high and their duration rather short. According to Scherer (2005), "as
emotions imply massive response mobilization and synchronization as
part of specific action tendencies, their duration must be relatively short
in order not to tax the resources of the organism and to allow behavioral flexibility" (p. 702). This echoes a point made earlier by Ekman
(1992):

It is not only adaptive for emotions to be capable of mobilizing the organism
very quickly (onset), but for the response changes so mobilized not to last very
long unless the emotion is evoked again. If one emotion-arousing event typically produced a set of response changes which endured for hours regardless of
what was occurring in the external world, emotions would be less responsive
than I think they are to rapidly changing circumstances. (pp. 185–186)

Because emotions are elicited *by* something, are reactions *to* something, and are generally *about* something, the cognitive appraisal
involved in the person–object transaction is considered a defining element (Lazarus, 1991a, 1991b). As noted earlier, the inclusion of appraisal
as one of the defining elements of emotion, let alone the main defining
element as in Lazarus' theory, is not universally agreed upon. Some
theorists prefer to consider emotion and cognition as independent
(albeit interacting) constructs. The endorsement of appraisal here as
one of several constituents of an emotion episode is a reflection of the
view many prominent emotion theorists now share. Davidson (2003),
criticizing those who believe that emotion and cognition are subserved
by separate and independent neural circuits, noted:

We now understand that emotion is comprised of many different subcomponents and is best understood not as a single monolithic process but rather as
a set of differentiated subcomponents that are instantiated in a distributed
network of cortical and subcortical circuits. Included within these subcomponents are different types of emotional cue recognition processes, processes involved in the production of behavioral, autonomic, and subjective
changes associated with emotion, processes that serve to regulate emotion
and processes that are required for remembering and retrieving emotional
events. (p. 129)

Several contemporary emotion theorists who subscribe to the cognitive paradigm have gone a step further, aligning their views with
Lazarus' claim that cognitive appraisal is a prerequisite and, therefore, a
defining element of emotions. For example, among many others, Frijda
(2008) wrote that "emotions can ... be defined as processes that involve
appraisal" (p. 71) and Clore and Ortony (2008) expressed the view that
"emotions are cognitively elaborated affective states" (p. 629).

Emotion theorists who consider each emotion a distinct entity have proposed appraisal *themes* that give rise to specific emotions. For example, according to Lazarus (1991a), the appraisal theme that corresponds to the emotion of anxiety is "facing uncertain, existential threat," the theme that underlies guilt is "having transgressed a moral imperative," the theme that characterizes shame is "failing to live up to an ego ideal," and the theme that is linked to pride is "enhancement of one's ego identity by taking credit for a valued object or achievement" (p. 122). Other theorists believe the appraisal themes proposed to underlie each distinct emotion have some noticeable commonalities (Ellsworth & Smith, 1988a, 1988b; Smith & Ellsworth, 1985). As a result, some emotions tend to cooccur and covary. Furthermore, evidence shows that some transitions from one emotion to another tend to occur more frequently than others. These phenomena imply some functional links. As an example, in the seminal study of Smith and Ellsworth (1985), responses along six dimensions of appraisal (pleasantness, anticipated effort, certainty, attentional activity, self–other responsibility/control, and situational control) could predict the correct emotion among 15 alternatives (happiness, sadness, fear, anger, boredom, challenge, interest, hope, frustration, contempt, disgust, surprise, pride, shame, and guilt) more than 40 percent of the time, a probability more than six times higher than chance.

Finally, a rich tradition that has contributed substantively to the understanding of emotion consists of functionalist accounts, namely theoretical efforts concerned not with what emotions are but rather with what emotions do (see review by Keltner & Gross, 1999). Some authors believe that only through an examination of functionalist accounts can we differentiate emotions from other affective phenomena. This is because the other attributes listed in this section may apply in some, but not all, cases, which may render them of dubious value as defining features from the standpoint of scientific inquiry (Davidson, 1994). According to the summary offered by Ellsworth (2009), the functions of emotions are to (a) direct attention to changes in the physical and social environment that have implications for the survival and well-being of the individual, (b) to motivate the individual to undertake appropriate action (such as to approach or avoid), (c) to connect the perception and interpretation of events to relevant behavioral responses, and (d) in the presence of several, potentially competing, goals, to set priorities by directing attention and action to those most important for survival and well-being.

What is mood?

Nowlis and Nowlis (1956) first identified two distinguishing features of emotion and mood that could be quantified, namely duration and intensity. Specifically, they noted that "mood is usually regarded as a more or less persistent state" and "the duration of emotion is shorter than that of mood" (p. 353). Furthermore, "the initial emotional response may be more intense and may be associated with explosive action," whereas "mood may be relatively less intense" (p. 353).

The element of duration, in particular, also became one of Ekman's (1992) oft-cited criteria for distinguishing basic emotions from moods. According to Ekman, "emotions usually last only for seconds, not minutes, hours or days," whereas moods "last for hours or days" (p. 186). Although emotions might give the impression of lasting for a long time (e.g., the fear of being fired in anticipation of a rumored corporate downsizing), Ekman suggested that such cases involve multiple episodes of emotion that occur in succession:

Examining the duration of both expressive and physiological changes during spontaneous emotional events suggests a short time span. When subjects have reported experiencing an emotion for 15 or 20 minutes, and I have had access to a videotaped record of their preceding behavior, I found that they showed multiple expressions of that emotion. My interpretation of such incidents is that people summate in their verbal report what was actually a series of repeated but discrete emotion episodes. (p. 186)

Other authors have emphasized that perhaps a more meaningful distinguishing feature of moods is that they are "diffuse and global" due to their "obscurity of origin" (Morris, 1992, p. 258). According to Frijda (2009), a mood is "an affective state of long duration, low intensity, and a certain diffuseness" (p. 258). This "diffuseness" is due to the fact that moods "are not about a particular object or event" (p. 258). Thus, *mood* is "the appropriate designation for affective states that are about nothing specific or about everything – about the world in general" (p. 258). Russell (2003, 2005) has argued that because frequently, though not always, moods lack an object (they are not *about* anything in particular), they may not seem much different from free-floating core affect. In many cases, however, moods may have a *vague* object. For example, when someone is in a "tense mood," the object might be something as general as one's whole future or as distant as one's happiness in 20 years. When in a "depressive mood," the object might be the totality of one's self. When in an "irritable mood," the object could be anything and anyone. In such cases, moods essentially do have a cause. However, unlike emotions, which follow their eliciting stimuli closely or even instantaneously, the cause of a mood is usually "temporally remote" (Morris, 1992) from the experience of the mood (e.g., when waking up in a "bad mood" in the morning as a result of a confrontation the previous evening). Consequently, the cause may not always be easily identifiable. According to Ekman (1994), "people usually can specify the event that called forth an emotion, and often cannot do so for a mood" (p. 57).

When a mood is *about* something, no matter how global, diffuse, or unspecific, then *mood* shares with *emotion* the fact that it stems from an appraisal. According to Lazarus (1991a), "both moods and acute emotions are reactions to the way one appraises relationships with the environment; moods refer to the larger, pervasive, existential issues of one's life, whereas acute emotions refer to an immediate piece of business, a specific and relatively narrow goal in an adaptational encounter with the environment" (p. 48). Lazarus (1994) elaborated further on what is appraised in the case of moods:

Moods ... are products of appraisals of the *existential background* of our lives. This background has to do with who we are, now and in the long run, and how we are doing in life overall. Although, if pressed, we might try to explain a mood by pointing to a specific event, when we are in a mood we rarely pin it down to anything specific, which is why moods are so vague and pervasive. However, the events we can legitimately point to in explaining a mood are apt to be profound in that they have major existential implications, such as the death of a loved one, loss of occupational roles, an assault on cherished lifelong beliefs, a life-threatening or disabling illness, and the like. When our mood is negative, it is not because a particular encounter has gone wrong but because life overall seems sour, which could be a partial result of that encounter; we denigrate ourselves and others, the world, the meanings on which our sense of self depend, our loved ones, our future, and we live out the scenario of the "theater of the absurd," which treats human existence as meaningless and ridiculous... On the other hand, when our mood is positive, it is because life seems good; our loved ones love and respect us, the world is just, the meanings on which we depend are reaffirmed, and our immediate and existential problems recede. (pp. 84–85)

Other authors who also accept that moods derive from appraisals have focused on more circumscribed questions but seem to converge on the postulates that (a) the appraisals refer to what the future might bring and (b) the exact point in the future at which the events in question might occur need not be specified. For example, Morris (1992, 1999) has proposed that the central appraisal theme that underlies the emergence of moods is whether one anticipates that she or he will have adequate resources to deal with challenges in the process of striving for one's goals. Batson et al. (1992) similarly link moods to the "expectation of future pleasure and pain" (p. 299).

As was the case with emotions, several functionalist accounts of mood can aid greatly in defining this construct and distinguishing it from emotion (Batson et al., 1992; Morris, 1992). According to Davidson (1994), the primary function of moods is to "modulate or bias cognition" (p. 52). Specifically:

Mood serves as a primary mechanism for altering information-processing priorities and for shifting modes of information processing. Mood will accentuate the accessibility of some and attenuate the accessibility of other cognitive contents and semantic networks. For example, individuals in a depressed mood have increased accessibility to sad memories and decreased accessibility to happy memories. (p. 52)

Perhaps associated with the empirically established phenomenon of mood-congruent memory, it appears that moods also facilitate appraisals of situational events in a way that is consonant with the mood. The result is that, while in a given mood, the threshold for the genesis of a related emotion is lowered and, thus, related moods and emotions frequently cooccur. For example, according to Frijda (2009), moods "appear to lower thresholds for mood-congruent event-elicited appraisals and emotions. Mood-consonant appraisals are facilitated; there is faster detection of mood-consonant events" (p. 258). Similarly, according to Ekman (1994):

Moods seem to lower the threshold for arousing the emotions, which occur most frequently during a particular mood. When a person is in an irritable mood, for example, that person becomes angry more readily than usual. Events that might ordinarily not be as likely to bring forth anger now do so easily. In an irritable mood people construe the world around them in a way that permits, if not calls for, an angry response. It is as if the person is seeking an opportunity to indulge the emotion relevant to the mood. (p. 57)

What does this mean and why should we care?

Table 2.1 summarizes some of the distinctions between affect, mood, and emotion outlined in the previous sections. The most important conclusion to draw from this summary is this: the era of considering affect, mood, and emotion as synonymous and interchangeable terms is approaching a long overdue finale. So, for authors, reviewers, and editors, this means a concerted effort must be made to move forward in line with this historically important development. The uncritical interchange of terms can no longer be considered innocuous or justified on the basis of precedent. Likewise, a measure developed to assess one construct (e.g., a measure of *emotion*) should not be used as a basis for drawing conclusions about another (e.g., *mood*).

Table 2.1 *Tentative distinctions between core affect, emotion, and mood*

	Core affect	Emotion	Mood
Present when?	Always	Rarely	Much of the time
Duration?	Constant	Short (seconds to minutes)	Long (hours or days – or longer in clinical cases, such as depression)
Intensity?	Variable (ebbs and flows)	High	Lower than emotion (but could be high in clinical cases, such as depression)
Multiple components?	No, elementary ("the most elementary consciously accessible affective feelings")	Yes (core affect, cognitive appraisal, bodily changes, vocal and facial expressions, action tendencies)	Yes but some components (e.g., peripheral physiology, facial expressions, action tendencies) are not as pronounced or distinct as in emotions
About something?	Not necessarily	Yes	Possibly, although not necessarily about something specific (could be "about everything, about the world in general")
Antecedent appraisal?	Not necessary in "free-floating" core affect (but may cooccur with an appraisal in emotion or mood)	Necessary	Necessary
Object of appraisal?	N/A	Specific stimulus, clearly identifiable	Varies but could be larger, "existential" issues or concerns or not easily identifiable
Temporal relation to stimulus?	Direct	Immediate or close	May be distant
Evolutionary origins?	Ancient, primitive	More recent than core affect	More recent than core affect
Cultural influence?	Limited	Presumed strong	Presumed strong

(cont.)

Table 2.1 (*cont.*)

	Core affect	Emotion	Mood
Function?	Approach useful and avoid harmful stimuli, prioritize multiple sensory stimuli, form valenced memories and preferences	Direct attention, coordinate response across multiple channels, communicate	Prepare or caution about what the future might bring, influence cognition, lower threshold for elicitation of congruent emotions
Examples?	Pleasure, displeasure, tension, relaxation, energy, tiredness	Anger, fear, anxiety, jealousy, pride, shame, guilt, love, sadness, grief, disgust	Dysphoria, euphoria, irritation, joyfulness, cheerfulness, grumpiness

Note: See text for additional explanations and references.

The distinctions enumerated here admittedly do not constitute an exhaustive or definitive list. In fact, an exhaustive or definitive system for differentiating affect, mood, and emotion may never emerge given the inherent "fuzziness" of these constructs. Moreover, the list of distinguishing features may evolve over time. However, it must be recognized that, at the present juncture, there seems to be enough convergence in the literature to characterize this tentative system as quasi-consensual. In any case, with all of its limitations notwithstanding, *this* system could arguably help bring some order where previously there was chaos. Measurement, and indeed the entire enterprise of scientific research, hinges on definitions. The need for a common system of demarcating constructs and communicating ideas is self-evident.

So, which construct should one study? This, of course, depends on the research question one wishes to investigate. In some research scenarios, the objective is to examine what, if any, effects certain manipulations have on how people feel (e.g., exposing individuals to different doses of alcohol or different degrees of sleep deprivation). In essence, these are descriptive or exploratory investigations. The most undesirable outcome in such cases would be for the experimental manipulation to impact how people felt in some way but for the measure to fail to register any changes. This situation would lead to the erroneous conclusion that there was no change when in fact a change did take place, albeit in a sector of the domain of interest not monitored by the researcher. In other words, the most prudent approach in such cases would be to employ a broad investigative scope, one that covers all possible variants of affect-ive experience (including, but not limited to, emotion and mood). Core affect seems the most appropriate construct to target in such scenarios. Focusing on the most general construct (i.e., core affect) implies that the researcher makes no assumptions about whether the resultant state is an emotion, a change in mood, or free-floating affect.

In other research scenarios, the objective is to examine the ability of an affective construct to predict concurrent or subsequent behav-ioral decision making (e.g., the decision to participate in physical activ-ity, smoke, drink, or abuse drugs). In this case, opinions diverge and a researcher would have to substantiate his or her decision. On one hand, some theorists have argued that what influences behavioral deci-sion making is the essential "goodness" or "badness" of how one feels (Kahneman, 1999). Empirical investigations based on this premise, for example, have measured the effects of pain experienced during medical procedures or discomfort felt while holding one's hand in a bucket of ice water (a common laboratory stressor). In this case, the appropriate con-struct would be the basic pleasure-displeasure dimension of core affect. On the other hand, some theorists have argued that specific emotions might play a much more salient role in behavioral decision making in real-life situations than pleasure-displeasure (Fredrickson, 2000; Lerner & Keltner, 2000). The main argument for this position is that pleasure or displeasure become much more potent influences on behav-ior if experienced as an integral component of a personally meaningful emotion compared to a situation in which the pleasure and displeas-ure occur in free-floating form (e.g., are purely somatic). A researcher would have to substantiate the focus on core affect or specific emotions after taking these arguments into account.

There are also research scenarios in which researchers are interested in the effects of manipulating specific environmental, interpersonal, or other situational conditions. In such studies, for example, researchers have examined the role of exercise in alleviating the appraisal of threat inherent in an academic examination (Doan, Plante, Digregorio, & Manuel, 1995), the role of inducing a negative self-appraisal by having women anxious about their physique exercise in front of a full-length mirror (Focht & Hausenblas, 2003), or the effects of manipulat-ing one's sense of physical self-efficacy (Marquez, Jerome, McAuley, Snook, & Canaklisova, 2002). Following the theoretical perspectives reviewed here, the appropriate construct to target in such cases would be emotion. In essence, these experimental manipulations are designed to induce specific patterns of cognitive appraisal. Theoretically, each pattern of appraisal should correspond to a specific emotion (e.g., fear, anxiety, or pride). Given the ample theorizing linking such manipulations to appraisals and ultimately to emotions, it is reasonable to hypothesize that changes in affect would emerge embedded within an emotional response.

To turn this point around, if we accept that cognitive appraisals are at the core of emotional responses, it follows that studies examining, for example, the state anxiety of individuals with high trait anxiety (e.g., Breus & O'Connor, 1998) lack an adequate theoretical rationale inasmuch as the cognitive appraisal presumed to underlie state anxiety is not manipulated. According to state-trait theories, which are based on interactional models of personality, a trait-like disposition does not necessarily mean that individuals characterized by low and high levels of a given trait will always exhibit state differences. For this to happen, a relevant situational stimulus (e.g., something or someone that could be appraised as posing a threat) is required. Likewise, studies based on the assumption that an emotion can be induced by changing one category of emotion-related symptoms also do not seem consistent with contemporary theories. For example, no theoretical basis exists for assuming that state anxiety can be induced by raising autonomic activity (e.g., by ingesting caffeine; Youngstedt, O'Connor, Crabbe, & Dishman, 1998) in participants without a clinical propensity for anxiety or panic.

Mood can also be a relevant object of study in health-behavioral research. For example, it would seem perfectly reasonable to examine whether the induction of specific moods by appropriate experimental manipulations (e.g., restlessness, depressed mood, or irritability) can influence the frequency of such behaviors as the consumption of alcohol or illicit drugs or whether an eight-week program of moderate physical activity lowers depression in individuals with a depression diagnosis. However, given the definition of mood discussed in this chapter, mood was probably not the most appropriate variable to target in many of the studies in which measures of mood were used. Except in individuals suffering from a mood disorder, moods are transient phenomena; they are not always present. Furthermore, it is important to keep in mind that the appraisals postulated to underlie moods are about large and pervasive issues (i.e., about "who we are, now and in the long run, and how we are doing in life overall," according to Lazarus, 1994, p. 84, or "about everything – about the world in general," according to Frijda, 2009, p. 258). So, unless a study is performed with a sample in which a mood is chronically present (e.g., individuals during a major depressive episode) or a particular mood is experimentally induced (e.g., by smoking abstinence), studies investigating changes in mood in response to a short intervention (e.g., drinking an alcoholic beverage, smoking a cigarette, or participating in a bout of physical activity) seem to lack a well-substantiated rationale. Moreover, considering the time course of moods (i.e., hours to days or longer), brief interventions (i.e., those lasting for just a few minutes) may not be long or powerful enough to change mood per se. What probably changes in such cases is core affect and it is the core affect that is reflected in self-reports of mood. To make a case that what changed was mood rather than core affect, a researcher would have to demonstrate that the change was enduring rather than immediately transient. In other words, the assessment protocol would have to be consistent with the slow and protracted time course of mood (i.e., extend for hours or days following the intervention).

Conclusion

As was argued in the introductory chapter, the first step toward a solution to the present crisis is realizing that there is a problem. If research on health behaviors continues along the path of freely interchanging the terms *affect*, *mood*, and *emotion*, it runs the risk of forming an insular camp, isolated from developments in affective psychology. However, arguably, this isolationism is unlikely to build a strong foundation for future growth. Since affective constructs seem to play important roles in many health behaviors, maintaining strong ties to affective psychology seems essential.

3   Should affective states be considered as distinct entities or as positioned along dimensions?

This book was based on the premise that the measurement of affective constructs, including core affect, mood, and emotion, within the domain of research investigating health behaviors would benefit from a thorough and critical reconsideration of concepts and practices. For this goal to be achieved, this domain of research must catch up to theoretical developments and contemporary measurement approaches in affective psychology. Numerous signs suggest that, over the years, certain methodological practices now shown to be either outdated or downright fallacious rose to the level of paradigm. For example, justifying the selection of a measure on the basis of the argument that "it has been used before" has appeared with such frequency in the literature that a tacit assumption must have developed that it represents an adequate or acceptable rationale. Likewise, interchanging terms or mislabeling constructs has become so common that these practices are widely emulated without eliciting criticisms from reviewers, editors, or readers.

To help overcome these problems, the previous chapter included a list of the essential features of affect, mood, and emotion that researchers can use as a guide in drawing the necessary distinctions between these constructs. Following the crucially important decision of which of these constructs should be targeted in a given investigation, the next question researchers will confront in their quest to establish a rationale for choosing a measure is how to best conceptualize or model the targeted construct (core affect, mood, or emotion). The options are many and their differences are anything but subtle. According to Russell and Feldman Barrett (1999), "some researchers use categories, some dimensions; some use bipolar concepts, some unipolar ones; some presuppose simple structure, some a circumplex, and some a hierarchy" (p. 805).

As an example, a researcher interested in studying the impact of a health behavior on emotion faces the dilemma of approaching each emotion as a distinct entity, considering some emotions as "basic" prototypes from which variants might emerge, or viewing the entire domain of emotion as defined by different sets of underlying dimensions (e.g., Ekman, Sorenson, & Friesen, 1969; Ellsworth & Smith, 1988a, 1988b; Fontaine, Scherer, Roesch, & Ellsworth, 2007; Russell & Bullock, 1985, 1986; Schlosberg, 1952, 1954). Likewise, a researcher about to embark on a study of the effect of a health behavior on mood must make a decision on whether to consider moods as bipolar dimensions (e.g., Lorr, McNair, & Fisher, 1982) or unipolar states (e.g., Rafaeli & Revelle, 2006). The arguments on each side are numerous and complex. Moreover, the implications of these decisions are crucial, so being adequately prepared to confront these dilemmas is imperative. It should be clear that, in the field of affect, mood, and emotion, no decision that touches on theory should be seen as obvious or de facto. All such decisions require a clearly articulated and adequately documented justification.

This chapter focuses on one of these critical modeling dilemmas, namely whether affective constructs represent distinct entities that should be considered independently of each other or they exhibit systematic interrelationships that can be modeled by a set of underlying dimensions. This is a question of central importance that will have a decisive impact on the choice of measure and, therefore, on the meaningfulness of the data to be collected.

Distinct entities or dimensions: why should we care?

When researchers choose a measure, they also, explicitly or implicitly, adopt the theoretical basis upon which that measure was developed. This implies that, during the measure selection process, it is extremely important to be aware not only of the theoretical basis of the measure itself but also of its limitations and arguments or evidence against it. However, in health-behavioral research, the selection of a measure is often not recognized for what it really ought to be, namely a profoundly theory-driven process.

Theoretical discussions on measurement issues in this literature are exceedingly rare. When researchers discuss the strengths and weaknesses of measures, the conversation tends to revolve mainly around practical rather than theoretical matters. For example, criticisms of the Profile of Mood States (McNair et al., 1971) have frequently centered on its length and the amount of time it takes to administer (e.g., Berger & Motl, 2000; Guadagnoli & Mor, 1989). However, one might argue that, from a broader perspective, these are rather secondary concerns. Arguably, a much more crucial question, for instance, is whether targeting the six distinct states assessed by the Profile of Mood States (i.e., Tension, Depression, Anger, Vigor, Fatigue, and Confusion) can truly capture the entire content domain of mood and, consequently, whether a researcher using this instrument would be justified in drawing conclusions about the effects of a certain intervention on the global domain of mood. Since we can all list several other veritable mood states not captured by the Profile of Mood States, is it not conceivable that changes might occur in those? In the case of exercise effects, for example, this potential problem of domain underrepresentation was pointed out early on by Morgan (1984), who wrote:

> Much, perhaps most, of the literature dealing with the psychologic effects of exercise has relied on the use of objective self-report inventories designed to measure constructs such as anxiety and depression … The extent to which these inventories can tap the psychometric domain of significance to the exerciser has not been evaluated. In other words, an investigator may employ an objective, reliable, valid test of anxiety or depression to quantify the psychologic effects of exercise, only to find that no "effects" have taken place when, in fact, there may have been numerous effects. (p. 134)

Researchers should know whether the measure they are about to use was designed to tap a global domain of content (such as the entire domain of *core affect, mood, or emotion*) or a specific state (such as *tension, calmness,* or *state anxiety*). Clearly, extrapolations from findings based on the assessment of a single, narrowly delimited state (such as *state anxiety*) to a global domain (such as *emotion* in general) would not be justified. Similarly, extrapolations from findings based on an assortment of distinct states (such as those assessed by the Profile of Mood States) to a global domain (such as *mood* in general) must be also be scrutinized. What is the evidence that this particular assortment of distinct states provides a comprehensive representation of the global domain?

Even when a measure explicitly promises to capture a global domain of content, researchers should critically evaluate this claim instead of accepting it passively. For example, a commonly employed measure, the Positive and Negative Affect Schedule (Watson, Clark, & Tellegen, 1988), has been presented as a measure of "the two primary dimensions of mood" (p. 1069). This statement seems to imply that, when combined, the dimensions of Positive Affect and Negative Affect can provide a comprehensive assessment of the global domain of mood. Presumably on the basis of this assumption, the Positive and Negative Affect Schedule has become one of the most widely used measures in many fields of basic and applied psychological research.

However, closer inspection reveals that the Positive and Negative Affect Schedule assesses only high-activation states and its scales "include no terms assessing fatigue and serenity" (Watson & Clark, 1997, p. 276). Given that both *fatigue* and *serenity* are probably of great interest to researchers examining the effects or the predictors of various health behaviors (e.g., Saxon, Skagerberg, Borg, & Hiltunen, 2010; Sonnentag et al., 2008), it seems that the decision to use the Positive and Negative Affect Schedule would require rigorous justification on this point. In essence, half of what most researchers would probably consider as the content domain of mood (containing all low-activation states) is actually missing from the Positive and Negative Affect Schedule. As Larsen and Diener (1992) explain, "for example, with the PANAS [Negative Affect] scale, a subject can only report having no emotional distress (zero on the [Negative Affect] scale). But from this we do not know whether that subject is feeling particularly calm and relaxed (the bipolar opposite of [Negative Affect]) or just average (the midpoint between the two ends of the dimension)" (p. 29). To reiterate the point made earlier, it is important for researchers to be fully aware of the strengths and limitations of the theoretical basis of the measures they select.

The distinct-states approach

One of the most important bifurcations in the measure selection algorithm researchers will confront is the question of whether to conceptualize and assess affective states as distinct entities or as positioned along dimensions. According to the "distinct-states" approach, each state is and should be examined as unique and distinct from all others (Izard, 1993; Roseman, Wiest, & Swartz, 1994). For example, the emotion of anxiety is associated with a unique pattern of antecedent appraisal (e.g., "facing uncertain, existential threat," according to Lazarus, 1991a); a unique experiential quality; characteristic attention-related biases (Eysenck, Derakshan, Santos, & Calvo, 2007); a possibly distinct "signature" of visceral and somatic symptoms (Levenson, 2003); tense facial, postural, and vocal expressions (Banse & Scherer, 1996); and a repertoire of coping responses (Folkman & Lazarus, 1985). For researchers specifically interested in anxiety, focusing on this one emotion and dissecting its components affords an unparalleled opportunity for a deep and detailed analysis.

In a variant of the distinct-states approach, several researchers initiated efforts to construct lists of so-called basic emotions (e.g., Ekman, 1992). These emotions are characterized as "basic" because they differ from each other in terms of criteria designated as important (e.g., antecedent appraisal, experiential quality, behavioral manifestations, psychophysiological patterns, regulatory efforts). However, the criteria considered important by different theorists vary. Since the criteria for judging the *basicness* of different emotions differ, not surprisingly, the emotions considered "basic" also differ (Ortony & Turner, 1990; for an excellent overview, see Power & Dalgleish, 2008, p. 65).

Although the distinct-states approach can highlight the unique features of different emotions or moods, it is also clear that some states resemble others (e.g., shame and guilt; envy and jealousy). Thus, another variant of the distinct-states approach further assumes that one can compose categories of states (hence the label "categorical" models), the members of which bear close resemblance to each other and a prototypical exemplar, but less resemblance to the members of other categories (e.g., Russell, 1991; Shaver, Schwartz, Kirson, & O'Connor, 1987). For example, the category of *anger* may comprise other members of this category, such as *rage, wrath*, and *annoyance*. These have similarities to the *anger* prototype but are different from the members of other categories, such as those defined by the prototypes *love* (e.g., *adoration, affection, fondness, tenderness*) or *fear* (e.g., *fright, horror, terror, panic*).

The dimensional approach

The main conceptual alternative to the distinct-states approach is the effort to identify elemental dimensions that account for the similarities and differences among affective states. The first seeds of the dimensional approach in the study of affective phenomena in modern psychology were planted by Wundt (1912, especially see pp. 60–61). Following Wundt, the most extensive empirical exploration of the dimensional structure of affective space was undertaken in the 1950s by a team of researchers led by Charles Osgood (Osgood, 1962; Osgood & Suci, 1955; Osgood, Suci, & Tannenbaum, 1957). Their analyses identified three dimensions that were orthogonal (i.e., unrelated) to each other: (a) an "evaluative" factor (later also termed *valence* or *pleasure-displeasure*) was characterized by scales like good–bad, pleasant–unpleasant, and positive–negative; (b) a "potency" factor (later also termed *dominance* or *control*) was characterized by scales like strong–weak, large–small, and hard–soft; and (c) an "activity" factor (later also termed *arousal* or *activation*) was characterized by scales like fast–slow, active–passive, and excitable–calm. Essentially the same three-dimensional structure later became the basis of Russell and Mehrabian's (1974, 1977) Semantic Differential Measures of Emotional State and Lang's Self-Assessment Manikin (Bradley & Lang, 1994; Hodes, Cook, & Lang, 1985; Lang, 1980), both of which include scales of pleasure, arousal, and dominance.

Subsequent reconsideration led to the elimination of the potency factor and the consolidation of a two-dimensional structure consisting of a *valence* (pleasure-displeasure) and an *activation* (arousal) dimension. According to Russell (1978), the potency factor may account for some additional variance but, in actuality, it refers to "antecedents or consequences of the affective experience, rather than the affect *per se*" and, thus, "dimensions beyond pleasure and arousal can ... perhaps best be discussed from a cognitive perspective" (p. 1166).

The two dimensions, valence and activation, have emerged from analyses done by several researchers who approached the problem from different perspectives, using different terminologies. On one hand, this convergence may be seen as compelling evidence of the robustness and reliability of the two-dimensional solution (Feldman Barrett & Russell, 1999). On the other, however, the diversity of viewpoints and, especially, the diversity of terms have contributed to some confusion and controversy in this area. There are at least four prominent variants of the two-dimensional structure, which are reviewed in more detail later in this chapter.

Russell's circumplex model

The circumplex model proposed by Russell (1980, 1989, 1997) is based on the idea that the affective space is defined by two orthogonal and bipolar dimensions, namely affective valence and perceived activation. The various affective states are conceived as combinations of these two basic ingredients in different degrees. As a result, affective states are arranged along the perimeter of the circle defined by the two dimensions (see Figure 3.1). States that are close together (e.g., happy and glad) represent similar mixtures of valence and activation. States positioned diametrically across from each other (e.g., happy and sad) differ maximally in terms of one or the other dimension (e.g., their valence). States separated by a 90° angle are independent of each other. According to Feldman Barrett and Russell (2009), "the term 'circumplex' literally means 'circular order of complexity' to indicate that the objects in question (in this case, affect-related items) are heterogeneous (can be decomposed into more basic psychological properties) and therefore cannot be easily ordered relative to one another in a simple linear fashion. Instead, their qualitative (or ordinal) similarity to one another is reflected in their proximity around the perimeter of the circle" (p. 87). An important difference of the circumplex compared to other two-dimensional conceptualizations is that the model does not predict a systematic clustering of states on or near the (orthogonal) axes and,

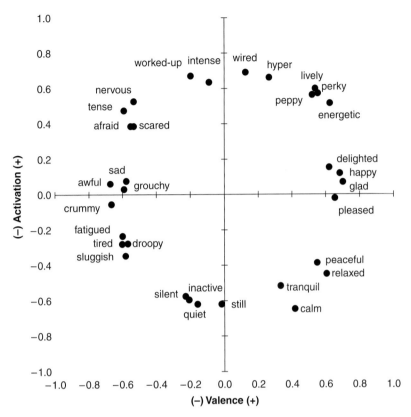

Figure 3.1. An example of the circumplex configuration of affective adjectives in a two-dimensional space defined by valence (pleasure-displeasure) and perceived activation (high-low). Data drawn from an unpublished study by the author.

thus, the spacing of states or clusters of states at equal intervals around the perimeter of the circle. According to Russell (1980), "affective space lacks 'simple structure.' Rather than clusters of synonyms falling near the axes, terms spread out more or less continuously around the perimeter of the space" (p. 1167).

Watson and Tellegen's Positive Affect – Negative Affect model

On the basis of factor analyses of inter- and intraindividual data from self-reports, Zevon and Tellegen (1982) and Watson and Tellegen (1985) also arrived at a two-dimensional solution (see Tellegen, 1985

for an overview). In agreement with Russell's analyses, they identified one dimension as reflecting affective valence (ranging from such
items as *happy* and *pleased* to *unhappy* and *sad*) and a second dimension as reflecting perceived activation, although they decided to label it
as "strong engagement – disengagement" (ranging from such items as
aroused and *astonished* to *quiescent* and *still*). However, the factor analyses
were followed by Varimax rotations, which tend to direct the (orthogonal) axes through areas with the highest concentration of items, thus
maximizing the accounted variance in the item pool. Most of the items
subjected to factor analysis did not reflect "pure" valence and activation
but rather mixtures of these two dimensions. As a result, one Varimax-
rotated axis extended from high-activation pleasant affect (e.g., *elated,
enthusiastic, excited*) to low-activation unpleasant affect (e.g., *drowsy,
dull, sluggish*) and the other from high-activation unpleasant affect (e.g.,
distressed, jittery, nervous) to low-activation pleasant affect (e.g., *calm,
placid, relaxed*). These rotated axes were chosen as primary (see Figure
3.2). Nevertheless, Watson and Tellegen (1985) emphasized that the
Varimax-rotated solution represents only "an alternative rotational
scheme," noting the "basic compatibility" (p. 222) of their model with
that proposed by Russell (see Figure 3.3). Watson and Clark (1997)
reiterated that the two models "essentially represent rotational variants
of one another" (p. 269).

Although the compatibility between the two models seems clear,
the presumed polarity and the labels given to the rotated dimensions
have caused considerable confusion (Larsen & Diener, 1992). As
described, the dimensions were clearly bipolar. Zevon and Tellegen
(1982) acknowledged that "the opposing ends of the two broad
dimensions are both associated with adjectival descriptors, a characteristic traditionally associated with bipolar structure" (p. 112).
Nevertheless, they chose to denounce bipolarity, stating that the
dimensions "are best characterized as *descriptively bipolar* but *affectively unipolar*" (p. 112). This enigmatic statement was based on the
argument that only "aroused-engaged states" can be conceived as
genuinely affective and, thus, the dimensions must be defined solely
by their high-arousal poles:

If one defines emotion or affect as a state of arousal or engagement, then only
the "high" ends are marked by adjectives describing the presence of affect ...
while the "low" ends are marked by adjectives that refer to the absence of affect
... As a matter of fact, the more "pure" or appropriate the low-end markers are
in reflecting the absence of the particular affect, the less they qualify as "emotions," since emotions are usually conceived of as almost inevitably associated
with some degree of arousal. (p. 112)

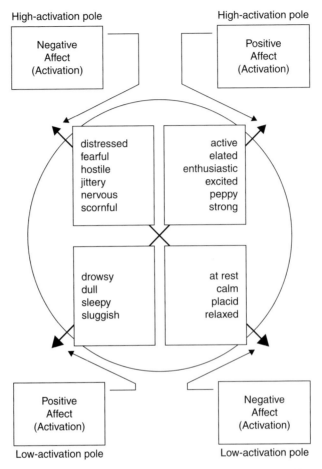

Figure 3.2. The two-dimensional model proposed by Watson and Tellegen (1985). One dimension, initially labeled Positive Affect and later renamed Positive Activation, extends from pleasant high activation to unpleasant low activation. The other, initially labeled Negative Affect and later renamed Negative Activation, extends from unpleasant high activation to pleasant low activation.

This position has been heavily criticized (Larsen & Diener, 1992; Mossholder, Kemery, Harris, Armenakis, & McGrath, 1994; Nemanick & Munz, 1994). For example, Carver (2001) made the following compelling point: "it is hard for me to imagine that sadness is not an affect; it is also hard for me to imagine sadness as involving much activation" (p. 351). Nevertheless, despite the criticisms, Watson and Tellegen have

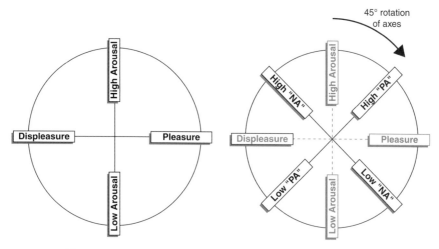

Figure 3.3. A side-by-side comparison of the sets of orthogonal dimensions from the models proposed by Russell (1980), on the left, and Watson and Tellegen (1985), on the right, illustrating their essential compatibility. As acknowledged by these authors, the two models represent rotational variants of each other.

insisted that the "descriptively bipolar" dimensions represent "truly unipolar constructs that essentially are defined by their high poles" because these "activated, high ends of the dimensions fully capture their essential qualities" (Watson, Wiese, Vaidya, & Tellegen, 1999, p. 827).

Consistent with Watson and Tellegen's position that the rotated dimensions should be defined solely by their high-arousal poles, the labels they gave to the dimensions denote unipolarity, concealing their actual bipolarity. Specifically, the dimension extending from high-activation pleasant affect (e.g., *elated*) to low-activation unpleasant affect (e.g., *drowsy*) was labeled Positive Affect and the dimension extending from high-activation unpleasant affect (e.g., *distressed*) to low-activation pleasant affect (e.g., *calm*) was labeled Negative Affect.

The potential for confusion created by these labels is readily apparent, since most people, for example, would consider *calm* an indicator of "positive" rather than "negative" affect. Perhaps the biggest problem was that many researchers mistakenly interpreted Watson and Tellegen's position that Positive Affect and Negative Affect are orthogonal (unrelated) to mean that pleasure and displeasure are orthogonal.

This would imply, for instance, that people could feel both happy and sad at the same time (Larsen, McGraw, & Cacioppo, 2001). Larsen and Diener (1992) cited several such cases of misinterpretation from the literature. However, as was explained, *happy* and *sad* were not indicators of the (orthogonal) Positive Affect and Negative Affect dimensions but rather indicators of the two opposite poles of the single bipolar dimension of pleasantness-unpleasantness in Watson and Tellegen's (1985) analyses. In fact, Watson and Tellegen (1985) closed their article warning researchers that "if pure Positive and Negative Affect markers are used ..., the mood scales will be orthogonal; however, if Pleasantness and Unpleasantness terms are selected, the resulting measures will be negatively correlated ... Not all positive and negative mood descriptors are uncorrelated, and so investigators must carefully consider the terms used to create their Positive Affect and Negative Affect measures" (p. 233).

Responding to a plea from other researchers to eliminate this source of confusion (Feldman Barrett & Russell, 1998), Watson et al. (1999) changed the names of the two dimensions to *Positive Activation* (instead of Positive Affect) and *Negative Activation* (instead of Negative Affect), to more clearly indicate that the dimensions (a) refer to something other than pleasure and displeasure and (b) are defined only by their high-arousal poles. These labels remain in use today (Gray & Watson, 2007) and should be preferred over the old labels.

Thayer's two-dimensional model

Thayer (1989) proposed a third variant of the two-dimensional structure. Initially, Thayer's goal in the late 1960s was to develop a self-report measure of arousal to be used instead of the more cumbersome psychophysiological measures. This effort was based on the assumption of a single, bipolar activation dimension ranging from extreme excitement to deep sleep. Factor analyses revealed the following four factors, which formed the basis of the measure later known as the Activation Deactivation Adjective Check List (AD ACL): (a) General Activation (e.g., *lively, full of pep, energetic*), (b) High Activation (e.g., *clutched up, jittery, stirred up*), (c) General Deactivation (e.g., *at rest, still, quiescent*), and (d) Deactivation-Sleep (e.g., *sleepy, tired, drowsy*). Thayer's (1967) initial interpretation was that these factors "approximate four different points on a hypothetical activation continuum" (p. 676).

Importantly, however, in addition to items he presumed to be pure indices of activation (e.g., *active, calm, sleepy*), Thayer also factor analyzed so-called nonactivation items taken from mood check lists, which "were included as a means of disguising the intent of the test" (Thayer, 1967, p. 665). This element was crucial for the subsequent evolution of the Activation Deactivation Adjective Check List, as it led to the observation that the four identified factors reflected more than just activation. This observation came in 1978: "the dimension suggesting positive affective tone is positively correlated with General Activation and negatively correlated with High Activation, ... while the negatively toned dimensions generally show the opposite relationships" (Thayer, 1978a, p. 750). From that point on, the Activation Deactivation Adjective Check List was considered not only a measure of arousal but also a measure of mood.

In 1978, Thayer outlined his theory of multidimensional activation (Thayer, 1978b), in which he denounced the idea of a single activation continuum and instead proposed two dimensions in constant, complex interaction. Activation Dimension A (later renamed *Energetic Arousal*) extends from feelings of energy (e.g., *energetic, vigorous*) on one end to feelings of tiredness (e.g., *drowsy, tired*) on the other. Thayer (1978b, 1987a, 1987b) recognized that a multitude of factors, including time of day, sleep deprivation, noise, incentive, various drugs, nutrition, and physical exercise can affect activation on this dimension. Activation Dimension B (later renamed *Tense Arousal*) extends from tension (e.g., *tense, jittery*) on one end to calmness (e.g., *calm, placid*) on the other. Unlike the developers of the other two-dimensional models reviewed earlier, Thayer was not only concerned with the static correlations between the two dimensions of his theory but also with their dynamic relationship and, in particular, how this relationship changes as a function of the level of energy expenditure. Thus, his position is more complex than a straightforward support for orthogonality. Specifically, he postulated that "the two dimensions form a curvilinear relationship":

[The two dimensions] ... are positively correlated at moderate levels and negatively correlated at higher levels of intensity. It is assumed that moderate tension enhances energy. But increased tension reduces energy and increases tiredness, while heightened energy states reduce feelings of tension. The prediction is also made that very low levels of energetic arousal (exhaustion) lead to a reduction in tense arousal. This complex relationship between the two dimensions results in the net appearance of orthogonality. (Thayer, 1986, p. 608)

The compatibility of the Activation Deactivation Adjective Check List and Thayer's factor-analytic data to other two-dimensional models of affect was noted early on by several authors (Meddis, 1972; Purcell, 1982; Russell, 1980; Russell & Mehrabian, 1977). In fact, commenting on Thayer's emphasis on arousal, Russell (1979) noted that "Thayer's scales are considerably mislabeled" because the difference between the scales "was as much the amount of pleasure as it was the degree of arousal" (p. 354). Thus, Russell suggested renaming General Activation (which combines pleasure with high arousal) as "vigor" or "excitement," General Deactivation (which combines pleasure with low arousal) as "calmness" or "relaxation," Deactivation-Sleep (which combines displeasure with low arousal) as "depression" or "tiredness," and High Activation (which combines displeasure with high arousal) as "distress." Indeed, in 1986, Thayer started using the terms Energy, Calmness, Tiredness, and Tension, respectively, to label the poles of the Energetic Arousal and Tense Arousal dimensions.

Russell (1980) first noted that Thayer's bipolar dimensions represent "rotational variants of pleasure and arousal" (p. 1171). Watson and Tellegen (1985) essentially agreed with this interpretation, suggesting that Thayer's Energetic Arousal dimension is compatible with their Positive Affect (now Positive Activation) dimension and his Tense Arousal dimension is compatible with their Negative Affect (now Negative Activation) dimension. Thayer (1989) himself concurred, noting that "the dimensions that Watson and Tellegen labeled as Positive and Negative Affect substantially overlap energetic and tense arousal as I have been discussing these mood dimensions" (p. 164). Nevertheless, he also insisted that his labels (emphasizing the arousal component rather than pleasure-displeasure) were superior because, although "the two dimensions do reflect differing affective tone, … considering extensive differential validational evidence associated with various criteria of arousal, and even on the basis of a simple analysis of apparent meaning, energetic and tense arousal would appear to be more appropriate names for these dimensions" (Thayer, 1986, p. 609). Perhaps in response to this point, when Watson et al. (1999) decided to change the labels of their dimensions to Positive Activation and Negative Activation, a main reason they cited was to "underscore the close affinity between the [Positive Activation] and [Negative Activation] dimensions and Thayer's (1989) influential constructs of Energetic Arousal and Tense Arousal, respectively" (p. 827).

The integrative circumplex of Larsen and Diener

A fourth variant of the two-dimensional model was proposed by Larsen and Diener (1992) on the basis of an extensive and critical review of the affect circumplex and similar conceptualizations. This variant, however, does not introduce any genuinely new conceptual elements but instead represents an attempt to bring together the aforementioned models, resolve terminological ambiguities, and highlight their commonalities. Larsen and Diener (1992) correctly argued that the use of factor analysis with Varimax rotation (as done by Zevon & Tellegen, 1982 and Watson & Tellegen, 1985) as a means of identifying the "best" orientation of the axes through the two-dimensional space is misleading. This approach is always dependent on how many (and how psychometrically strong) items have been chosen to represent each sector of this space. Following the rotation, the axes will always run through the most densely populated areas. So all one has to do to turn the axes through a given sector is to oversample items from that sector.

Furthermore, Larsen and Diener (1992) emphasized that "the circumplex model is also a measurement model" (p. 33), not just a conceptual model intended to depict fundamental differences and similarities among affective states. Wanting to highlight the potential for using the circumplex as a basis for measurement, they took a practical position in between Russell's (1980) view that affective states are arranged in a more or less continuous fashion around the circle and Watson and Tellegen's (1985) view that there are distinct clusters representing Positive Affect and Negative Affect. Specifically, Larsen and Diener (1992) proposed that the two-dimensional space can be divided into octants (on the notion of distinct but adjacent segments within the circumplex, also see Haslam, 1995). These octants can be demarcated by two sets of orthogonal axes, with one set a 45° rotational variant of the other. One set would represent Russell's (1980) valence (ranging from such items as *happy* and *glad* to *unhappy* and *sad*) and activation dimensions (ranging from *active* and *aroused* to *still* and *quiet*). The second set would represent Watson and Tellegen's (1985) and Thayer's (1989) 45° rotated versions, but with the labels simplified as (a) Activated Pleasant Affect (e.g., *enthusiastic, elated*) to Unactivated Unpleasant Affect (e.g., *dull, tired*) and (b) Activated Unpleasant Affect (e.g., *distressed, annoyed*) to Unactivated Pleasant Affect (e.g., *relaxed, content*). Thus, Larsen and Diener (1992) envisioned a measure that would form "eight composite scores to represent the octants of the circumplex (or four bipolar scores to represent the four major bipolar dimensions of the circumplex)" (p. 50).

The compatibility of contemporary dimensional models

The arguments presented so far for the compatibility of the four variants of the two-dimensional model reviewed here were mainly

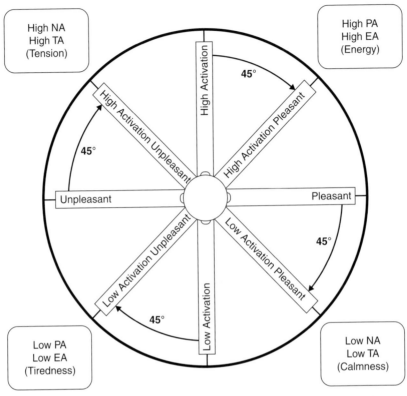

Figure 3.4. Integrative schematic depicting the compatibility of the four variants of the two-dimensional structure of core affect (i.e., Russell's, Watson and Tellegen's, Thayer's, and Larsen and Diener's). Of central importance for understanding this idea is the fact that the dimensions of Positive Affect / Positive Activation (PA) and Negative Affect / Negative Activation (NA) proposed by Watson and Tellegen (1985) and Energetic Arousal (EA) and Tense Arousal (TA) proposed by Thayer (1986, 1989) represent 45° rotational variants of the dimensions of Pleasure (valence) and Arousal (activation) proposed by Russell (1980). For an empirical demonstration, see Yik et al. (1999).

conceptual (see Figure 3.4). As is often the case, however, demonstrating the validity of these conceptual arguments empirically has been more challenging. Some researchers have examined the correlations between measures based on the different variants and have reported failures to find support for compatibility (Hutchison et al., 1996; Schimmack & Reisenzein, 2002). However, taking a much more comprehensive approach designed to control for as much random and systematic measurement error as possible, Yik, Russell, and Feldman Barrett (1999) showed that scales based on the four two-dimensional models fit well within the space defined by valence and activation. Specifically, for unipolar constructs (e.g., Thayer's Energy scale or Watson and Tellegen's Positive Affect), valence and activation explained between 53 percent and 90 percent of the variance, with a mean of 72 percent. For bipolar dimensions (e.g., Thayer's Energetic Arousal or Larsen and Diener's Activated Pleasant Affect to Unactivated Unpleasant Affect), valence and activation explained between 73 percent and 97 percent of the variance, with a mean of 84 percent. Yik et al. (1999) offered two explanations for the finding that valence and activation did not account for 100 percent of the variance. First, despite the best efforts to control for random and systematic measurement error, some error surely remains. Second, there is undoubtedly more in the richness and diversity of our affective lives than valence and activation. This important point is examined in more detail in the next section.

The hierarchical structure of the affective domain: an integrative framework

Pronk, Crouse, and Rohack (1995) reported that, in a sample of women (30 to 66 years of age), a maximal treadmill test induced postexercise increases in both *fatigue* and *self-esteem*. Vocks, Hechler, Rohrig, and Legenbauer (2009) found that a group of women (mean age 28.58 ± 6.78 years) showed a postexercise increase in *positive mood* and a decrease in *state body dissatisfaction*. From a measurement perspective, these interesting findings pose a challenge. Fatigue or a global index of positive mood could be captured well by existing self-report instruments based on some of the aforementioned dimensional models. However, self-esteem and body dissatisfaction, despite their obvious interest to researchers and practitioners alike, cannot. They represent qualitatively different constructs that do not fall under the rubrics of either *affect* or *mood*. They are probably closer relatives to the emotion of pride. According to Lazarus (1991a), the key generative cognitive appraisal underlying this emotion (i.e., the "core relational theme" in his terms) refers to an "enhancement of one's ego-identity by taking credit for a valued object or achievement" (p. 122). Can dimensional models adequately deal with states such as these? Can *pride* "fit" into a circumplex? The simple answer is no.

Recall that, initially, Russell and Mehrabian (1977) advocated incorporating a third dimension, namely dominance/submissiveness, in their model (besides pleasure and arousal), on the basis of the argument that "only dominance makes it possible to distinguish angry from anxious, alert from surprised, relaxed from protected, and disdainful from impotent" (p. 292). Soon thereafter, however, Russell (1978) supported a two- rather than a three-dimensional structure based on the argument that the dominance dimension represents cognitive antecedents or consequences of affect rather than a dimension underlying affect per se.

Many authors over the following years identified this as a problem in the circumplex model. The fact that *anxious* and *angry* are placed side by side in the high-activation unpleasant quadrant of the circumplex does not seem satisfactory to most psychologists. Particularly motion theorists with a strong cognitive orientation attacked the idea of dimensional models with fervor. In the words of Smith and Ellsworth (1985), two-dimensional models are "both theoretically sterile and experientially implausible" (p. 814). Similarly, according to Clore, Ortony, and Foss (1987):

Dimensions of this kind are so general that they are quite uninformative with respect to identifying features that distinguish emotions from other things. They reveal no principled definitive differences between emotions (e.g., *sympathy*) and things having nothing whatsoever to do with emotions (e.g., *food*). Nor are they informative with respect to distinguishing one type of emotion, say, *anger* ... from another type, say *fear*. (p. 752)

Lazarus (1991a) expressed a similar view:

Much of value is lost by putting these reactions into dimensions, because the simplifying or reductive generalizations wipe out important meanings about person–environment relationships, which the hundreds of emotion words were created to express. If we want to know what makes people or any given person *angry*, for example, the task is not facilitated – in fact, it is actually undermined – by a preoccupation with the so-called underlying response dimensions, which supposedly transcend emotion categories. *Anger*, then, becomes only a kind of unpleasant activation, when in reality it is a complex, varied, and rich relational pattern between persons, one that is distinctive and powerful in its effects on the participating persons and the larger social setting. (pp. 63–64)

Numerous other authors, both some of those favoring and some of those opposing the idea of dimensional models, have launched similar critiques (Carver, 2001; Fontaine et al., 2007; Larsen & Diener,

1992; Reisenzein, 1994; Schimmack & Grob, 2000). There can be little doubt that dimensional models, as heuristically useful as they are, "fail to capture the rich tapestry given to the emotions by cognitive labeling" (Larsen & Diener, 1992, p. 45). So, after decades of referring to dimensional models as models of *emotions*, it is now widely recognized that the true usefulness and heuristic value of dimensional models does not extend that far. For example, in their extensive reanalysis of published data sets to investigate the extent to which they conform to a circumplex (and the factors that influence their compatibility with the model), Remington, Fabrigar, and Visser (2000) identified a number of terms whose position in circumplex space was characterized as ambiguous. Not surprisingly, these included emotions with specific cognitive antecedents (i.e., *confident, proud, guilty*). Likewise, following their analysis of 24 emotion terms in three European cultures, Fontaine et al. (2007) concluded that at least four dimensions, not two, would be required to adequately account for the differences and similarities between them (i.e., valence, activation, potency-control, and novelty-unpredictability recovered 75.4 percent of the variance).

Recognizing this limitation, Russell and Feldman Barrett (1999) wrote: "we now believe that this dimensional structure [i.e., the two-dimensional circumplex] represents and is limited to the core affect involved" (p. 807). Agreeing with the critics, they noted that "qualitatively different events can appear as if the same when only this dimensional structure is considered," offering the typical examples of *fear* and *anger*, which "fall in identical places in the circumplex structure." In essence, the pleasure and arousal dimensions represent only one component of these states (i.e., the core affect involved) but not other important components (e.g., cognitive appraisal of meaning and implications, attributions, future projections, action tendencies). However, it is those other components that can differentiate *fear* from *anger*. Thus, Russell and Feldman Barrett warned that "assessment devices based on the dimensional-circumplex approach capture core affect but miss the other components" (1999, p. 807). Along the same lines, Russell (2003) acknowledged that "by themselves, pleasure and arousal do not fully account for most emotional episodes" and the circumplex "does not provide a sufficiently rich account of prototypical emotional episodes" because it "fails to explain adequately how fear, jealousy, anger, and shame are different." He concluded that "the dimensional perspective must be integrated with the categorical perspective" (2003, p. 150). In essence, this was a call for the conceptualization of the affective domain as hierarchically organized, with the more basic and relatively simpler

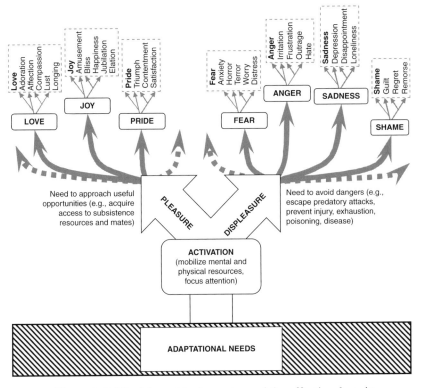

Figure 3.5. The hierarchical structure of the affective domain.
In an evolutionary sense, the basic dimensions of core affect (i.e.,
pleasure-displeasure and activation) preceded and formed the basis
for the evolution of distinct emotions. In turn, prototypical emotions
further evolved into more subtly differentiated derivatives. While
constructs at all levels of the hierarchy serve the common purpose
of promoting adaptation, constructs at higher levels reflect a higher
degree of differentiation. The most likely driving force behind the
transition from the lower to the higher levels of the hierarchy has
been the emergence of increasingly larger and more complex social
structures. The figure was inspired by similar schematics in Nesse
(2004), Shaver et al. (1987), and Schimmack and Crites (2005).

construct of core affect at the base and the increasingly more differentiated repertoire of individual mood and emotion states at the top (see
Figure 3.5).

The critical insight that led to this important development is the distinction between *core affect* and *emotions* (what Russell calls "prototypical emotional episodes"). Once again, this underscores the importance

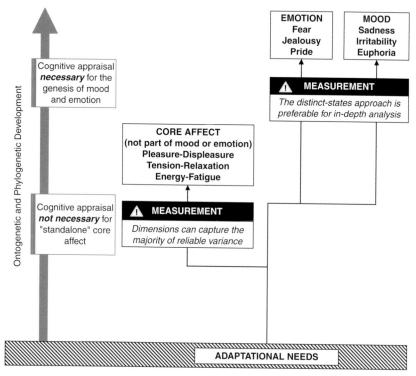

Figure 3.6. Implications of the hierarchical structure of the affective domain for measurement. Free-floating or stand-alone core affect can be efficiently and effectively measured using the dimensional approach. On the other hand, if the focus of a particular study is on a specific mood or emotional state (or a set of specific mood or emotional states), then the distinct-states approach is generally preferable.

of what was considered here "the crucial first step" of recognizing the differences between the various affective phenomena. If a researcher is interested in core affect (e.g., *fatigue* in the example given in the beginning of this section), then a dimensional perspective would be an appropriate choice. If, on the other hand, a researcher is interested in emotions (e.g., *pride*), then he or she should approach that emotion as a distinct entity, taking into account its unique cognitive (and other) features (see Figure 3.6).

It is important to point out that consensus among theorists is developing on this issue. In the article presenting their own version of a two-dimensional model (i.e., Positive Affect, Negative Affect), Watson and Tellegen (1985) wrote:

Although we restrict ourselves to an examination of these dominant dimensions, we are not thereby suggesting that all emotional experience can be reduced to only two variables. Positive and Negative Affect, although accounting for about one half to three quarters of the common variance, do not exclude the operation of additional systematic sources of variance. The two-dimensional framework, in other words, is complementary to, rather than competitive with, multifactorial structures. In fact, we show that Positive and Negative Affect are hierarchically related to the more numerous and circumscribed "discrete-emotion" factors posited by other investigators. (p. 220)

These authors continued to pursue the idea of a hierarchical arrangement through the 1980s (e.g., Watson & Clark, 1984) and 1990s (Watson & Clark, 1992, 1997), providing not only theoretical arguments but also empirical evidence to support it. Describing an idea essentially similar to that outlined by Russell (2003), Watson and Clark (1997) wrote:

We want to emphasize that these two basic approaches – dimensions and discrete affects – are not incompatible or mutually exclusive; rather, they essentially reflect different levels of a single, integrated hierarchical structure … That is, each of the higher order dimensions can be decomposed into several correlated yet ultimately distinct affective states, much like a general factor of personality (e.g., neuroticism) can be subdivided into several narrower components or "facets" (e.g., anxiety, vulnerability). In this hierarchical model, the lower level reflects the unique descriptive/explanatory power of the individual discrete affects (i.e., specificity), whereas the general dimensions reflect their shared, overlapping qualities (i.e., nonspecificity). (p. 269)

This two-level hierarchy was later expanded into an empirically derived three-level hierarchy (Tellegen, Watson, & Clark, 1999a, 1999b). The tip of the pyramid is defined by a bipolar dimension of pleasure versus displeasure. The intermediate level reflects Watson and Tellegen's (1985) orthogonal dimensions of Positive Affect and Negative Affect. Finally, at the base of the pyramid, one can find discrete states such as *fear*, *anger*, and *sadness*.

Conclusion

What are the practical implications of these integrative, hierarchical models for researchers? Perhaps the most important point is that both the distinct-states (or categorical) and the dimensional approach have their place, so one should not think of this issue as an either-or dichotomy. Which one is more suitable for a given study depends on the specific aim of the study. If a study involves an experimental manipulation likely to induce a pattern of cognitive appraisal underlying a specific emotion, then the investigation should focus on that particular emotion (i.e., using a distinct-states or categorical perspective). For example, if a study places sedentary women or women highly anxious about their physical appearance in front of mirrors while they exercise (in other words, if the study involves a manipulation of a very specific pattern of cognitive appraisal), then the appropriate target would be the distinct emotion of anxiety (i.e., the specific emotional state theorized to emerge from that particular appraisal; e.g., Focht & Hausenblas, 2003; Martin Ginis, Jung, & Gauvin, 2003) rather than general affect (e.g., Martin Ginis, Burke, & Gauvin, 2007). If, on the other hand, the purpose of a study is to examine the effects of a more general manipulation (e.g., the effects of different doses of alcohol or different degrees of sleep deprivation) or a manipulation the impact of which cannot be anticipated on the basis of current theory (e.g., dehydration, a high dose of caffeine, or glucose supplementation during a long run), then it would make more sense to expand the investigative scope by focusing on the broad domain of core affect (Backhouse, Ali, Biddle, & Williams, 2007; Backhouse, Biddle, Bishop, & Williams, 2011; Backhouse, Bishop, Biddle, & Williams, 2005). This can be done effectively and efficiently by using a two-dimensional model such as the circumplex.

To be clear, measurements based on a dimensional model will certainly lack the high degree of specificity that can only be afforded by the distinct-states approach. Were the participants anxious or tense? Did they feel exhilaration or enthusiasm? The dimensional approach cannot make these types of differentiations (which could be a critical shortcoming, depending on the research question). What it promises instead is an encompassing and balanced perspective that should capture the essence of most major changes in affective experience (so that important changes should not go undetected) while requiring the assessment of no more than two constructs. As Fontaine et al. (2007) aptly put it, "The optimal number of dimensions to be included in a study depends on the question the researcher is asking. For a researcher interested in the effects of sympathetic activation, one dimension (arousal) may be sufficient. For a researcher interested in the subtle distinctions among related emotions such as shame, guilt, embarrassment, and self-anger, four dimensions might not be enough" (p. 1056). For measurement based on the dimensional perspective to be most meaningful, researchers should recognize both the unique strengths and the important limitations of such models.

At the same time, it should be kept in mind that the decision to choose emotions as the object of a given study should not necessarily be taken to imply the use of a distinct-states or categorical approach. Some authors maintain that a dimensional approach to the study of the domain of emotions is viable, as long as additional dimensions (besides valence and activation) are used to account for elements besides core affect (Fontaine et al., 2007). However, since the majority of the variance in emotions comes from the complex patterns of underlying appraisal processes, other authors have focused specifically on these appraisal themes. Two important observations have emerged: (a) certain themes exhibit considerable similarities (e.g., between fear and anxiety; shame and guilt; or envy and jealousy) and (b) some transitions from one emotion to another occur quite frequently. On the basis of these observations, efforts have been undertaken to understand the dimensional structure of the appraisal themes that give rise to emotions (Ellsworth & Smith, 1988a, 1988b; Smith & Ellsworth, 1985). In the seminal study by Smith and Ellsworth (1985), responses along six dimensions of appraisal (pleasantness, anticipated effort, certainty, attentional activity, self–other responsibility/control, and situational control) could predict the correct emotion among 15 alternatives (happiness, sadness, fear, anger, boredom, challenge, interest, hope, frustration, contempt, disgust, surprise, pride, shame, and guilt) more than 40 percent of the time, a probability more than six times higher than chance. The extension of Weiner's (1985) theory dealing with the dimensions of causal attributions (i.e., locus, stability, and controllability) to the domain of emotions also falls in this category. According to Weiner (1985), "the emotion of pride and feelings of self-esteem are linked with the locus dimension of causality; anger, gratitude, guilt, pity, and shame all are connected with the controllability dimension; and feelings of hopelessness (hopefulness) are associated with causal stability" (p. 561).

In sum, the previous sections have hopefully illustrated the profound importance of distinguishing between the distinct-states and the dimensional approaches to the study of affective constructs. Given the implications of these distinctions for measurement, it seems reasonable to suggest that authors should directly and consistently address this issue in substantiating their choice of measure. To return to the examples offered in the introduction, the choice of the Profile of Mood States should be accompanied by an explanation of the reasons why a distinct-states approach was preferred in the specific context of a given investigation and, furthermore, why the distinct states of Tension, Depression, Anger, Vigor, Fatigue, and Confusion (as opposed to some other assortment of distinct states) were deemed of interest. Likewise, the choice of the Positive and Negative Affect Schedule should be accompanied by an explanation of the reasons why a dimensional approach was preferred and, furthermore, why Watson and Tellegen's specific dimensional model was chosen over alternative conceptualizations (addressing such factors as the appropriateness of the rotation and the polarity of the dimensions).

4   Are pleasant and unpleasant states independent or polar opposites?

The aim of this chapter is to survey the evidence pertaining to another important theoretical question researchers interested in measuring affect, mood, or emotion will have to confront during the process of selecting a measure. This question is whether pleasant and unpleasant states should be conceptualized as independent (unrelated to each other, which implies that people could feel both happy and sad at the same time) or as polar opposites.

Questions of bipolarity versus independence: what complexities lurk beneath the surface?

Readers may have encountered in the literature studies that employed the original unipolar version of the Profile of Mood States (McNair et al., 1971) and others that employed the more recent bipolar version (McNair, Lorr, & Droppleman, 1992). Most have probably never seen, however, a substantive explanation for why the unipolar or the bipolar version was preferred or what the implications would be of using one instead of the other. In the rare occasions on which a reason is given, it usually refers to issues, such as the relative popularity of the two measures, that are unrelated to the profound conceptual differences between them. For example, researchers have stated that their decision to focus on the unipolar version was based on the fact that it "remains the more commonly selected version of POMS by contemporary researchers of sport and exercise in preference to the POMS–Bi" and thus a study based on the unipolar version would have "relevance to a larger number of researchers" (Terry & Lane, 2000, p. 97).

Similarly, readers may have encountered studies that employed the Activation Deactivation Adjective Check List (Thayer, 1989), which taps two bipolar dimensions (Energetic Arousal, Tense Arousal), and studies that employed the Positive and Negative Affect Schedule (PANAS; Watson, Clark, & Tellegen, 1988), which measures two unipolar dimensions (Positive Affect, Negative Affect). Other studies employed both simultaneously (e.g., Bartholomew & Miller, 2002; Lochbaum, Karoly, & Landers, 2004). Again, readers have probably never seen any reference to the uni- or bipolarity of the factors among the reasons considered by authors in deciding to use one versus the other (or both).

Likewise, the theorized relations between the dimensions of a theoretical model (or the factors of a measure based on a theoretical model) are extremely important. In some cases, such as the Feeling Scale (Hardy & Rejeski, 1989), pleasure ("feel good") and displeasure ("feel bad") are theorized to lie on the two opposite ends of a single bipolar dimension of "affective valence." In other cases, such as the Positive and Negative Affect Schedule (Watson, Clark, & Tellegen, 1988), "positive affect" and "negative affect" are theorized to be statistically independent (at a 90° angle). Although some researchers exhibit a preference for bipolarity and others for independence, the conceptual arguments supporting these preferences remain unclear. For example, some authors have expressed the view that "the good / bad bipolarization of affect during exercise appears to be assessing the pleasure / displeasure core of emotions" (Hardy & Rejeski, 1989, p. 308). Others have favored models in which positively and negatively valenced states are represented by separate, independent dimensions because "the presumption of affect as bipolar and therefore unidimensional (i.e., positive and negative affect are at opposite ends of the same continuum) is troublesome from both conceptual and theoretical perspectives" (McAuley & Courneya, 1994, p. 165). Authors in the latter camp maintain there is "considerable evidence to support the notion that positive and negative affect are distinct constructs and not just opposite ends of a continuum" (Mermelstein, Hedeker, & Weinstein, 2010, p. 222).

There are also signs that the exact meaning and the implications of bipolarity and independence have not been fully appreciated. For example, Tomarken, Davidson, Wheeler, and Doss (1992) computed the algebraic difference between the Positive Affect and the Negative Affect scores on the Positive and Negative Affect Schedule (Watson, Clark, & Tellegen, 1988), claiming that "this difference is equivalent to the pleasure-displeasure dimension that Russell ... has argued is basic to emotion" (p. 682). Following their lead, Petruzzello, Jones, and Tate (1997) computed an "affective valence" variable by subtracting the score of the Psychological Distress scale of the Subjective Exercise Experiences Scale (McAuley & Courneya, 1994) from the score on the Positive Well-Being scale of the same questionnaire. The authors considered Psychological Distress an analogue of the Negative Affect scale and Positive Well-Being an analogue of the Positive Affect scale of the Positive and Negative Affect Schedule (Watson, Clark, & Tellegen, 1988). Thus, they stated that the Positive Well-Being – Psychological Distress difference "yields a measure of the relative balance of positive and negative affect and is also consistent with Solomon's bipolar hedonic state" (p. 207). More recently, citing Petruzzello et al. (1997), Lochbaum et al. (2004) computed an "affect balance" variable by subtracting the score on the Tense Arousal scale of the Activation Deactivation Adjective Check List from the score on the Energetic Arousal scale, characterizing this difference as reflecting "affective valence."

Is the derivation of these difference scores conceptually justified? The Positive Affect/Energetic Arousal and Negative Affect/Tense Arousal factors can be thought of as vectors in dimensional space. Based on the rules of vector algebra, to subtract one vector from another, simply computing the algebraic difference would be incorrect – unless the two vectors were perfectly parallel (e.g., if the "positive" and the "negative" vectors were aligned). When the two vectors are not parallel, trigonometry must be used instead, taking into account the angles between the vectors.

The relevance of the issue of bipolarity versus independence should now be apparent. If Positive Affect, Positive Well-Being, or Energetic Arousal and Negative Affect, Psychological Distress, or Tense Arousal, are theorized to be polar opposites (in the same way that pleasure and displeasure are the opposite poles of the same bipolar dimension), then the algebraic difference between scores on these scores would make sense. If, on the other hand, these dimensions are theorized to be orthogonal (at 90° angles), then a difference score would be algebraically improper. As explained in the previous chapter, the Positive Affect and Negative Affect dimensions in Watson, Clark, and Tellegen's (1988) model of the Positive and Negative Affect Schedule and the Energetic Arousal and Tense Arousal dimensions in Thayer's (1978a, 1989) model of the Activation Deactivation Adjective Check List are conceptualized as orthogonal, not as polar opposites.

In this chapter, the issue of the relationship between positively and negatively valenced affective states is examined in more detail. It is probably fair to characterize this as one of the most intensely debated topics within the affect literature. Perhaps an important reason for this level of interest is the rather counterintuitive (and, therefore, highly intriguing) implication that, if pleasant and unpleasant states can be shown to be independent, this would entail that people could feel both *happy* and *sad* at the same time. Consider, for example, a question that has arisen in the exercise psychology literature. Seasoned runners sometimes report that exercise "hurts so good" (Acevedo, Kraemer, Haltom, & Tryniecki, 2003). This phrase refers to affective states that seem oppositely valenced; on one hand, there seems to be displeasure ("hurt") but, on the other, this allegedly feels "good." What is the current thinking within affective psychology about such seemingly contradictory statements? The answer is not simple.

Although emotion theorists and social psychologists have had an enduring interest in the question of whether people can feel both happy and sad at the same time, the controversy surged following Watson and Tellegen's (1985) suggestion that Positive Affect (which most researchers erroneously took to mean *pleasure* or *happiness*) and Negative Affect (which most researchers erroneously took to mean *displeasure* or *sadness*) were orthogonal. As explained in the previous chapter, in Watson and Tellegen's (1985) model, Positive Affect (notice the capital initials) does not refer to pleasure (e.g., *happy, pleased*) but rather to states combining pleasure and high activation (e.g., *elated, enthusiastic*). Likewise, Negative Affect does not refer to displeasure (e.g., *sad, unhappy*) but rather to states combining displeasure and high activation (e.g., *distressed, jittery*). In Watson and Tellegen's (1985) model, pleasure and displeasure clearly represent the two opposite poles of a single bipolar dimension. According to Watson and Tellegen (1999), "this apparent conflict actually is a pseudocontroversy that emerged because of continuing sources of confusion in the field" (p. 602). More specifically:

The terms "positive affect" and "negative affect" have been used inconsistently by different writers. In early studies of self-rated affect, researchers tended to use the terms indiscriminately to refer to any positively and negatively valenced feeling states ... This produced widespread confusion in the literature, because ... different types of mood descriptors actually show substantially different intercorrelations. (p. 602)

Nevertheless, the empirical demonstration of the bipolarity of pleasure and displeasure has been difficult (Ekkekakis & Petruzzello, 2001a). At this point, it has become clear that certain methodological elements can elucidate or obscure the bipolar relationship (also see Remington et al., 2000).

The crucial role of methodological factors

First, the sector of affective space from which items are sampled can make a substantial difference (Carroll, Yik, Russell, & Feldman Barrett, 1999; Russell & Carroll, 1999a, 1999b; Watson, 1988; Watson & Tellegen, 1985, 1999). Items that denote "pure" pleasure and "pure" displeasure (e.g., *happy* and *sad*) tend to show bipolarity (i.e., evidence of strong negative correlations). On the other hand, items that reflect mixtures of pleasure with activation (what Watson and Tellegen have called *Positive Affect* or *Positive Activation*) and mixtures of displeasure with activation (what Watson and Tellegen have called *Negative Affect* or *Negative Activation*) tend to show weak or near-zero correlations (i.e., evidence of independence). This is fully predicted on the basis of the dimensional models reviewed in the previous chapter.

Second, random and systematic measurement error attenuates the strength of the negative correlation between indices of pleasure and displeasure, thus biasing these correlations toward ostensibly supporting independence. Although this point was first made decades ago (Bentler, 1969) and reiterated several times (Lorr et al., 1982; Lorr & Shea, 1979; Lorr, Shi, & Youniss, 1989; Russell, 1979), not until a compelling publication by Green, Goldman, and Salovey (1993) did it receive broader attention in affective psychology (Feldman Barrett & Russell, 1998; Green & Salovey, 1999; Green, Salovey, & Truax, 1999; Russell & Carroll, 1999a, 1999b; Watson & Clark, 1997). Green et al. (1993) boldly asserted that "in our view, the independence of positive and negative affect is a statistical artifact" (p. 1029). Indeed, in a series of studies, they convincingly demonstrated that "when random and nonrandom measurement error is taken into account, the independence of positive and negative affect, however defined, proves ephemeral" (p. 1029). As one example, a correlation between happiness and sadness changed from -0.25 based on the raw scores to -0.85 after controlling for the effect of random measurement error.

Besides the unreliability of measurement, the attenuating impact on correlation coefficients which is broadly appreciated, another type of common measurement error that has this type of effect is the use of asymmetrical scales (e.g., response scales that provide an unequal number of options for rejection versus acceptance, such as "not at all," "a little," "quite a bit," "extremely"). Long ago, Meddis (1972) drew attention to the fact that "the asymmetrical scales were suppressing negative correlations and prejudicing the factor analysis against the discovery of bipolar factors" (p. 180). Svensson (1977) and Diener and Iran-Nejad (1986) made the same point. Finally, Russell and Carroll (1999a, 1999b) showed that two items from opposite ends of a single bipolar continuum, if assessed by unipolar response scales (e.g., ranging from "not at all" to "very much"), cannot have a perfect -1.00 correlation. A perfect negative correlation, considered by some the litmus test of bipolarity, could only occur if the information provided by the two items were completely redundant. However, when one is, for example, moderately *happy* (e.g., 3 on a 5-point scale ranging from "not at all" to "very much"), one is not also moderately *sad* (e.g., also 3 on the same 5-point scale) but rather "not at all" *sad*. Therefore, the correlation between two such items can never reach −1.00.

Third, if the instructions given to respondents refer to extended periods of time (e.g., "how you felt last week") instead of a single point in time (e.g., "how you are feeling right now"), they may possibly report feeling, for example, both *happy* and *sad* but this could simply refer to responses that took place at different times rather than concurrently (Russell, 1979). For example, in a study by Warr, Barter, and Brownbridge (1983), binary (*Yes* or *No*) responses to questions alluding to positive (e.g., "Have you ever felt that things were going your way?") and negative affect (e.g., "Have you ever felt very worried?") were found to be uncorrelated ($r = -0.07$). However, this cannot be seen as surprising given that the responses referred to "How have things been going in the past few weeks?" and, during that period of time, the number of desirable and undesirable life events were also found to be uncorrelated ($r = 0.07$). Diener and Emmons (1984) explored this issue further. They reported that based on within-subject analyses of daily reports, correlations between positive and negative affect were −0.10 over a three-week period, −0.31 over the course of a single day, −0.57 for momentary ratings, and −0.85 at moments during which the participants were experiencing some form of affective excitation. Thus, Diener and Emmons (1984) concluded:

The relation between positive and negative affect depends on the time period being considered. Positive and negative affect states do vary inversely, but only over short time spans; the two are unlikely to occur together within the same person at the same moment. Our results clearly show that the strongest inverse correlations are found when one feels strongly emotional, and that the correlation between positive and negative affect decreases in a linear fashion as the logarithm of the time span covered increases. (p. 1114)

Fourth, as also noted by Diener and Emmons (1984), although the relationship may be unclear when the respondents are in an affectively mundane, neutral, or ambiguous situation, evidence of bipolarity emerges during affectively charged episodes. According to Diener and Emmons (1984), "when a person is experiencing either positive or negative affect, he or she is less likely to experience the other type of affect" (p. 1111). Folkman and Lazarus (1985) found that the correlation between "positive affect" (*exhilarated, pleased, happy, relieved*) and "negative affect" (*angry, sad, disappointed, guilty, disgusted*) became increasingly more negative as a situation turned from highly ambiguous to highly unambiguous. Specifically, the correlation was 0.08 before an academic examination, -0.25 after the examination but before the grades were announced, and -0.50 after the grades were announced. Diener and Iran-Nejad (1986) similarly concluded that "people do not simultaneously experience both positive and negative affect at intense levels" (p. 1036). These findings have been replicated (Brehm & Miron, 2006; Schimmack, 2001; Scollon, Diener, Oishi, & Biswas-Diener, 2005). Based on previous studies and their own research (Potter, Zautra, & Reich, 2000; Reich & Zautra, 2002; Zautra, Berkhof, & Nicolson, 2002; Zautra, Potter, & Reich, 1998; Zautra, Reich, Davis, Potter, & Nicolson, 2000), Reich, Zautra, and Davis (2003) proposed a Dynamic Model of Affect, according to which stress tends to induce a more simplistic mode of cognitive processing and, as a result, when under stress, the relationship between positive and negative affect tends to conform to bipolarity.

Finally, several authors have questioned whether the commonly employed factor analytic model, which is based on the product-moment correlation matrix, is truly the most appropriate for analyzing bipolar data (Sjöberg, Svensson, & Persson, 1979). For example, van Schuur and Kiers (1994) and van Schuur and Kruijtbosch (1995) argued for the use of a unidimensional unfolding model. Schmukle and Egloff (2009) proposed the use of polychoric rather than product-moment correlations and showed that, with the use of a polychoric correlation matrix, even data collected with unipolar response scales yield evidence of bipolarity.

Although the effects of these methodological factors are relatively straightforward and some are widely known (e.g., the attenuating effect of unreliability on correlation coefficients), their implications for the question of bipolarity versus independence is rarely considered. However, it should be clear that, if these issues were taken into serious consideration, they could place many of the findings that seem to point toward independence under a very different light.

Evaluative Space Model and "emotionally complex" situations

Despite the growing appreciation for the bipolarity of pleasure and displeasure, the relationship between positively and negatively valenced affective states remains a complex issue with some interesting hidden wrinkles. One such issue, which is receiving increasing attention, is the relationship between positively and negatively valenced affect under so-called emotionally complex situations. One example would be "After exercising for a year, I've lost 5 pounds. I am proud of that but I am also disappointed because I thought I would have lost more than 15 pounds by now." In this example, the pleasure of pride and the displeasure of disappointment can apparently coexist, pointing toward a relationship of independence rather than bipolarity. Some authors use these types of scenarios as evidence that the independence of positively and negatively valenced affect is not only possible but frequent.

In the 1990s, Cacioppo and Berntson (1994; Cacioppo, Gardner, & Berntson, 1997, 1999) proposed a bivariate, as opposed to bipolar, model for attitudes and evaluative responses to stimuli. According to these authors, the reciprocal activation of positive and negative attitudes and evaluations (i.e., one increasing, the other decreasing, as predicted by bipolar models) is possible but represents only one mode of activation, the others being a nonreciprocal (i.e., both increasing or both decreasing) and an independent mode (i.e., one changing without a corresponding change in the other): "the question is not whether such processes are reciprocally activated but under what conditions they are reciprocally, nonreciprocally, or independently activated" (Cacioppo & Berntson, 1994, p. 401). An example of the kinds of responses Cacioppo and Berntson originally had in mind include the mixed feelings one may have toward one's parents (e.g., a child's love may be combined with frustration or resentment for the parents' overprotectiveness) or toward a political candidate (e.g., someone liking the economic plan but not the position on civil liberties). However, their writings also explored implications for affect without always making the distinction between affect and attitude or evaluative responses as clear as it should be.

For example, Ito, Cacioppo, and Lang (1998) elicited (bipolar) valence and activation, as well as (unipolar) positivity, negativity, and ambivalence, in response to viewing slides from the International Affective Picture System. Of 253 participants, the overwhelming majority ($n = 239$ or 94.5 percent) provided reciprocal ratings, and only a very small group ($n = 8$ or 3 percent) provided uncoupled ratings (the remaining six participants were inconsistent). There was no evidence of cooccurrence of positive and negative responses. Across all slides, the correlation between positivity and negativity ratings was strongly negative ($r = -0.78$). Nevertheless, Ito et al. (1998) concluded that "most but not all participants demonstrate a reciprocal relation in their positivity and negativity ratings" (p. 876) and speculated that evidence for nonreciprocal activation may occur if respondents are presented with more emotionally complex situations.

In a follow-up study, Larsen et al. (2001) acknowledged that "individuals typically feel either happy or sad a great deal of the time" but set out to examine "whether individuals can ever feel both happy and sad" using scenarios that involved "more emotionally complex situations" (p. 687). Such situations included watching the film *Life Is Beautiful* (which contains both happy and sad scenes) or moving out of one's college dormitory (at which moment one may feel happy for the beginning of summer but sad for losing contact with roommates and friends). The researchers found that, whereas only 10 percent of participants reported feeling both happy and sad before the film, 44 percent reported feeling both happy and sad after the film. Similarly, whereas only 16 percent of the students said they felt both happy and sad on a typical day, 54 percent said they felt both happy and sad on move-out day. Similar results were obtained with scenarios of disappointing wins (winning a certain amount when you could have won more) and relieving losses (losing a certain amount when you could have lost more; Larsen, McGraw, Mellers, & Cacioppo, 2004). These scenarios are analogous to the weight loss example mentioned earlier.

Can such findings be reconciled with dimensional models positing a bipolar relation between pleasure and displeasure? Although Cacioppo and his collaborators ask whether respondents feel *good* or *bad* (or *happy* or *sad*), what these questions tap into in those particular situations is not really affect but rather a cognitive evaluation. According to Russell and Feldman Barrett (1999), in arguing for a bivariate evaluative space, Cacioppo and his collaborators "discuss not core affect, but evaluative reactions to a stimulus" (p. 813). One can easily accept the possibility of someone recognizing advantages and disadvantages in a given behavioral decision, agreeing with some parts of what someone else is saying but disagreeing with others, or finding some scenes in a film romantic and sweet but others violent or crude. We all have both good and bad memories of our childhood and we see both positive and negative aspects in ourselves. That does not necessarily mean, however, that our core affect at a precise point in time can be both positive and negative simultaneously. Larsen et al. (2001) acknowledged that, although they agree that evaluative reactions and affect are distinct constructs, they "do not draw such sharp divisions between classes of affect" (p. 687). However, as explained in this book (see Chapter 2), such divisions are important and can often help resolve theoretical issues that may initially seem perplexing.

When a runner says that "exercise hurts so good," a likely explanation is that the "hurt" represents a core affective reaction that emerges directly from the body, unmediated by cognition, whereas the "good" may reflect the result of a cognitive appraisal (e.g., that fatiguing exercise can only be "good" for your physical conditioning or that one just met a personal challenge that has boosted his or her self-esteem). Alternatively, the "hurt" and the "good" simply did not occur at precisely the same time but instead one followed the other in quick succession. For example, a well-established phenomenon in exercise psychology is the "affective contrast" (or "rebound") phenomenon that occurs upon the termination of an exercise bout (i.e., the quick reversal from a lower-than-baseline level of pleasure seconds before the termination of the bout to a higher-than-baseline level seconds after). According to Solomon's (1980, 1991) opponent process model, affective valence (or "hedonic tone" in his terminology) is jointly determined by two processes (the a–process and the b–process), which have opposite valence signs. In the case of vigorous exercise, the a–process is charged with negative affective valence (possibly reflecting intense interoceptive cues) whereas the b–process is charged with positive affective valence (possibly reflecting the function of endogenous opioids or endocannabinoids). The affect experienced at any point during and following the exposure to a stimulus (such as an exercise bout) is assumed to reflect the algebraic sum of the two processes. Solomon attributed this operation to a hypothetical "affect summator" that constantly computes this algebraic sum. Invoking a mechanism of this sort was deemed necessary because, although two independent processes appear to codetermine the pattern of affective responses to a stimulus, the experience of affect at any given point is unitary. When exercise stops, so does the (negatively charged) a–process, leaving the (positively charged) b–process to dominate conscious awareness. For the runner, exercise may "hurt" during the bout but feel "so good" afterward.

Neural considerations

In their efforts to substantiate the position that positively and negatively valenced affective states are independent, theorists have also used arguments based on neuroanatomy and neurophysiology. Thus, discussions of the neural bases of pleasant and unpleasant affect have become an important and integral part of this debate. Specifically, proponents of the notion of independence have utilized the argument that the brain has separate, specialized areas for positively and negatively valenced affects. According to their reasoning, this type of neural architecture points to distinct evolutionary histories and creates the possibility that oppositely valenced affective states can be aroused concurrently. If, on the other hand, positive and negative affective responses were only meant to be aroused reciprocally or in a mutually exclusive fashion, then the brain would probably process both positive and negative affective responses within the same area or system. Two main variations of this argument have appeared, one referring to hemispheric lateralization and the other to more specific brain areas. These two variations are examined in more detail.

Watson et al. (1999) cited research and theorizing by Richard Davidson on the specialized role of the left and right prefrontal cortices. For several decades, Davidson (1992a) has maintained that "the anterior regions of the left and right hemispheres are specialized for approach and withdrawal processes, respectively" (p. 127). Moreover, since, in his view, approach-oriented motivational tendencies are inherently intertwined with positive affect and, conversely, withdrawal-oriented motivational tendencies are inherently intertwined with negative affect, Davidson also predicts that the left and right prefrontal cortices also play specialized roles in positive and negative affect, respectively: "In adults and infants, the experimental arousal of positive, approach-related emotions is associated with selective activation of the left frontal region, while arousal of negative, withdrawal-related emotions is associated with selective activation of the right frontal region" (Davidson, 1992b, p. 39).

Indeed, several studies in a systematic line of research conducted by Davidson and his colleagues have demonstrated both that baseline measures of frontal asymmetry assessed by electroencephalography are associated with self-reports of positive and negative affect and that changes in left and right prefrontal activity are associated with the experimental induction of positive and negative affect. However, not all attempts to independently replicate such findings have been successful. In the context of physical activity (Hall, Ekkekakis, & Petruzzello, 2010; Lochbaum, 2006) and in other contexts (Hagemann, Naumann, Becker, Maier, & Bartussek, 1998; Hagemann, Naumann, Lürken, Becker, Maier, & Bartussek, 1999), there have been null findings and findings contrary to predictions (but see Davidson, 1998, for a response). Perhaps more importantly, authors have begun to question whether the asymmetrical activation of the prefrontal cortices is truly reflective of affect. In a series of intriguing electroencephalography studies, Harmon-Jones showed that greater left than right prefrontal activity was positively associated with anger, a negatively valenced emotion which, however, is approach oriented (Harmon-Jones, 2007a; Harmon-Jones & Allen, 1998; Harmon-Jones & Sigelman, 2001). These data have led theorists to reject the long-held belief that approach-oriented motivation is isomorphic with positive affect and withdrawal-oriented motivation is isomorphic with negative affect (Carver & Harmon-Jones, 2009b; Harmon-Jones, 2004, 2007b). Furthermore, researchers are increasingly accepting that the conceptual model, according to which the left frontal brain region is involved in the experience and expression of positive affect and the right frontal brain region is involved in the expression and experience of negative affect, "is no longer viable" (Harmon-Jones, 2007b, p. 151).

Watson (2009) has found this evidence convincing. He has not only denounced the notion of isomorphism but also conceded that the left and right prefrontal cortices are not specialized for the processing of positively and negatively valenced affect. Specifically, Watson (2009) wrote:

In recent years, researchers increasingly have emphasized the isomorphism between the psychometrically defined, phenotypic dimensions of negative affect (or activation; NA) and positive affect (or activation; PA) – that is, the extent to which one experiences negative and positive moods, respectively – and the underlying motivational systems regulating avoidance and approach behaviors, respectively ... My colleagues and I have made this same basic point in some of our work ... arguing that self-reported NA essentially represents the subjective component of the withdrawal-oriented [behavioral inhibition system], whereas the PA dimension basically reflects the operation of the approach-regulating [behavioral activation system] ... Carver and Harmon-Jones (2009b) have challenged the validity of this isomorphism, and they have presented a broad range of data to refute it. I applaud their efforts to bring clarity to this extremely important issue. Moreover, several aspects of their analysis are praiseworthy. In particular, I found their review of the anterior cortical asymmetry evidence to be persuasive, and I basically agree with their conclusion that "such asymmetry reflects direction of motivational engagement (approach vs. withdrawal)." (p. 205)

Cacioppo and his collaborators also made a notable attempt to link positively and negatively valenced affect to separate brain areas. Cacioppo and Berntson (1994, p. 407), Cacioppo, Gardner, and Berntson (1997, p. 7), Cacioppo and Gardner (1999, p. 203), and Cacioppo, Gardner, and Berntson (1999, p. 845) have argued that affective positivity and negativity are served by separable neural systems, thus making it possible for positive and negative affective responses to be induced concurrently. According to Cacioppo et al. (1999):

Early work on the neural systems mediating reward and aversion revealed that reinforcing and punishing effects could be induced by stimulation of differentiated brain areas ... This work spearheaded efforts to elucidate the neural and neurochemical substrates of hedonic processes. Recent studies have focused on the role of the mesolimbic dopamine pathway in reward ... and on the amygdala as a substrate for aversion ... The mesolimbic dopamine pathway originates in the ventral tegmental area of the midbrain and projects to the nucleus accumbens. Activation of this system has been shown to function as a reward ... In contrast. the amygdala has been implicated in negative affect. (p. 845)

Along the same lines, the first argument presented under the title "Evidence for separability of positive and negative affect" by Larsen et al. (2001) was the following:

Consistent with the hypothesis that the experience of positive and negative affect can be separable, evidence from the neurosciences suggests that the neural processes involved in positive and negative affect are partially distinct ... Specific neural structures also appear to be differentially involved in positive and negative affect. The amygdala, for example, has often been implicated in negative affect ... In contrast to the role of the amygdala in negative affect, the mesolimbic dopaminergic pathway projecting from the ventral tegmental area of the midbrain to the nucleus accumbens has been implicated in positive affect. (p. 687)

This line of reasoning has been widely echoed and portrayed as supporting the thesis of independence. In exercise psychology, for example, Gauvin and Rejeski (2001) alluded to "data suggesting that the neurological processes underlying positive and negative affect are distinct" (p. 76) to substantiate the argument that the notion of bipolarity represents an oversimplification. Despite such strong claims, however, extensive neuroscientific work has convincingly demonstrated that both the portrayal of the nucleus accumbens as the seat of positive affect and the portrayal of the amygdala as the seat of negative affect must be rejected (for a more extensive summary of this evidence and references, see Ekkekakis, 2008, pp. 147–151). This new evidence has prompted the following admission by Berntson and Cacioppo (2008):

Historically, the amygdala has been recognized as a primary integrative site for aversive reactions and negative affect, whereas the nucleus accumbens has been implicated in incentive motivation and positive affect ... The contemporary picture is somewhat more complex than a simple dissociation between the amygdala and nucleus accumbens, however; the latter, for example, has now been implicated in both positive and negative affect. (p. 197)

These authors also noted that "there may be some inhibitory interaction between positive and negative substrates [which] probably accounts for the fact that whereas positive and negative substrates can be coactivated, one does not generally observe strong concurrent positive and negative activations" (p. 198). This means that two anatomically distinct neural systems may well be activated reciprocally (activation of one automatically inhibiting the other) rather than concurrently. This raises what is perhaps a larger and more important issue. Even if one were to accept that positive and negative affect are served by distinct neural systems, there is no evidence that the presence of separable neural substrates necessarily entails the simultaneous conscious experience of conflicting (i.e., pleasant and unpleasant) affects. Neurophilosophers have argued that, even if consciousness relies on an anatomically distributed network of brain areas, it remains experientially unitary at any given point in time (Greenfield, 1995, see pp. 88–91). Making essentially the same point, Russell and Feldman Barrett (1999) have noted that "[although] core affect might involve multiple and functionally independent neural mechanisms that need not themselves be bipolar ... bipolarity may emerge in forming conscious affective feelings" (p. 813).

Current status of the bipolarity versus independence debate

Although it would be premature to declare the bipolarity versus independence debate settled (Larsen & McGraw, 2011; Norris, Gollan, Berntson, & Cacioppo, 2010), some points of convergence have nevertheless become apparent. Most importantly, there is now consensus that the relation between *pleasure* and *displeasure* (or *happiness-sadness*) is best modeled by a single bipolar dimension. Thus, Russell and Carroll (1999a) have asserted that "for the routine assessment of affective feelings, bipolar response formats are justified" (p. 25). Importantly, Watson and Tellegen (1999) have agreed with this position, although only in reference to the *pleasure* versus *displeasure* dimension; they remain unconvinced about the bipolarity of other pairs that have been suggested to be bipolar, such as *elated* versus *bored*. It should be noted, however, that their own earlier analyses (Tellegen, 1985; Watson & Tellegen, 1985; Zevon & Tellegen, 1982) had shown that states like *elated* and *enthusiastic* were the polar opposites of states like *dull* and *sluggish*.

The statement that a consensus is emerging in favor of the bipolarity of pleasure and displeasure must nevertheless be accompanied by a series of caveats, the importance of which cannot be overemphasized. First, not all positively valenced and negatively valenced affective states are expected to show a bipolar relation. Items reflecting a combination of pleasure with high activation (such as *elated, enthusiastic, excited*), described as Positive Affect (Watson & Tellegen, 1985) or Positive Activation (Watson et al., 1999) are theorized to be orthogonal to items reflecting a combination of displeasure with high activation (such as *distressed, jittery, nervous*), described as Negative Affect (Watson & Tellegen, 1985) or Negative Activation (Watson et al., 1999). Likewise, items reflecting a combination of pleasure with low activation (such as *calm, relaxed, placid*) are also theorized to be orthogonal to items reflecting a combination of displeasure with low activation (such as *sluggish, sleepy, dull*). Watson and Tellegen (1999) have stressed that "the correlation between positive and negative feelings varies substantially as a function of the descriptors that are used" and added that "this is an extremely important point" (p. 602). Given the unfortunate history of confusion on this point, researchers are urged to consider the strong warning by Watson and Tellegen (1999) that, in their model, "positive affect" is not synonymous to pleasure (or happiness) and "negative affect" is not synonymous to displeasure (or sadness). Rather, these terms have a very specific meaning:

The terms "positive affect" and "negative affect" were reserved for relatively pure markers of the two valenced activation dimensions that were hypothesized to be 45° removed from Russell's dimensions ... The primary purpose of these restrictive definitions was to eliminate the confusion that had plagued the earlier literature: In this more precise terminological scheme, markers of positive affect and negative affect should consistently show weak negative correlations, whereas terms reflecting pleasantness and unpleasantness should tend to be strongly negatively correlated (and, hence, define a single bipolar dimension). In recent years, researchers have increasingly ignored these conceptual/terminological distinctions and have reverted to using the terms "positive affect" and "negative affect" indiscriminately ... Now, we again face the extremely confusing situation that researchers may report low, moderate, even strong–negative correlations between measures of positive affect and negative affect because of substantial differences in the descriptors used to create the scales. The literature is so confused at this point that the terms "positive affect" and "negative affect" perhaps should indeed be used only as inclusive terms referring to any positive and negative feeling states. (pp. 602–603)

Second, bipolarity should only be expected to apply to pleasant and unpleasant "core affect" (as defined in Chapter 2) and for a single point in time. It should not be expected to apply to states defined by cognitive antecedents (such as emotions) or with a strong cognitive or evaluative component (such as attitudes). As Russell and Feldman Barrett (1999) noted in response to Cacioppo, "it is possible that positive and negative *evaluations* are independent, whereas core affect is bipolar" (p. 813, italics added). For example, purely cognitivistic models, in which affect is seen strictly as a response to judgments of how successfully people move toward incentives and away from threats, can comfortably accommodate the concurrent elicitation of positively and negatively valenced responses (e.g., Carver, 2001; Carver & Scheier, 1990). Carver and Harmon-Jones (2009a) explain:

People often have multiple goals in mind simultaneously, with one at a time receiving the most processing resources and thus occupying consciousness. If humans are organized in such a way that progress on multiple goals is tracked simultaneously, affect can exist with regard to each such goal. A person can be happy about one thing at a wedding (e.g., "The bride is so happy"), sad about another (e.g., "I never was that happy"), and anxious about another (e.g., "The bride's parents hate the groom") ... If there are multiple simultaneous goals, there can be multiple affect states, creating the clear potential for mixed feelings. (p. 217)

Furthermore, bipolarity is not necessary for reports of affective experiences referring to extended periods of time, since these may include numerous oscillations between positively and negatively valenced states. As one can easily appreciate, human beings are capable of processing conflicting or contradictory cognitions about the same object (e.g., physical activity can both benefit and hurt my arthritic knee) but it is highly unlikely that they could experience both pleasant and unpleasant affect at the exact same point in time. The reason why this is unlikely is adaptational; living systems that use affect as the main guide for their behavioral decisions would be faced with possibly lethal dilemmas at every turn. Bipolarity is also not necessary in cases in which even just one of the two states whose relationship is being investigated is defined by cognitive antecedents or has a strong cognitive component. This can help resolve the apparent paradox in the example in which strenuous exercise is said to "hurt so good." As noted earlier, the "hurt" probably reflects cognitively unmediated (purely somatic) core affect, whereas the "good" probably reflects the outcome of a cognitive appraisal of strenuous exercise as constituting the accomplishment of a personal challenge or the accrual of a training benefit.

Third, the evidence offered by Cacioppo and coworkers (e.g., Larsen et al., 2001, 2004), as well as others (e.g., Hemenover & Schimmack, 2007; Schimmack, 2001, 2005), has compelled many researchers to accept the possibility of "mixed emotions" (i.e., both pleasant and unpleasant) in "emotionally complex situations." Russell and Carroll (1999a) have acknowledged that, although usually bipolar, positively and negatively valenced states "might be separable in specific circumstances" (p. 26). These circumstances might be rare and indeed complex but are nonetheless within the realm of possibility in modern life. Furthermore, researchers have pointed out that the tendency to view pleasant and unpleasant affective states as bipolar or independent might be an individual difference variable (Rafaeli, Rogers, & Revelle, 2007; Vautier & Raufaste, 2003).

What does this all mean and why should we care?

The foregoing review, despite offering only a rudimentary summary of the multifaceted debate surrounding the issue of bipolarity versus independence, should suffice to convince readers that choosing a measure in which pleasant and unpleasant affective states are conceptualized as bipolar as opposed to independent (or vice versa) requires at least a basic explanation. The arguments for and against each point of view have been discussed so extensively in the literature and the implications of the two positions are so critical that to simply present a measure without explicitly stating why bipolarity or independence was preferred seems arbitrary.

What is at stake? First, using a measure in which pleasant and unpleasant states are conceptualized as representing the two opposite poles of a single dimension essentially ensures that measurement will be balanced with respect to valence. In other words, respondents will be given an equal chance to report that they are experiencing a pleasant or an unpleasant state. Having this type of balanced measurement approach can protect the research enterprise from bias. This is a real concern, as illustrated by the fact that some researchers have criticized the overemphasis on negative affective states (e.g., "the [Profile of Mood States] is heavily skewed toward measuring negative states"; McAuley & Courneya, 1994, p. 165; "most existing measures and related research have been preoccupied with negative affect"; Gauvin & Rejeski, 1993, p. 404) and others have criticized the inadequate coverage of negative affective states (e.g., "tiredness or fatigue ... probably do not suffice to capture the entire range of negatively valenced states induced by exercise"; Backhouse, Ekkekakis, et al., 2007, pp. 501–502).

As noted in the introduction, mood has been assessed with the unipolar version of the Profile of Mood States in some studies and with the bipolar version in others. Typically, this has been done without offering explicit arguments in support of one or the other option. If a researcher chooses the unipolar version of the Profile of Mood States, the respondents are asked, among other states, whether they feel tension (with items such as *tense*, *nervous*, or *anxious*). They are not asked whether they feel the polar opposite, namely calmness. On the contrary, if a researcher uses the bipolar version of the Profile of Mood States, respondents are not only asked whether they feel tension but also whether they feel calmness (with items such as *composed*, *relaxed*, or *serene*). According to Lorr et al. (2003), despite the fact that "with few exceptions, nearly all mood adjective check lists and rating scales measure monopolar dimensions," "common sense and semantics suggest that each feeling state must have a bipolar opposite" (p. 5). Furthermore, in an excerpt of profound importance, they state:

Most other instruments used in clinical settings (e.g., standard POMS) measure only the negative affects, such as anxiety, distress, depression, and hostile feelings. Since these instruments neglect the more positive affects such
as cheerfulness, agreeableness, composure, and sense of potency, they are
appropriate for assessing only clients with psychiatric problems. POMS–Bi,
however, is appropriate not just for clients with psychiatric problems, but also
for normals. (p. 1)

The implications of this excerpt for studies in the domain of health
behavior, an overwhelming number of which have been conducted with
the "standard" (i.e., unipolar) Profile of Mood States and participants
without any mental health problems, should be apparent. It should
also be clear that, when deciding between measures based on unipolar
versus bipolar conceptualizations of affective constructs, the previous
popularity of one or the other within a given domain of inquiry is not
the best guide. Such matters should be decided on the basis of conceptual considerations. If the developers of the Profile of Mood States
themselves have explicitly recommended the use of the bipolar over the
unipolar version for use with nonpsychiatric samples, researchers who
choose to employ the unipolar version in spite of this recommendation
should explain the rationale that led to their decision.

One might counter that there is no need to directly assess both poles
of a bipolar dimension since changes at one pole can be inferred by
changes at the other. For example, when one feels less tension, it might
seem reasonable to assume that one also experiences more calmness at
the same time. This, however, is untrue when the response scales used
are unipolar (e.g., from "not at all" to "extremely"), as is usually the
case. As Diener and Iran-Nejad (1986) and Russell and Carroll (1999a)
explained, if pleasure and displeasure are bipolar (180° apart), we can
assume that the distribution of true scores follows a normal distribution from pleasure (+) to displeasure (−), with a mean at a zero or "neutral" point. If an item from one pole (e.g., "I feel pleasure") is assessed
with a unipolar response scale (i.e., from "slightly" to "extremely"), its
relation to an item from the opposite pole (e.g., "I feel displeasure") is
nonlinear and thus can never be −1.00. It is important to remember
that, although when one reports feeling "very pleasant" (e.g., 5 on a
5-point scale), one is likely to feel "not at all unpleasant," when one
feels "moderately pleasant" (e.g., 3 on a 5-point scale), one does not feel
"moderately unpleasant" but rather, again, "not at all unpleasant." In
other words, instead of being perfectly negative linear (i.e., −1.00), the
relation between two such items would be approximately "L" shaped (in
fact, if the distributions are non-normal and the relation is nonlinear,

the correlation coefficient would not be the appropriate statistic to use). Russell and Carroll (1999a) estimated that, theoretically, if measurement is error free and the response scales are strictly unipolar, the correlation can only be as low as -0.467. Thus, simply put, when unipolar response scales are used, a score representing one pole of a theoretically bipolar dimension can never be perfectly redundant with a score representing the opposite pole. Therefore, assessing just one pole would leave out a considerable portion of the variance compared to assessing both poles.

This may seem too abstract and theoretical to be of practical significance but it is. Consider, for example, the position expressed by Watson and Clark (1997) that "unipolar scales [are] quite capable of measuring the underlying [bipolar] dimensions" (p. 277) and subsequently by Watson et al. (1999) that they find it unnecessary to also measure the low-activation ends of their Positive Affect and Negative Affect dimensions because the "activated, high ends of the dimensions fully capture their essential qualities" (p. 827). If the reasoning in the previous paragraph is correct, then the Positive and Negative Affect Schedule, which purports to measure bipolar dimensions by tapping only the high-activation poles and using a unipolar response scale (from "very slightly or not at all" to "extremely"), would be a questionable choice. This should be an important consideration for health behavior researchers since the polar opposites of high Positive Affect (i.e., fatigue, tiredness, depression, boredom) and high Negative Affect (i.e., calmness, relaxation, serenity, tranquility) are probably of great interest in a wide range of settings. Researchers interested in including these low-activation states within the scope of their investigations (and most probably are) should directly explain (a) the reasons for endorsing Watson et al.'s (1999) conceptual position that low-activation states such as "sluggishness and relaxation" are non-affective (p. 827) and (b) whether and why the Positive and Negative Affect Schedule was thought the best available option.

Although the weight of the evidence at this point seems to tilt the scale in favor of a bipolar relation between pleasure and displeasure, supporting Russell and Carroll's (1999a) statement that "bipolar response formats are justified" (p. 25) for routine assessments, exceptions may also be justified (e.g., Rafaeli & Revelle, 2006). Russell and Carroll (1999a) and Watson and Tellegen (1999) agree, for example, that, in cases in which the question of bipolarity versus independence is to be empirically tested, unipolar scales are the only option. The reason is that bipolar scales assume and thus impose bipolarity, precluding any tests of the alternative possibility, namely independence. Larsen, Norris, McGraw,

Hawkley, and Cacioppo (2009) have raised this issue again, reminding researchers that there are such emotionally complex scenarios as disappointing gains or relieving losses. Examples from health-behavioral research might include experiencing health benefits of smaller magnitude compared to what one had expected or, after a fainting incident, finding out that one has impaired glucose tolerance but has not suffered any myocardial damage. Clearly, when investigating such scenarios, researchers should opt for the independent assessment of positively and negatively valenced affect.

5   Selecting a measure: a proposed three-step process

The process of selecting a measure should ideally include the following steps (see Ekkekakis, 2008, 2012). The first step involves deciding which construct to target among the three main constructs that comprise the global domain of affective phenomena, namely *core affect, mood,* and *emotion.* This difficult question must be answered with clarity before one can move further along the process of selecting a measure.

The second step in the process entails a series of complex decisions and is thus at least as intellectually demanding as the first step. It involves choosing from among the different theoretical models proposed for conceptualizing the chosen construct. As explained in Chapters 3 and 4, measures do not (or, at least, *should not*) evolve in a theoretical vacuum; when one chooses a measure, one presumably also accepts or endorses the theoretical infrastructure upon which the measure was built. Arguably, it should be deemed inconceivable to choose a measure without having a firm understanding of the underlying theory or without being able to articulate the theoretical reasoning behind this choice. Researchers must recognize that, within the domain of affect, mood, and emotion research lies a multitude of theoretical perspectives. This cannot be ignored; researchers will encounter multiple bifurcations in the decision-making algorithm and must be prepared to argue in favor of one or the other option. These decisions have a defining impact on the data that will be collected, and, by extension, on the overall quality and meaningfulness of any study. As described in the previous two chapters, the differences between the options one must face are not slight or trivial. They typically represent diametrically opposite conceptual viewpoints and are often surrounded by intense intellectual battles that span several decades and dozens of published articles.

Once a researcher has pinpointed the construct she or he wishes to target, and has selected among the various theoretical models proposed for conceptualizing this construct, the third step is to choose among the available measures based on the selected theoretical model. At this point, the researcher must evaluate the technical-psychometric information available on each measure (i.e., whether a measure meets or surpasses established criteria for evaluating the various facets of reliability and validity). This step also involves contemplating more practical matters, such as the length of the measure (i.e., single-item rating scale versus a multi-item questionnaire).

This third step is also a demanding one, requiring considerable experience and expertise in psychometrics to carry out effectively. However, it is crucial to recognize that this step should be considered only as the *last* step in this multistep process, and never as the *sole* step. Its meaningfulness evaporates if the previous two steps are missing. As demonstrated by the numerous examples discussed in Chapter 1, what could be the value of identifying an internally consistent scale when the researcher does not have a clear idea about the construct she or he wants to target and, as a result, ends up interpreting a measure of one construct (e.g., emotion) as a measure of another (e.g., mood)? Similarly, how meaningful would it be to cite a goodness-of-fit index of 0.95 unless one had an informed and critical perspective on whether the theoretical basis of the measure was adequate or whether the model being tested in a confirmatory factor analysis was truly consistent with the theory in all of its (perhaps seemingly esoteric but nevertheless crucial) details?

The three-step system proposed here (see Figure 5.1) is consistent with the recommendations offered by experts in affective psychology. For example, Larsen and Fredrickson (1999), focusing their discussion specifically on the measurement of emotion, noted that, first, researchers should "construct a working definition of emotion(s) that best fits their research agenda prior to selecting measures" (p. 40). In other words, they recommended that "those embarking on emotions research first consider what they take emotions to be" (p. 42) and, by extension, how emotions differ from other states that fall under the broad umbrella of affective phenomena. They explained that they recommend this step for two reasons: "First, it can limit the possible misinterpretations of your results. Second, and perhaps more critically, it can make choosing among various emotion measures an easier task" (p. 41).

Similar to the present proposal, the second step they recommended was to consider and choose among the various theoretical models put forth for conceptualizing the domain of emotion. For example, addressing the issue examined in Chapter 3, Larsen and Fredrickson (1999) wrote that deciding whether to conceptualize emotions as "discrete and/or dimensional ... can impinge directly on emotion measurement" (p. 41). Similarly, addressing the issue discussed in Chapter 4, they noted:

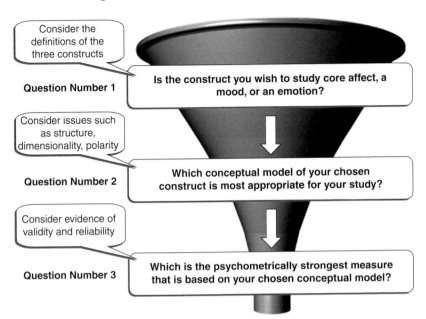

Figure 5.1. The three-step system for choosing (and justifying the selection of) a measure of affect, mood, or emotion.

One question concerns the relation between pleasure and pain, between positive and negative emotions. Are the conditions that give rise to pleasant emotions simply the opposite of those that produce unpleasant emotions? Can circumstances that bring about pleasantness cancel unpleasant states and vice versa? Should we think of pleasure and pain as end points on a continuum, or as completely separate and independent dimensions? (p. 40)

The third step recommended by Larsen and Fredrickson (1999) was to consider "the traditional measurement issues of reliability and validity" (p. 42). The analogies to the three-step approach proposed here should be evident.

Although the recommendations outlined in this guidebook are merely suggestions, it might be worth contemplating what the literature might look like in five or ten years if the editorial boards of journals decided to require that authors include this type of three-tiered documentation of their measure-selection process in all manuscripts. Arguably, this would represent a strong stimulus for progress as it would offer a framework for systematizing and clarifying the complex decision-making process leading to the choice of measures.

Justifying the selection of a measure: some examples

The material reviewed so far provides a glimpse of the conceptual issues that have dominated the scientific discourse on the conceptualization and assessment of affective phenomena in recent decades. The primary aim of the review was to act as a stimulus and basic guide to this literature. Under no circumstances can it serve as a substitute for conducting one's own meticulous and critical analysis of the primary sources. Similarly, the examples offered in this section do not constitute an endorsement of a particular measure and should not be considered as prototypes to be emulated in any strict sense; rather, they are meant to illustrate how the selection of a measure can be justified using the proposed three-tiered system.

The proposal for adopting this three-tiered justification is tantamount to a banishment from Methods sections as irrelevant and uninformative of such features as the popularity of a measure as criteria that led to its selection. Researchers must become accustomed to treating the selection of a measure as a profoundly theory-driven process. It should be clarified that, although in the following examples all the information is presented in one contiguous section, authors could easily distribute parts of the necessary material to the Introduction and Method sections.

Let us first consider an imaginary study aimed at examining the effects of a bout of physical activity on experimentally induced state anxiety. Since it makes little sense to examine the effectiveness of any intervention in reducing a state that is absent, researchers first induce state anxiety by having participants prepare for a 20-question quiz on a topic described only as "world geography" in front of a microphone, a video camera, and an austere-looking three-member panel. The progression from specifying the target construct (Tier 1) to describing and justifying the chosen conceptualization of the construct (Tier 2) and, finally, identifying the appropriate measure (Tier 3) should be evident but the sections have been marked for easier reference.

State Anxiety. The emotion of state anxiety was selectively targeted as the outcome variable in this investigation. The reason is that the experimental manipulation (preparing for the quiz) was specifically designed to elicit the pattern of cognitive appraisal theorized to stimulate a state anxiety response, namely a perception of personal inadequacy in the face of an impending threat to one's ego (Beck & Clark, 1997; Lazarus, 1991a; Spielberger, 1985). **[Tier 1]** At the level of self-report, a state anxiety response can be indexed by various clusters of symptoms commonly theorized to manifest as a coordinated syndrome (e.g., Spielberger, 1985). However, given the application of a physical activity intervention in the present study, it was necessary to distinguish somatic symptoms (such as the perception of respiratory, cardiocirculatory, or sudomotor changes) from cognitive symptoms (such as worry or apprehension, thoughts of negative consequences, and inability to concentrate). Previous studies have demonstrated that cognitive and somatic items can form separate factors (Ekkekakis, Hall, & Petruzzello, 1999) and change in a non-coordinated fashion (Rejeski, Hardy, & Shaw, 1991) in response to physical activity. This distinction is also supported by extensive psychometric evidence in educational, clinical, and psychotherapeutic contexts (Lehrer & Woolfolk, 1982; Liebert & Morris, 1967; Schwartz, Davidson, & Goleman, 1978). **[Tier 2]** On the basis of this conceptual framework, the state anxiety scale of the State-Trait Inventory for Cognitive and Somatic Anxiety (STICSA; Ree, French, MacLeod, & Locke, 2008) was used in this study. The 10 cognitive (e.g., "I think the worst will happen") and 11 somatic items (e.g., "My muscles are tense") were accompanied by a 4-point response scale (not at all; somewhat; moderately so; very much). Ree et al. (2008) showed that, although a model with two correlated factors ($r = 0.59$ to 0.73) fit the data well and the scores on both scales were elevated prior to an academic examination, only the somatic scale score significantly increased after CO_2 inhalation. Furthermore, Ree et al. (2008) and Grös, Anthony, Simms, and McCabe (2007) found that, in samples of students and anxiety patients, the scales of the STICSA were more closely related to measures of anxiety than measures of depression. In the present study, the cognitive and somatic scales of the STICSA exhibited adequate internal consistency (alphas > 0.75). **[Tier 3]**

The second example refers to the measurement of core affect. Let us suppose that the purpose of this imaginary study was to investigate an "affective competition hypothesis," according to which physical activity can compete against and eventually replace addictive substances by eliciting comparable affective responses to them. Thus, the study compared the affective responses to a 15-minute bout of self-paced walking and to the smoking of two cigarettes in a sample of smokers initiating a quitting attempt. Since the most salient experiential features of the affective responses to physical activity and smoking remain shrouded in mystery and may well vary greatly from person to person, a study like this would benefit from a broad and balanced approach to measurement (i.e., one not biased in favor of or against any particular, positive or negative, variant of affective experience).

Affective responses. Consistent with the aim of the present study, the targeted construct was core affect (Russell, 2003, 2005; Russell & Feldman Barrett, 1999). Core affect is defined as "the most elementary consciously accessible affective feelings" (Russell & Feldman Barrett, 1999, p. 806). As such, core affect is generally considered "the most general" (Batson, Shaw, & Oleson, 1992, p. 298) construct in the hierarchy of affective constructs, being broader than mood and emotion. **[Tier 1]** Under the present combination of experimental conditions, it was not possible to predict the exact nature of affective responses that would be elicited from physical activity and smoking. Thus, instead of focusing on a few distinct varieties of affect, it was deemed preferable to attempt to capture this global domain of content in a more encompassing fashion. To this end, core affect was conceptualized as a domain defined by a set of basic dimensions. Specifically, the measurement approach was based on the circumplex model (Feldman Barrett & Russell, 2009), according to which the domain of core affect can be defined by two orthogonal and bipolar dimensions, namely affective valence (pleasure to displeasure) and perceived activation (Carroll, Yik, Russell, & Feldman Barrett, 1999; Remington, Fabrigar, & Visser, 2000; Russell & Carroll, 1999a). **[Tier 2]** To operationalize these dimensions, we used the composite short form (Västfjäll & Gärling, 2007) of the Swedish Core Affect Scales (SCAS; Västfjäll, Friman, Gärling, & Kleiner, 2002). The circumplex structure of the original multi-item SCAS was supported by multidimensional scaling analysis and a circumplex-specific confirmatory procedure (Browne, 1992) yielding satisfactory fit indices (RMSEA = 0.07, AGFI = 0.89, CFI = 0.92). The composite short form consists of two bipolar scales, one assessing valence (with the terms *displeased-pleased, sad-glad, depressed-happy*) and one assessing activation (with the terms *sleepy-awake, passive-active, dull-peppy*). The two scales exhibited strong correlations ($r > 0.90$) with the corresponding scales of the Self-Assessment Manikin (Bradley & Lang, 1994) but an intercorrelation of only -0.10, supporting their orthogonality. The bipolar rating format (-4 to +4) was used in this investigation. **[Tier 3]**

These examples illustrate that a principled and organized system for justifying the choice of a measure is possible. They also show that resorting to such superficial arguments as the popularity of a measure is superfluous and detracts attention from more substantive considerations. The value of the three-tiered system can be appreciated mainly when these examples are juxtaposed to excerpts from the published literature, in which measures are presented unaccompanied by a supporting rationale. Following the three-tiered system not only encourages authors to think systematically about their measurement options but also provides readers with greatly needed information with which they can meaningfully evaluate the conceptual basis and methodological rigor of published works.

6   The old classics: measures of distinct states

The previous chapters described the nature and the severity of some of the problems associated with the measurement of affect, mood, and emotion in health-behavioral research (Chapter 1), outlined a framework for defining and distinguishing between these three constructs (Chapter 2), and summarized certain issues of fundamental significance for the conceptualization and assessment of affective constructs, namely whether these states should be considered as distinct entities or as positioned along dimensions (Chapter 3) and whether pleasure and displeasure are independent or polar opposites (Chapter 4). This review culminated in a proposal for a three-tiered system for justifying the selection of a measure (Chapter 5).

In this and the remaining chapters, the background provided so far will be used in critiquing some of the most frequently used measures in health-behavioral research. Emphasis is placed on the conceptual bases and the developmental histories of the measures, the significance and implications of which are all too often overlooked. The aim of this presentation is to sensitize researchers to approach each measure critically, raise awareness of the relative strengths and limitations of each measure, and offer key references for further study.

The Multiple Affect Adjective Check List

The Multiple Affect Adjective Check List (Zuckerman & Lubin, 1965a) was one of the first self-report measures designed to assess transient affective states as opposed to stable traits. Furthermore, it was primarily aimed at the general population rather than clinical groups. These characteristics made the Multiple Affect Adjective Check List a pioneering development in the study of affective phenomena. Its development history is an interesting example of the distinct-states approach described in Chapter 3.

The predecessor of the Multiple Affect Adjective Check List was the Affect Adjective Check List (Zuckerman, 1960), a 21-item check list measure of anxiety consisting of 11 anxiety-present (e.g., *afraid*, *fearful*) and 10 anxiety-absent items (e.g., *calm*, *cheerful*). The anxiety score increased for every anxiety-present item checked and for every anxiety-absent item left unchecked. In the last sentence of the 1960 article, Zuckerman noted that the same general format could also be used to develop other tests, with depression and hostility being "two obvious possibilities" (p. 462). So, a few years later, the first version of the Multiple Affect Adjective Check List appeared, combining scales for anxiety, depression, and hostility (Zuckerman, Lubin, Vogel, & Valerius, 1964). Readers should note how fundamentally different this distinct-states approach is from approaches based on dimensional views of the global affective space. Essentially, the Multiple Affect Adjective Check List was developed as a measure of three distinct states that its developers considered important, without making any claims whatso-ever about covering a global domain of content (such as affect, mood, or emotion).

The added Depression scale consisted of 20 depression-present (e.g., *blue*, *discouraged*) and 20 depression-absent items (e.g., *alive*, *enthusiastic*) that were all different from those used in the Anxiety scale. Similarly, the Hostility scale consisted of 16 hostility-present (e.g., *angry*, *bitter*) and 12 hostility-absent items (e.g., *agreeable*, *amiable*). Several add-itional items were retained for further testing, for a total of 132 items. Zuckerman and Lubin (1965b) provided normative data.

A problem that quickly became apparent was that the scales were highly intercorrelated and lacked discriminant validity, possibly because the check list format increased the influence of acquiescent response sets (i.e., a person with a tendency to check many items would receive lower negative affect scores). When factor analysis became more readily available, the 132-item pool was factor analyzed (Zuckerman, Lubin, & Rinck, 1983) and a new structure emerged. Specifically, anxiety-present, depression-present, and hostility-present items formed three separate factors, while the positively worded items formed two factors (one named Positive Affect and the other Sensation Seeking). However, given the strong intercorrelations among factors within each category, Zuckerman et al. (1983) proceeded to also merge Anxiety, Depression, and Hostility into a Dysphoria (DYS) factor and Positive Affect (PS) and Sensation Seeking (SS) into a combined PASS factor.

A subsequent independent factor analysis confirmed that the items formed separate factors consisting of the positively and the negatively worded items, respectively (Gotlib & Meyer, 1986). The influence of response sets was again presented as the most likely explanation, lead-ing to the following warning: "investigators who use the Multiple Affect

Adjective Check List scales as measures of affect should be aware of the potential problems with this questionnaire" (p. 1165). The hierarchical structure (five first-order factors and two second-order factors) formed the basis for the revised edition of the Multiple Affect Adjective Check List, the Multiple Affect Adjective Check List – Revised (Lubin et al., 1986; Zuckerman & Lubin, 1965a), which comprised 66 scored and 66 filler items. However, an independent factor analysis again yielded just two factors, separating the positively and the negatively worded items (Hunsley, 1990).

The Multiple Affect Adjective Check List has been used in thousands of studies in many areas of psychology. However, its popularity has declined in recent years. Nevertheless, it was important to review it here to illustrate two crucial points. First, the history of the Multiple Affect Adjective Check List essentially parallels the conceptual developments in the field of affective psychology, highlighting the progression from distinct-states to dimensional and, eventually, to hierarchical models. Second, to set the background for the review of newer measures, it was important to remind readers of the history of one of the most popular measures of affect. In particular, it is worth pondering whether a measure initially intended to assess three distinct constructs (anxiety, depression, hostility) can be considered an encompassing measure of the global domain of "affect." Even when it is scored in terms of the higher-order dimensions of DYS and PASS, a measure initially developed to target three distinct states will always be limited by the scope and representativeness of its item pool. Factor analysis cannot uncover the structure of a content domain; it can only help uncover the structure of a given item pool.

The Profile of Mood States

The Profile of Mood States is one of the most popular self-report measures, not only in health-behavioral research but in psychology in general. However, few of the researchers using the Profile of Mood States offer specific reasons for their selection (other than its enormous popularity) and few seem fully aware of the history of this measure.

What seems to have been the earliest draft of what later became known as the Profile of Mood States appeared in a study designed to assess the effects of tranquilizers (meprobamate and chlorpromazine) in a sample of male veterans receiving psychotherapy on an outpatient basis (Lorr, McNair, Weinstein, Michaux, & Raskin, 1961). The measure, which did not yet have a name, was described as a collection of "55 common adjectives describing feeling states" (p. 383) grouped in five categories (anxiety, hostility, depression, inertia, and activity). In a subsequent publication with a similar aim (i.e., investigating the effects of chlordiazepoxide), the measure (which still did not have a name) was described as a "feeling and attitude scale, which has been shown to be sensitive to change in several studies" (Lorr, McNair, & Weinstein, 1963, p. 261). The number of items had been increased to 60, each accompanied by a 4-point response scale ("not at all," "a little," "quite a bit," "extremely"). The measure purportedly assessed "six moods," namely Tension-Anxiety, Anger-Hostility, Depression, Vigor, Fatigue-Inertia, and Thinking-Confusion.

The now famous initials POMS appeared for the first time in 1964, although they did not originally stand for Profile of Mood States but rather for Psychiatric Outpatient Mood Scale (McNair & Lorr, 1964). The stated goal of the developers of the POMS was to "construct and develop a useful method for identifying and assessing mood states in psychiatric outpatient populations" (p. 620). They now hypothesized six mood states "on the basis of clinical observation and a review of previous studies" (p. 620). Those six were Tension, Anxiety, Anger, Depression, Vigor, and Fatigue.

It is very important for current and prospective users of the Profile of Mood States to understand that the item pool was composed of items drawn from various adjective lists, a dictionary, and a thesaurus with the purpose of matching them to the six targeted mood states (which were slightly different from those in the present-day six-factor structure). Furthermore, the items were retained only if "four psychologists concurred in judging [them] to be descriptive of the six hypothesized mood states" (McNair & Lorr, 1964, p. 621). In other words, as was the case with the Multiple Affect Adjective Check List, there was again no intention to develop an item pool that would reflect the global content domain of mood. The goal of McNair and Lorr was to assess certain specific states they deemed of interest for the study of psychiatric outpatients.

It is also important to note that the reference to "previous studies" as the basis for hypothesizing six factors seems to point to the highly influential analyses by Nowlis and Nowlis (1956). These investigators were studying the effects of drugs but also hoped to develop a measure "that is applicable to a wide variety of situations not involving drugs" (p. 352) and to discover "generally applicable categories" of mood states (p. 354). They had originally hypothesized that they would uncover four bipolar dimensions (level of activation, level of control, social orientation, and hedonic tone), but, when their empirical analysis was completed (Green & Nowlis, 1957), they found eight unipolar and correlated factors (concentration, aggression, pleasantness, activation-deactivation, egotism, social affection, depression, and anxiety). When Nowlis (1965, 1970) later developed the Mood Adjective Check List, the number was raised to 12 (aggression, anxiety, surgency, elation, concentration, fatigue, social affection, sadness, skepticism, egotism, vigor, and nonchalance). Clearly, neither the eight nor the twelve factors agreed fully with the six factors proposed by McNair and Lorr (1964). Thus, their insistence on these six factors was driven more by their clinical judgment and experience than by previous empirical findings.

McNair and Lorr (1964) conducted a series of factor analyses with data gathered from neurotic psychiatric outpatients, during which some items were deleted and new ones added. In the process, the Tension and Anxiety items were found to form a single factor. A Confusion factor did not emerge initially but did emerge after new items were added (presumably, the interest in this factor was due to confusion being an important variable when investigating the effects of psychotropic drugs). For researchers who have questioned whether "confusion" is a mood state, it is important to note that McNair and Lorr (1964) were also unsure whether this factor represented "cognitive inefficiency, a mood state, or both" (p. 624). Furthermore, a weak Friendliness factor appeared unexpectedly out of items added to strengthen the Anger factor. Confidence in a five-factor grouping was later increased based on findings from factor analyses by other investigators but on similar item pools (Lorr et al., 1967). The five factors were labeled Depression, Vigor-Activity, Fatigue-Inertia, Tension-Anxiety, and Anger-Hostility. A sixth factor "variously called Concentration, Thoughtful, Confusion, and Clear Thinking" (p. 89) was also considered possible. However, when 62 items given to samples of undergraduate students (for the first time to a nonclinical sample) were factor analyzed, eight rather than five or six factors emerged. The additional factors were Cheerful, Thoughtful (similar to Confusion), and Relaxed-Composed.

Interestingly, Lorr et al. (1967) examined whether these eight factors could be ordered in a circular fashion, as would be predicted by the circumplex model. Indeed, they found some support but also some discrepancies (e.g., the correlation between Inert-Fatigued and Composed-Relaxed was negative). They concluded that "while the present data offer some support for the hypothesis, further trial will be necessary before a circular order can be established" (p. 94). Furthermore, based on a visual inspection of the scale intercorrelations, they noted that even the eight scales did not suffice to cover the entire circle without leaving large gaps: "it is evident that at least one mood variable is missing between Composed-Relaxed and Inert-Fatigued" and possibly another one "between Energetic and Angry-Irritable" (p. 94).

Despite these highly interesting observations, the version of the POMS that became commercially available in 1971 under the new name "Profile of Mood States" was offered with a six-factor structure comprising Tension-Anxiety, Depression-Dejection, Anger-Hostility, Vigor-Activity, Fatigue-Inertia, and Confusion-Bewilderment (McNair et al. 1971). Soon thereafter, Spielberger (1972b) began his critical review of the Profile of Mood States with what is clearly its most serious limitation (and yet a point largely absent from discussions of the Profile of Mood States in the applied psychology literature to date):

The POMS test manual suggests that the POMS factors emerged from the test construction procedures. This is somewhat misleading in that, for the initial item pool and subsequent additions to the pool, adjectives with semantic connotations that reflected the factors the authors wished to assess were selected. Put differently, factor analysis was employed to refine the mood dimensions the authors wished to assess rather than to sort out or map the mood domain. While the authors have been successful in defining six mood factors, a different set of mood dimensions might have resulted if other adjectives had been included in the item pool in addition to those selected by the authors on a priori grounds as fitting their conceptual definition of the mood dimensions they wished to measure. (p. 387)

Years later, Thayer (1989) made a similar point, criticizing the Profile of Mood States for grouping items without "sufficient theoretical guidance" and for proposing "distinctions among mood dimensions" without offering a theoretical model for "the ways in which these factors interact" (p. 16). Current and prospective users of the Profile of Mood States are urged to consider these warnings. From a practical perspective, these experts are suggesting that one cannot generalize from data collected with the Profile of Mood States to the global domain of "mood," only to the six distinct states this measure includes (see Figure 6.1). The reason is that no theoretical or empirical basis supports the idea that the particular assortment of factors that make up the Profile of Mood States provides an encompassing representation of this global domain of content. One can easily think of mood states not included in the Profile of Mood States that might be of interest to investigators in the domain of health-behavioral research (e.g., cheerfulness or joviality, peacefulness or serenity). Recall, for example, that Relaxed-Composed was identified in earlier analyses by Lorr et al. (1967) but was not included in the commercial version of the Profile of Mood States.

Independent investigations of the factor structure of the Profile of Mood States have yielded inconsistent results. Norcross, Guadagnoli,

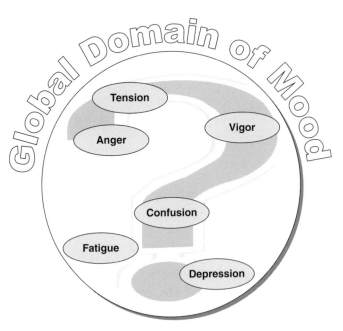

Figure 6.1. There is no conceptual argument or empirical evidence that the six distinct states assessed by the Profile of Mood States can provide comprehensive coverage of the global domain of mood. Therefore, extrapolations from assessments based on the Profile of Mood States to the global domain of mood are unwarranted.

and Prochaska (1984), examining responses from a sample of psychiatric outpatients and a sample of adult smokers, found that the Anger-Hostility, Vigor-Activity, and Fatigue-Inertia factors were reproduced in both samples. However, the Tension-Anxiety and Confusion-Bewilderment factors were not reproduced in either sample and the Depression-Dejection factor was reproduced in the outpatient sample but not in the smoker sample. Because of some very high inter-factor correlations (up to 0.81), the authors warned that "caution is recommended in the separate scoring and interpretation of these scales" (p. 1277). Boyle (1987) found evidence of nine factors, including the standard six plus a second Depression factor, a Friendliness factor, and an Arousal-Alertness factor (each accounting for approximately 2 percent of the variance). Focusing on the loadings of individual items, Reddon, Marceau, and Holden (1985) found that, while the factors had satisfactory homogeneity and internal consistency, less than two-thirds of the items were discriminantly valid in any given sample (i.e., had higher loadings on their own scales than on irrelevant scales) and less than half of the items were consistently (i.e., across different samples) discriminantly valid. Thus, these authors noted that "possibly the test constructor, clinician, or researcher in the mood domain may or may not wish to consider a more articulated assessment of moods than that available through the standard form of the POMS" (p. 257).

It is also important to consider the evolution of the Profile of Mood States after its initial commercial version and the developments that led to the publication of the newer, bipolar version. Prompted by Osgood's (1962) famous analyses of the structure underlying affective meaning, which revealed bipolar dimensions, Bentler's (1969) demonstration that measurement error tends to conceal bipolarity, and Meddis' (1972) influential work on the role played by unipolar response formats in the same regard, Lorr and Shea (1979) started exploring the question "are mood states bipolar?" For example, they noted that because the Profile of Mood States uses a unipolar response format, its scales "are more subject to extreme response bias" (p. 469). They postulated that nine states (cheerful, energetic, grouchy, anxious, dejected, tired, agreeable, composed, and confidence/potency) would exhibit circular ordering, similar to a circumplex. An advantage they saw in this type of modeling was that it would provide "a definition of the universe of content" (p. 469), something clearly missing from the Profile of Mood States.

In a sample using a unipolar response format, after partialling out an extreme response style score, four of the five factors that emerged were bipolar (Composed-Anxious, Energetic-Tired, Agreeable-Angry, Optimistic-Pessimistic), whereas only Cheerful remained unipolar. In a second sample using a bipolar response format, three of the six factors that emerged were bipolar (Composed-Anxious, Energetic-Tired, Agreeable-Angry) and three were unipolar (Confident, Dejected, Cheerful). Lorr and Shea (1979) also found some support for circular ordering and wondered whether the dimensions of Pleasantness-Unpleasantness and Arousal would be found to explain this phenomenon. Lorr et al. (1982) followed up on these findings, this time hypothesizing five bipolar factors (Composed-Anxious, Agreeable-Hostile, Energetic-Tired, Elated-Depressed, Clear-thinking-Confused). Using a slightly modified version of the Profile of Mood States (with the addition of items measuring friendliness and elation), they performed a factor analysis on data from psychiatric patients. After partialling out the variance due to extreme response bias from the interitem correlations, they found evidence for four of the five hypothesized bipolar factors (Elated-Depressed, Agreeable-Hostile, Energetic-Tired, Clear-thinking-Confused). The fifth factor (Composed-Anxious) could not emerge as bipolar for the simple reason that there was a very unbalanced representation of the two poles in the item pool, with nine items representing the Anxious pole but only one representing the Composed pole. The authors also mentioned that, in a separate study, they derived a bipolar Confident-Unsure factor. Thus, since the 1980s, the bipolar version of the Profile of Mood States includes the following factors: Composed-Anxious, Agreeable-Hostile, Elated-Depressed, Confident-Unsure, Energetic-Tired, and Clearheaded-Confused.

Continuing to work on this topic and convinced of the bipolar nature of mood states, Lorr developed a measure that used the semantic differential format (Lorr & Wunderlich, 1988). The new measure was named the Feeling and Mood Scales and later the Semantic Differential Mood Scale to avoid any interference with the commercial success of the Profile of Mood States. Lorr and Wunderlich (1988) hypothesized six bipolar factors (Cheerful-Dejected, Energetic-Tired, Relaxed-Anxious, Good-natured-Grouchy, Confident-Unsure, and Excited-Bored) and found factor-analytic evidence for five (Cheerful-Dejected, Relaxed-Anxious, Confident-Unsure, Energetic-Tired, and Good-natured-Grouchy), whereas items hypothesized to form the Excited-Bored factor were grouped with Cheerful-Dejected.

Closing this long cycle, Lorr et al. (1989) made one more attempt to identify the "five or six mood states [that] can account for most of the inter-individual variation in affect" (p. 156). The attempt, however, was unsuccessful. Lorr et al. hypothesized six bipolar factors: Relaxed-Anxious, Agreeable-Grouchy, Joyful-Depressed, Confident-Unsure, Energetic-Tired, and Excited-Apathetic. With what is now known about the content and structure of the affective domain (see Chapters 1–3), it is clear that some of the hypothesized factors cover the same space (e.g., from high-activation pleasant to low-activation unpleasant affect: Joyful-Depressed and Energetic-Tired), whereas others refer to cognition rather than affect (i.e., Confident-Unsure). So the resultant factor structure did not agree with the hypothesis (bipolar factors for Hostile Depression versus Satisfied Pleasure, Energetic versus Fatigued/Drowsy, Composure versus Anxiety, Confidence versus Self-doubt, and a unipolar Active Arousal factor). Important, however, even without the benefit of a guiding theoretical framework, most of the factors were found to be bipolar after the removal of variance due to extreme response bias.

Furthermore, Lorr et al. (1989) examined the first two principal components after a Varimax rotation and found that one represented Pleasant versus Unpleasant Affect and the second represented Energetic Arousal versus Drowsy Fatigue. Although this solution did not align with either Russell's (1980) or Watson and Tellegen's (1985) model due to the unbalanced composition of the item pool, the important conclusion is that, after almost 30 years of exploring the nature of mood, Lorr et al. (1989) produced data that converged with the universal two-dimensional model of affect presented here (for more on the endorsement of the circumplex model, see Lorr, 1989, 1997).

Given this history, it might seem surprising that even the original unipolar version of the Profile of Mood States, long rendered outdated by the theoretical developments in affective psychology, continues to be used with great regularity in health-behavioral research. The main (if not the only) argument put forth by researchers for their choice of measure is that the Profile of Mood States has been very popular. For example, as noted in Chapter 1, in exercise studies, researchers have claimed that they chose this measure because it "has been used extensively to assess the acute effects of exercise on mood" (Hoffman & Hoffman, 2008, p. 359), or "has been widely utilized in exercise research" (Bryan et al., 2007), or is "one of the most frequently used mood measures in sport and exercise psychology" (Johansson et al. 2008, p. 201), or is "historically the most frequently used measure in exercise and mood state studies" (Hansen et al. 2001, p. 269).

Critiques of the Profile of Mood States in health-behavioral research are rare and have concentrated on issues of secondary importance, such as its length and the inclusion of only one positive scale, namely Vigor (Berger & Motl, 2000; Gauvin & Rejeski, 1993; Guadagnoli & Mor, 1989; McAuley & Courneya, 1994). At this stage of knowledge development, the argument that a measure is used because it has been used before cannot be deemed compelling. Researchers who select the Profile of Mood States for a particular study should explain this decision in light of the issues raised in the literature. Furthermore, it is important that researchers avoid generalizations from the six distinct states to the global domain of mood, as such extrapolations are clearly unjustified by the history, the scope, and the structure of this measure.

The State-Trait Anxiety Inventory

The State-Trait Anxiety Inventory (Spielberger et al., 1970; Spielberger, 1983) was based on Spielberger's highly influential theory of state and trait anxiety developed in the 1960s and 1970s (Spielberger, 1966, 1972a). According to this theory, state anxiety is defined as a "transitory psychobiological emotional state or condition that is characterized by subjective, consciously experienced thoughts and feelings relating to tension, apprehension, nervousness, and worry that vary in intensity and fluctuate over time" (Spielberger & Reheiser, 2004, p. 70). In contradistinction, trait anxiety is defined as "relatively stable individual differences in anxiety proneness as a personality trait" or "differences in the strength of the disposition to respond to situations perceived as threatening with elevations in state anxiety" (pp. 70–71). Spielberger's theory was influenced by the advent of "trait by situation" interactionism in personality psychology, as well as the rise of appraisal-based approaches in the study of emotion. The theory thus predicts that high-trait-anxious individuals will tend to interpret a larger proportion of situations as entailing some type of threat than low-trait-anxious individuals. The perception of threat will depend on appraising a higher level of threat in each situation, a lower level of coping capabilities, or both.

The State-Trait Anxiety Inventory includes two scales, each consisting of 20 items: one assesses state anxiety (with items such as "I am worried" and "I feel frightened") and the other assesses trait anxiety (with items such as "I worry too much over something that really doesn't matter" and "I lack self-confidence"). The state-anxiety items are accompanied by a four-point scale of intensity, ranging from "not at all" to "very much so." The trait anxiety items are accompanied by a four-point scale of frequency, ranging from "almost never" to "almost always." For example, the state-anxiety scale has been used in exercise psychology to investigate the anxiolytic effects of single bouts of activity (e.g., Bodin & Martinsen, 2004), whereas the trait anxiety scale has been used as a measure of the effects of exercise training studies lasting for weeks or months (e.g., DiLorenzo et al., 1999).

The original version of the State-Trait Anxiety Inventory was published in 1970 and designated as Form X-1 for the state version and Form X-2 for the trait version (Spielberger et al., 1970). A revision, designated as Form Y-1 (for state anxiety) and Form Y-2 (for trait anxiety), was published in 1983 (Spielberger, 1983). The purpose of the revision was to replace "several items with poor psychometric properties" (Vagg, Spielberger, & O'Hearn, 1980, p. 212). For example, the item *anxious* was replaced by *frightened* because some respondents interpreted it to mean "eager" (Spielberger, 1985, p. 12). Furthermore, Spielberger (1983) noted that the development of Form Y was driven by the desire to make the questionnaire more "consistent with theoretical refinements in our concept of anxiety" by giving "greater emphasis to the cognitive or 'worry' aspects of anxiety than the original items" (p. 12).

Primarily because it incorporated the important conceptual distinction between states and traits and its items were appropriate for use with respondents without clinical levels of anxiety, the State-Trait

Anxiety Inventory became (and continues to be) exceptionally popular. However, it has also received a fair amount of criticism. Current and prospective users of this questionnaire should be aware of the limitations discussed in the literature and these should inform their measurement decisions. Critics have primarily focused on two important issues, namely the factor structure and the content overlap with depression.

Factor-analytic results of both Form X and Form Y have been inconsistent in terms of the nature and composition of the resultant factors but have been consistent in showing that the state and trait anxiety scales contain more than one factor each (Bernstein & Eveland, 1982; Caci, Baylé, Dossios, Robert, & Boyer, 2003; Endler, Magnusson, Ekehammar, & Okada, 1976; Mook, Kleijn, & van der Ploeg, 1991; Mook, van der Ploeg, & Kleijn, 1992; Sherwood & Westerback, 1983; Vagg et al., 1980).

The most commonly reported finding has been the separation of the positively worded (or "anxiety-absent") and negatively worded (or "anxiety-present") items into different factors. Initially, Spielberger et al. (1970) selected items intended to differ in terms of their "item intensity specificity." This psychometric concept refers to a property of different items to discriminate better at one level of anxiety than at another. According to Spielberger (1985), in constructing the state-anxiety scale, "the main goal was to measure a continuum of increasing intensity on which low scores indicated feeling calm and serene, intermediate scores were associated with moderate levels of tension and worry, and high scores reflected intense fear, approaching terror and panic" (p. 11). For example, the item "I feel rested," which is positively worded (i.e., denotes the absence of anxiety), was selected because it was thought more sensitive to fluctuations in state anxiety at the low end of the state-anxiety continuum than at the high end. In actuality, an empirical investigation of the location of the items along the state and trait anxiety continua using Rasch modeling revealed several weaknesses, including parts of the continua not represented by any items, parts covered by multiple items, and several badly fitting items that misrepresented the respondents' level of anxiety (Tenenbaum, Furst, & Weingarten, 1985). Nevertheless, in general, the anxiety-absent items were located near the bottom and the anxiety-present items were located near the top of the continua.

Spielberger's position regarding these findings was that they do not necessarily indicate multidimensionality:

While the consistent finding of anxiety-present and anxiety-absent factors could be interpreted as evidence of the multidimensionality of the [state anxiety] and [trait anxiety] scales, it seems more plausible to interpret these factors as resulting from either "item-method variance" (i.e. the STAI consists of two distinctive types of items, anxiety-present and anxiety-absent), or to "item-intensity specificity" (i.e. the anxiety-present items appear to be more effective in measuring higher levels of state and trait anxiety, whereas the anxiety-absent items are more sensitive at lower levels. (Vagg et al., 1980, p. 213)

However, other researchers have been more critical, since it is indeed uncommon for a supposed unidimensional construct to be represented by multiple factors, regardless of any effects of item-method variance or item-intensity specificity. For example, Bernstein and Eveland (1982), on the basis of their confirmatory factor analysis, concluded that the "worst feature" of the State-Trait Anxiety Inventory "is that differences between positive and negative items are approximately as great as the differences between State and Trait items" (p. 372). They aptly noted that, although the separation of anxiety-present and anxiety-absent items is "interesting in its own rights, ... it should not obscure the appropriateness of the state-trait distinction" (p. 372). In other words, method-related factors should not preclude the straightforward interpretation of the factors meant to be substantive.

Adding further evidence that this is problematic, Mook et al. (1991) showed that, when the items of the State-Trait Anxiety Inventory and those from a depression questionnaire were factor analyzed together, the distinction that emerged was between symptom-present and symptom-absent items rather than between anxiety and depression items. Especially if the formation of separate factors can be attributed to the influence of such factors as denial and social desirability (e.g., Bonke, Smorenburg, van der Ent, & Spielberger, 1987; Mook et al., 1991), the presence of multiple factors has clear implications for validity and, therefore, cannot be seen as a benign phenomenon.

Of particular relevance to many of the studies in health-behavioral research, in which the respondents are young, healthy, and non-anxious college students, is the observation that, while respondents score very low in anxiety-present items (indicating a low degree of anxiety), scores on anxiety-absent items tend to cover a wide range (Bonke et al., 1987). It has often been noted that healthy college students give total scores only a few points above the bottom of the range (Dishman, 1995) and rate anxiety-present items (e.g., *frightened*), in particular, so close to the bottom of the range that their variance approaches zero (Ekkekakis et al., 1999). This phenomenon raises the possibility that anxiety-present and anxiety-absent items indeed reflect different sources of variance.

The second major criticism directed toward the State-Trait Anxiety Inventory relates to its conspicuously high content overlap with depression. Although anxiety and depression frequently occur as comorbid conditions (Mineka, Watson, & Clark, 1998; Watson & Kendall, 1989), a measure of anxiety should remain as "uncontaminated" by depression as possible. Replacing items that seemed more relevant to depression than anxiety (e.g., "I feel blue," "I feel like crying") was one of the main reasons cited for revising Form X of the State-Trait Anxiety Inventory and developing Form Y (Spielberger, 1985; Vagg et al., 1980). However, the revision did not seem to solve the problem, since Form Y (both the state and trait scales) continues to show very strong overlap with measures of depression (Bieling, Antony, & Swinson, 1998; Endler, Cox, Parker, & Bagby, 1992; Gotlib, 1984). It is clear that some of the remaining items also reflect depression more than anxiety (e.g., "I feel like a failure").

In the late 1980s, Watson and Clark (Clark & Watson, 1991; Watson, Clark, & Carey, 1988) began developing a so-called tripartite model to distinguish between symptoms of anxiety and depression. According to this model, negative affect is common to both anxiety and depression, low positive affect and anhedonia are specific to depression, and physiological tension and hyperarousal are specific to anxiety. Empirical tests of the tripartite model have been supportive (Mineka et al., 1998) and the model has stimulated renewed efforts to improve the discriminant validity of measures of anxiety and depression. However, having been developed and revised prior to the emergence of the tripartite model, the State-Trait Anxiety Inventory has not incorporated this important conceptual advance. According to Bieling et al. (1998):

The construction of the STAI, in both its original and revised forms, predated recent advances in the understanding of the relationship between anxiety and depression. Indeed, the items of the trait scale that represent the "anxiety-absent" dimension may possibly reflect depression (i.e. low positive affect) rather than anxiety. Based on content, these items appear to assess high levels of dysphoric mood and harsh self-judgements, both of which are more typically associated with depression than anxiety (e.g. *I wish I could be as happy as others seem to be*; *I feel like a failure*). (pp. 778–779)

The weaknesses of the State-Trait Anxiety Inventory brought to the forefront in other areas of psychology have not attracted much attention within the domain of health-behavioral research. The popularity of the questionnaire remains very high. As is the case with the Profile of Mood States, the selection of the State-Trait Anxiety Inventory is typically justified precisely on the basis of its prior popularity by suggesting that extensive prior use is tantamount to validation or de facto evidence of psychometric merit. For example, as noted in Chapter 1, in exercise psychology, authors have chosen to use the State-Trait Anxiety Inventory because it is the "most widely used measure of anxiety in exercise research" (Knapen et al., 2009) or the "most widely used anxiety measure in exercise studies" (Youngstedt, 2010), it has been "employed in nearly 50% of studies on exercise and anxiety" (Motl et al., 2004, p. 98), or is "the most often employed measure of state anxiety in the exercise literature" (Bartholomew & Linder, 1998, p. 208).

Research in the context of exercise (Rejeski et al., 1991) has also uncovered an important limitation of the state-anxiety portion of the State-Trait Anxiety Inventory that had not been noticed in other contexts. The State-Trait Anxiety Inventory was developed based on the assumption that, when a state-anxiety response occurs, the various characteristic symptoms of anxiety (i.e., affective, cognitive, behavioral, and physiological) manifest themselves more or less in unison. In fact, this coordinated symptomatology was thought to define the occurrence of a state anxiety "syndrome" (Spielberger, 1972a). As a result, the state-anxiety portion of the State-Trait Anxiety Inventory is scored as a unidimensional instrument despite the fact that it includes items referring to affective (e.g., *I feel pleasant*), cognitive (e.g., *I feel self-confident, I am worried*), behavioral (e.g., *I am jittery*), and perceived physiological symptoms (e.g., *I feel calm, I am tense*). In most cases (e.g., when facing an academic exam or a job interview), these diverse symptoms do exhibit a coordinated response and do form a relatively tight cluster.

Exercise and other arousal-inducing stimuli (e.g., caffeine, chronotropic drugs), however, are different in a very important respect; they can induce noticeable or even substantial changes in perceived physiological activation independently of an appraisal of threat (which is the defining element of a state-anxiety response in Spielberger's and other cognitive theories). Rejeski et al. (1991) showed that, near the end of a 20-minute bout of treadmill exercise at 75 percent of heart rate reserve, scores on items indicative of perceived physiological activation (e.g., *calm, relaxed*) increased (i.e., participants felt less calm and less relaxed, which are scored as indicating increased state anxiety), whereas scores on items indicative of cognitive components of anxiety (e.g., *worried*) decreased. This divergent pattern of responses suggested that, during exercise, the different items of the State-Trait Anxiety Inventory became indices of different constructs rather than a unitary construct of *state anxiety*. Weakened item intercorrelations led to a collapse of the internal consistency of the scale (alpha coefficient of 0.33). Multiple laboratories have since replicated the same pattern of item responses using different exercise modalities and intensities (Bartholomew & Linder, 1998; Ekkekakis et al., 1999; Focht & Hausenblas, 2003; Katula, Blissmer, & McAuley, 1999; McAuley, Mihalko, & Bane, 1996).

These data have important implications for the validity of research investigating changes in state anxiety in response to stimuli that cause changes in perceived physiological activation based on the State-Trait Anxiety Inventory. Treatments that *increase* state-anxiety scores may not necessarily be anxiety inducing and, conversely, those that *decrease* state-anxiety scores may not necessarily be anxiolytic. Such changes could in fact reflect, at least in part, increases and decreases in items indicative of perceived physiological activation. Thus, the most likely reason the participants in the study by Rejeski et al. (1991) reported feeling less *calm* and *relaxed* during vigorous exercise was not that they became more anxious (after all, they reported feeling less *worried*) but rather that they had been exercising vigorously. Likewise, when the participants reported feeling more *calm* and *relaxed* 10 minutes after exercise, this probably did not reflect a decrease in state anxiety per se but rather, at least to some extent, the typical postexercise decrease in perceived physiological activation as their bodies returned to home-ostasis. The fact that state-anxiety scores derived from the State-Trait Anxiety Inventory increase as exercise intensity increases (Katula et al., 1999) supports this conjecture. Likewise, the fact that the postexercise decrease in state-anxiety scores is delayed as exercise intensity increases (e.g., Raglin & Wilson, 1996) may reflect a delay in physiological recovery rather than a true "delayed anxiolysis," as the phenomenon has been labeled in the exercise literature (Cox, Thomas, Hinton, & Donahue, 2004; Raglin, 1997). Nevertheless, the widely touted phenomenon of exercise-induced anxiolysis remains a reasonable possibility since items indicative of what Spielberger (1972a) considered the core of the state-anxiety response, namely the cognitive appraisal of threat (e.g., *I am worried*), have been found to decrease with exercise (Ekkekakis et al., 1999).

Besides these inherent limitations of the State-Trait Anxiety Inventory as a measure of anxiety, additional problems have emerged regarding how this measure is used and interpreted by researchers. In many studies in the field of health-behavioral research, the State-Trait Anxiety Inventory is simply misused. First, as noted in Chapter 1, it is not uncommon to see this questionnaire used as a measure of mood, stress, relaxation, general well-being, or "how people feel" in general. Clearly, these uses are incompatible with the stated scope of the measure, which was developed to assess a specifically defined and delimited emotional state (state anxiety) and disposition (trait anxiety).

Second, given that the cognitive appraisal of (primarily ego-related) threat is theorized to be the defining element of the anxiety process in Spielberger's (1972a) theoretical model, using the State-Trait Anxiety Inventory with samples of young, healthy, and non-anxious college students in studies that do not involve any experimental manipulation of anxiety-associated appraisals of threat presents some interpretational challenges. Is one really studying anxiety when the participants are non-anxious and anxiety is not experimentally induced? On a scale ranging from 20 to 80, does a score change from 25 to 22 really constitute evidence of "anxiolysis" with meaningful practical implications? Some researchers have argued that such studies are still instructive as they constitute cases of "analogue research" (Martinsen & Morgan, 1997). However, as commonly defined, analogue research involves providing treatment to individuals who manifest a certain problematic trait, such as anxiety proneness, albeit to a nonclinical degree and/or inducing a problematic state, such as fear, albeit transiently and without the risk of causing trauma to the participants. With few exceptions, in which either the participants are selected to manifest high trait anxiety (e.g., Breus & O'Connor, 1998; Focht & Hausenblas, 2003) or anxiety is transiently elevated by an experimental manipulation (e.g., Acevedo, Dzewaltowski, Kubitz, & Kraemer, 1999; Crocker & Grozelle, 1991; Doan et al., 1995; Evatt & Kassel, 2010), these conditions are not frequently met and, therefore, the label "analogue research" does not seem suitable. Given this situation, a first step before choosing the State-Trait Anxiety Inventory should be to contemplate whether one is genuinely interested in studying anxiety, as this construct is defined and delineated within the conceptual framework upon which this measure was based.

After deciding that anxiety is their true target, the next step for researchers should be to consider whether Spielberger's model of anxiety, which formed the conceptual basis of the State-Trait Anxiety Inventory, is the most appropriate for their study among alternative conceptualizations (particularly those that have emerged in the four decades that have passed since the State-Trait Anxiety Inventory was first introduced). Clearly, to make this determination, any researcher studying anxiety should have a good grasp of conceptual developments in the anxiety field since that time.

With this in mind, it is very important to point out that, during the "formative" period of the State-Trait Anxiety Inventory (i.e., in the late 1960s and throughout the 1970s), the first models of anxiety that distinguished between cognitive and somatic components began to appear in the test anxiety (e.g., Liebert & Morris, 1967; Morris,

Davis, & Hutchings, 1981) and psychotherapy literatures (e.g., Lehrer & Woolfolk, 1982; Schwartz et al., 1978). Interesting, before the 1983 development of Form Y of the State-Trait Anxiety Inventory, Spielberger fully endorsed the idea that anxiety is a multidimensional construct comprising cognitive and somatic elements. Accordingly, he developed the Test Anxiety Inventory (Spielberger, Golzalez, Taylor, Algaze, & Anton, 1978) as a questionnaire that contained both a "worry" (i.e., cognitive concerns about consequences of failure) and an "emotionality" scale (i.e., perceived reactions of the autonomic nervous system evoked in response to the perception of threat). However, without directly addressing this inconsistency, the State-Trait Anxiety Inventory was never revised to incorporate this crucial conceptual advance. Thus, by continuing to reflect the conceptualization of anxiety as a unidimensional construct, the State-Trait Anxiety Inventory has essentially been rendered obsolete from a conceptual standpoint. Modern measures of anxiety, including the Endler Multidimensional Anxiety Scales (Endler, Edwards, Vitelli, & Parker, 1989; Endler, Parker, Bagby, & Cox, 1991), the Four-System Anxiety Questionnaire (Koksal & Power, 1990), and the State-Trait Inventory for Cognitive and Somatic Anxiety (Grös et al., 2007; Ree et al., 2008), distinguish between cognitive and somatic components. This distinction is clearly more than a subtle refinement, as it has direct relevance to the critique by Rejeski et al. (1991) discussed here. A measure that distinguishes between cognitive and somatic symptoms would avoid the confound identified by these authors, enabling researchers to observe independent or divergent changes in these two components. Thus, it is important to note that, in the first known study to employ the Endler Multidimensional Anxiety Scales in conjunction with a bout of exercise, Blanchard, Rodgers, Bell, Wilson, and Gesell (2002) found that exercise induced significant changes in the autonomic-emotional scale (e.g., "Hands feel moist," "Heart beats faster," "Perspire") but not in the cognitive-worry scale (e.g., "Unable to focus on task," "Unable to concentrate," "Feel self-conscious").

A third problem with how the State-Trait Anxiety Inventory is used in health-behavioral research pertains to the use of shortened versions. This trend may be driven in part by convenience (since short scales are easier to administer repeatedly during an experimental session) and in part by the desire to circumvent the cost associated with using a copyrighted and commercially distributed measure. If a shortened scale is used, it is important to ensure that it is empirically derived (i.e., that published data support the selection of the specific items) and that the items that are used are from Form Y rather than from the now defunct Form X. The reason is that Form X "included several items with poor psychometric properties" (Vagg et al., 1980, p. 212), which were replaced in Form Y. Researchers are also cautioned to only draw item lists from the original articles reporting the derivation of the shortened scales because item lists that have appeared in some studies do not always match those in the cited original sources.

In closing this critique, it is useful to point out that one issue that complicates the evaluation of the State-Trait Anxiety Inventory by researchers is its undeniable popularity across a wide range of scientific fields and over an extended period of time. This type of extreme popularity creates two significant problems. First, it tends to "automate" the selection of certain measures, creating the false impression that, to measure a certain variable, there is de facto only one choice. Popular measures seem like a "safe bet," unlikely to be questioned by reviewers. When a popular measure exists, regardless of its flaws, the selection of a less popular measure often requires rigorous justification. For example, authors have summarily rejected criticisms against the State-Trait Anxiety Inventory as "not compelling," urging researchers to continue measuring anxiety "by means of existing measures such as the STAI … that are known to possess construct validity" (Raglin, 1997, p. 111) since it has been used in a "large body of research" (O'Connor et al., 2000, p. 138).

Second, extreme popularity means that the measure has been historically the basis for a large amount of data. Given the reliance of the research process on the measure, investigators and practitioners working in that field usually accept these data as an established body of evidence. Therefore, questioning the measure that formed the basis of this body of evidence (as one would have to do, directly or indirectly, in supporting and selecting an alternate measure) is often seen as an iconoclastic attack against what is considered the orthodox knowledge base of the field, against previous studies, or even against the scientific credibility of investigators who have used the popular measure. Naturally, most researchers, young and established ones alike, are unlikely to risk creating such undesirable impressions.

7   Dimensional measures

Dimensional models of core affect, mood, and emotions have maintained a prominent position in psychology for decades. Accordingly, such models have provided the conceptual foundation for the development of an array of measures (see Figure 7.1), some of which (like the Positive and Negative Affect Schedule) have been used in thousands of studies and some whose use is less widespread. For the former, the aim of this chapter is to highlight strengths and limitations that have become apparent through years of extensive use. For those in the latter category, the aim of the chapter is to bring them to the attention of researchers who may not be aware of them and to describe their basic features.

The Self-Assessment Manikin

The Self-Assessment Manikin (SAM) was developed by Lang (1980; Hodes et al., 1985) on the basis of Mehrabian and Russell's (1974) three-dimensional model of "emotion" (which would now be considered a model of core affect). The three dimensions of the model, which were theorized to be bipolar and orthogonal, were pleasure-displeasure, arousal-nonarousal, and dominance-submissiveness (also referred to as potency, self-efficacy, or control). Accordingly, the Self-Assessment Manikin consisted of scales measuring each of these three dimensions. The Self-Assessment Manikin is unique in that each scale consists of a series of cartoon-like characters with expressions ranging from happiness (smiling face) to sadness (frowning face), from sleepiness (eyes closed) to high arousal (shaking and heart pounding), and from submissiveness (small size) to dominance (large size). The original version of the Self-Assessment Manikin was computer based. Users could manipulate the expressions interactively through a series of 30 progressively different images using a joystick. A paper-and-pencil version became available later (Bradley, Greenwald, & Hamm, 1993; Bradley & Lang, 1994), consisting of strips of five images for each scale. Users

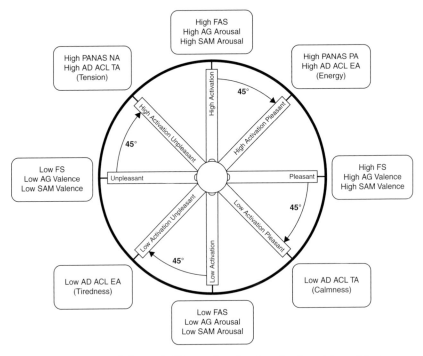

Figure 7.1. Schematic illustrating the theorized position of factors from various dimensional measures on two-dimensional affective space (as discussed in Chapter 3). Included in the figure are the Positive Affect/Activation (PA) and Negative Affect/Activation (NA) scores derived from the Positive and Negative Affect Schedule (PANAS; Watson, Clark, & Tellegen, 1988), the Energetic Arousal (EA, energy versus tiredness) and Tense Arousal (TA, tension versus calmness) scores derived from the Activation Deactivation Adjective Check List (AD ACL; Thayer, 1989), the Valence and Arousal scales of the Self-Assessment Manikin (SAM; Lang, 1980), the Valence and Arousal scales of the Affect Grid (AG; Russell, Weiss, & Mendelsohn, 1989), the Feeling Scale (FS; Hardy & Rejeski, 1989), and the Felt Arousal Scale (FAS; Svebak & Murgatroyd, 1985).

could also select the spaces in between the images (i.e., a nine-point response scale in total). The Self-Assessment Manikin has been used in some studies in the domain of health-behavioral research (e.g., Ekkekakis, Hall, Van Landuyt, & Petruzzello, 2000; Ong, Cardé, Gross, & Manber, 2011; Ostafin, Marlatt, & Greenwald, 2008; Smith et al., 2002), yielding results generally consistent with those derived from other similar instruments. Because the Self-Assessment Manikin does not rely on verbal descriptors but rather on universally recognized facial and bodily cues, researchers have suggested it would be appropriate for cross-cultural research (Morris, 1995).

One question users of the Self-Assessment Manikin will have to contemplate is whether they accept the inclusion of the dominance-submissiveness dimension as one of the basic constituents of affective state. As explained previously (see Chapter 3, section entitled "The dimensional approach"), this has been and remains an interesting and, to some extent, unresolved conceptual question. On one side of the argument is considerable evidence that the addition of a third dimension (MacKinnon & Keating, 1989; Mehrabian, 1995, 1997; Mehrabian & Russell, 1974; Morgan & Heise, 1988; Osgood & Suci, 1955; Russell & Mehrabian, 1974, 1977), or even a fourth (Fontaine et al., 2007), contributes unique variance in distinguishing between different *emotions*, beyond that accounted for by valence and arousal. Therefore, if the objective of the research is to make such differentiations and, importantly, if the construct under investigation is *emotion* rather than *core affect*, then the incorporation of the dominance-submissiveness dimension would make sense. Remember, however, that the researcher should then explain the reasons for approaching the study of different emotions from a dimensional, as opposed to a distinct-states or categorical, perspective, since the distinct-states perspective would inevitably attain an even more fine-grained degree of differentiation. On the other side of the argument, as Russell (1978, 1980, 1989) has maintained since the late 1970s, dominance-submissiveness (and associated appraisals of potency, self-efficacy, or control) should not be considered a constituent dimension of affect because they are not inherently *affective*, but rather *cognitive*, in nature; they are not a component of the core affective experience but rather, strictly speaking, an antecedent or a consequence of the affective experience. Therefore, according to this line of reasoning, if an investigation targets core affect, the dimension of dominance-submissiveness should be considered outside its scope.

Another important conceptual and psychometric issue users of the Self-Assessment Manikin should consider pertains to the arousal scale. According to two-dimensional models such as the circumplex, the arousal scale should be unrelated (orthogonal) to the valence scale. However, in the case of the Self-Assessment Manikin, the two scales may show a negative intercorrelation, indicating that, as arousal ratings increase, they tend to be coupled with lower pleasure ratings (e.g., Bradley & Lang, 1994). This reflects two interrelated problems.

First, reducing the concept of arousal to the perception of physiological symptoms raises concerns over the validity of the scale (i.e., whether it faithfully reflects the construct it is supposed to reflect). According to Russell (1989), there is a problem in "speaking of arousal in strictly physiological terms" (p. 105), since arousal as a constituent dimension of affect is more than just a physiological construct.

Second, respondents tend to interpret the images toward the high end of the arousal scale (i.e., heart pounding, as if coming out of the chest) as negatively valenced. This issue received considerable attention prior to the development of the Self-Assessment Manikin but was evidently not taken into account in the planning and design of this measure. As it became apparent from the critiques of Schachter and Singer's (1962) famous experiment on the cognitive modifiability of epinephrine-induced physiological arousal, very high levels of physiological arousal are not affectively neutral but rather inherently unpleasant (Marshall & Zimbardo, 1979; Maslach, 1979). Schachter and Singer (1979) fully acknowledged this point and described their own experiences when they injected themselves with high doses of epinephrine: "We might have been convinced by someone that we were about to die, but no amount of social psychological tomfoolery could have convinced us that we were euphoric, or angry, or excited, or indeed anything but that something was very wrong and that we felt lousy" (p. 991). Conveying the broader meaning of the construct of arousal – beyond its strict physiological connotations – through a cartoon character is difficult. However, limiting the scope to physiological symptoms entails an underrepresentation of the intended domain of content. In that sense, the validity of the arousal scale must be viewed with skepticism.

The Affect Grid

The Affect Grid (AG; Russell, Weiss, & Mendelsohn, 1989) was developed on the basis of Russell's (1980) circumplex model of affect. Accordingly, it provides two scores, one for pleasure-displeasure and one for low-to-high arousal. Its format was designed to make this instrument "the instrument of choice when subjects are called on to make affective judgments in rapid succession or to make a large number of judgments, especially when those judgments are to be aggregated" (Russell et al., 1989, p. 499). The Affect Grid is a 9 by 9 grid, with the horizontal dimension representing affective valence (from unpleasantness to pleasantness) and the vertical dimension representing the degree of perceived activation (ranging from sleepiness to high arousal). Respondents place a single "X" mark in one of the 81 cells of the grid and this response is scored along both the valence and the arousal dimensions. To facilitate comprehension, anchors are provided at the extremes of the two orthogonal dimensions ("pleasant feelings" versus "unpleasant feelings" and "high arousal" versus "sleepiness"), as well as at the four corners: "excitement" (pleasant high arousal), "relaxation" (pleasant low arousal), "depression" (unpleasant low arousal), and "stress" (unpleasant high arousal). An independent modification extended the dimensions of the grid to 99 by 99 cells (Kuppens, Oravecz, & Tuerlinckx, 2010), presumably to allow the expression of more interindividual variability.

The Affect Grid has been used in health-behavioral research (e.g., Apolzan, Flynn, McFarlin, & Campbell, 2009; Ekkekakis et al., 2000; Wardell, Read, Curtin, & Merrill, 2012), although not extensively. One possible explanation for its relatively low popularity is that some respondents may find the grid format somewhat confusing. For this reason, the Affect Grid is accompanied by lengthy instructions. Although these instructions are clear and informative, they also underscore the point that, in order for the Affect Grid to be used effectively, research participants need to invest some time and effort in familiarizing themselves with what the instrument is asking, as well as with its layout.

The Circular Mood Scale

The Circular Mood Scale (CMS; Jacob, Simons, Manuck, Rohay, Waldstein, & Gatsonis, 1989; Jacob et al., 1999) is another brief self-report measure developed on the basis of Russell's (1980) circumplex model. It is a circle surrounded by a series of verbal descriptors anchoring each of the eight octants of the circle (clockwise from the top): *active / attentive, euphoric / elated, happy / friendly, calm / relaxed, uninvolved / inactive, bored / sluggish, unhappy / grouchy, alarmed / angry.* A later version (Jacob et al., 1999) provides a series of eight corresponding stylized faces in addition to the verbal anchors. To indicate their affective state, respondents draw a line connecting the center of the circle to a point in the periphery that is closer to how they feel. The angular location of the mark can then be converted to pleasure and activation scores by trigonometric equations. Furthermore, to indicate the intensity of that affective state, respondents mark a point on the line connecting the center to the periphery.

Researchers have used the Circular Mood Scale in a limited number of studies so far (e.g., Jacob et al., 1999; Räikkönen et al., 2004). As was the case with the Affect Grid, concerns about the unfamiliarity of respondents with the format and the constructs being assessed might be the culprit for its relatively low impact. Jacob et al. (1989) noted the need to (a) allow respondents to practice by marking a standard list of affective states on the circle and (b) apply quality controls by checking whether responses on the Circular Mood Scale are consistent with other self-reports of affective states (e.g., an adjective check list). Furthermore, Jacob et al. (1989) pointed out an inherent difficulty of measurement instruments requiring a single response to reflect possible cases of "mixed feelings" (e.g., *bittersweet*).

The Feeling Scale and the Felt Arousal Scale

Although neither the Feeling Scale (FS) nor the Felt Arousal Scale (FAS) were originally developed with the affect circumplex in mind, researchers in exercise psychology have extensively used them to measure the dimensions of valence (pleasure-displeasure) and activation (low-high arousal), respectively, during exercise sessions. The Feeling Scale (Hardy & Rejeski, 1989) is an 11-point bipolar scale ranging from −5 to +5. Anchors are provided at zero ("Neutral") and at all odd integers, ranging from "Very Bad" (−5) to "Very Good" (+5). According to Hardy and Rejeski (1989), "rather than dealing with various categories of emotion (e.g., anger, joy, depression, anxiety, vigor), the scale was designed to evaluate the core of emotions: pleasure / displeasure" (p. 305). The Felt Arousal Scale is one of the scales of the Telic State Measure (Svebak & Murgatroyd, 1985). It was originally developed as a measure of the construct of felt arousal (in contradistinction to preferred arousal) in the context of reversal theory. It is a 6-point, single-item scale, ranging from 1 to 6, with anchors only at 1 ("Low Arousal") and 6 ("High Arousal"). It is worth noting that the Feeling Scale and Felt Arousal Scale have been adapted for children with the addition of a series of stylized drawings of faces ranging from very happy to very sad and from very sleepy to very alert (Hulley et al., 2008). In turn, these were modeled after similar scales long used in clinical settings for the measurement of pain in children (e.g., McGrath, de Veber, & Hearn, 1985).

The difference in the format of the Feeling Scale and Felt Arousal Scale (e.g., number of possible response options, number of anchors) is a desirable feature when the two scales are administered together, side by side. This is because using identical formats for scales intended to measure different constructs tends to artificially inflate their intercorrelation (adding so-called common method variance). To the contrary, the use of different formats generally strengthens discriminant validity by forcing respondents to consider their answers independently for each scale. Furthermore, anecdotally, respondents tend to find the familiar rating-scale format of the Feeling Scale and Felt Arousal Scale easier to understand compared to the Self-Assessment Manikin, Affect Grid, and Circular Mood Scale.

On the other hand, there is a common challenge associated with all these scales. It pertains to the difficulty associated with explaining the concept of perceived activation or arousal to respondents (Ekkekakis & Petruzzello, 2002; Parfitt, Rose, & Burgess, 2006). According to Watson and Vaidya (2003), although "it is relatively easy to develop reliable measures of Pleasantness and Unpleasantness," the assessment of the arousal dimension "has proven to be much more problematic" (p. 356). For example, it is critical to convey that activation should be considered as something distinct from pleasure-displeasure. Someone in a state of high activation could be experiencing either a pleasant state (e.g., *excitement, ecstasy*) or an unpleasant state (e.g., *distress, tension*). Likewise, someone in a state of low activation could be experiencing either a pleasant state (e.g., *calmness, serenity*) or an unpleasant state (e.g., *melancholy, tiredness*). However, very few terms exist in the English language for "pure" low and high arousal (e.g., *quiet, worked up*) and even these almost always acquire unambiguous positive or negative connotations when used in conversational context. Therefore, respondents are essentially asked to perform the difficult and unfamiliar mental operation of "extracting" or "isolating" the activation component from what they are feeling, quantify it, and report it. When proper care is taken to ensure that participants have comprehended these concepts, most are able to use the scale effectively. Because the instructions that accompany the Felt Arousal Scale are correct but overly succinct, researchers may find that adapting the more detailed instructions of the Affect Grid (Russell et al., 1989) could be helpful.

Lishner, Cooter, and Zald (2008) raised an additional issue that pertains to all rating scales of affect, including the Feeling Scale and Felt Arousal Scale. These authors noted that the verbal anchors used in such scales are typically selected without empirical study of their scaling properties. This can lead to various problems, including floor and ceiling effects, the inability to interpret scores in an absolute (e.g., what a rating of +3 means) as opposed to a relative sense (e.g., a drop of three units from baseline), and the inability to carry out intergroup or cross-cultural comparisons. For example, because the typical response to the question "how are you feeling?" in many Western cultures is "good," the baseline Feeling Scale rating is usually +3 (which is anchored by the adjective "good"). In other cultures, however, the rather bold statement "I feel good" is reserved for only those cases in which a preceding positive event would justify "feeling good." Otherwise, average baseline ratings remain closer to zero ("neutral") than +3.

Furthermore, in the case of the Feeling Scale, no empirical reason exists for having equal spacing (two units) between, for example, feeling "fairly good" (+1) and "good" (+3) as between "good" and "very good" (+5). To address these issues, Lishner et al. (2008) developed a valence rating scale (named the Empirical Valence Scale) with verbal anchors and spacing between the anchors that was based on empirical study. Researchers currently using non-empirically derived rating scales such as the Feeling Scale should consider the advantages of the Empirical Valence Scale.

The Evaluative Space Grid

The aforementioned measures were based on the two-dimensional model combining affective valence (pleasure-displeasure) and activation (arousal). The Evaluative Space Grid (Larsen et al., 2009) was based instead on the bivariate model of evaluative space developed by Cacioppo and Berntson (1994; Cacioppo et al., 1997, 1999) and described in Chapter 4. An important point to underscore is that the Evaluative Space Grid was designed as a measure of the positivity or negativity of "evaluative reactions," which according to Larsen et al. (2009) includes affective responses but also extends into other domains, such as attitudes. The format of the Evaluative Space Grid was modeled after the Affect Grid, in that it is also presented as a grid (5 by 5 cells in the case of the Evaluative Space Grid, compared to 9 by 9 cells in the case of the Affect Grid). Respondents are asked to mark any of the 25 cells, responding to the questions "How POSITIVE do you feel about the stimulus?" along the x-axis and "How NEGATIVE do you feel about the stimulus?" along the y-axis. The response scale is unipolar (not at all, slightly, moderately, quite a bit, extremely). In validation studies, Larsen et al. (2009) used the Evaluative Space Grid to rate the positivity and negativity of gambling outcomes (wins, losses); attitudes toward positive, negative, and ambivalent verbal stimuli; and the positivity and negativity of pictures, sounds, and words. According to these authors, a major advantage of the Evaluative Space Grid is that it can detect ambivalence (i.e., it does not assume the reciprocal activation of positive and negative evaluations). To return to a point made while discussing Cacioppo and Berntson's model, it seems that the Evaluative Space Grid might be useful when participants are asked to express responses based, at least in part, on cognitive evaluations (such as attitudes or attribution-based emotions) or when asked to reflect about their experiences over extended periods of time (which might have included both pleasant and unpleasant episodes).

The Semantic Differential Measures
of Emotional State

The Semantic Differential Measures of Emotional State (Mehrabian & Russell, 1974) was the first self-report measure based on a dimensional model. Specifically, its structure was based on the following premise: "Various emotional states are considered to be derivative concepts and are definable as regions in a three-dimensional space. The dimensions of this space are the bipolar and independent factors of pleasure-displeasure, arousal-nonarousal, and dominance-submissiveness" (Russell & Mehrabian, 1974, p. 79). Such a model, for example, permitted Russell and Mehrabian to distinguish between anger and anxiety in terms of the three dimensions as follows: "anger consists of feelings of displeasure, high arousal, and dominance; whereas anxiety consists of feelings of displeasure, high arousal, and submissiveness" (p. 79). Accordingly, the Semantic Differential Measures of Emotional State consisted of three scales, with six semantic-differential items each, accompanied by 9-point response scales: Pleasure (e.g., *happy-unhappy, pleased-annoyed*), Arousal (e.g., *stimulated-relaxed, excited-calm*), and Dominance (e.g., *controlling-controlled, influential-influenced*).

This structure is well supported from a factor-analytic perspective (Russell, Ward, & Pratt, 1981). Using scores from these three scales (as well as their interactions and an acquiescence score), Russell and Mehrabian (1977) showed that they could account for the majority of reliable variance in scores from 42 other scales from the literature (including those of the Multiple Affect Adjective Check List, Profile of Mood States, and Activation Deactivation Adjective Check List). The multiple correlation coefficients ranged from 0.51 to 0.88. For example, the multiple correlation coefficients were 0.81 for Tension, 0.88 for Depression, 0.85 for Anger, 0.76 for Vigor, 0.72 for Fatigue (from the Profile of Mood States), 0.76 for Energy, 0.75 for Calmness, 0.65 for Tiredness, and 0.82 for Tension (from the Activation Deactivation Adjective Check List). Russell and Steiger (1982) subsequently replicated these findings for the scales of the Profile of Mood States using both intraindividual and interindividual data. These results have been widely cited as evidence of the strength of the dimensional approach.

Furthermore, the Pleasure scale of the Semantic Differential Measures of Emotional State has been found to correlate 0.77 with the Pleasure scale of the Affect Grid, 0.97 with the Pleasure scale of the paper-and-pencil version of the Self-Assessment Manikin, and 0.96 with the computer version. Similarly, the Arousal Scale of the Semantic Differential Measures of Emotional State has been found to correlate

0.80 with the Arousal scale of the Affect Grid, 0.94 with the Arousal scale of the paper-and-pencil version of the Self-Assessment Manikin, and 0.95 with the computer version (Bradley & Lang, 1994; Russell et al., 1989).

While these are good indications of psychometric merit, some terms used to form the pairs of semantic differential items in the Semantic Differential Measures of Emotional State raise concerns. For example, the Pleasure factor, in addition to standard exemplars of the pleasure-displeasure dimension (e.g., *happy-unhappy*), also includes items with significant activation content, such as *relaxed-bored*. Similarly, the arousal scale includes the seemingly "pure" marker item *aroused-unaroused*, but also includes the item *excited-calm*, which represents a mixture of arousal and pleasure.

The Positive and Negative Affect Schedule

The Positive and Negative Affect Schedule (Watson, Clark, & Tellegen, 1988) was developed as the operationalization of the orthogonal dimensions of Positive Affect (now called Positive Activation) and Negative Affect (now called Negative Activation) that emerged from the analyses of Zevon and Tellegen (1982) and Watson and Tellegen (1985). Since its publication, the Positive and Negative Affect Schedule has become one of the most widely used affective measures, cited in thousands of studies. It consists of 20 items, 10 for the Positive Affect scale (e.g., *interested, excited*) and 10 for the Negative Affect scale (e.g., *distressed, upset*). Each item is accompanied by a 5-point scale, ranging from "very slightly or not at all" to "extremely."

A fundamental consideration in the construction of the Positive and Negative Affect Schedule was to derive two scales (Positive Affect and Negative Affect) that would be as close to statistically independent (orthogonal) as possible. This was achieved by selecting items that showed loadings of $|.40|$ or higher on one factor and $|.25|$ or lower on the other. Indeed, the intercorrelation when the questionnaire was administered with the instruction "indicate to what extent you feel this way right now, that is, at the present moment" was only -0.15. Furthermore, Watson, Clark, and Tellegen (1988) reported that "the [Positive Affect] scale (but not the [Negative Affect] scale) is related to social activity and shows significant diurnal variation, whereas the [Negative Affect] scale (but not the [Positive Affect] scale) is significantly related to perceived stress and shows no circadian pattern" (p. 1069). Other investigators have also reported data supporting this statistical independence (e.g., Crocker, 1997; Egloff, 1998;

Goldstein & Strube, 1994; Hillerås, Jorm, Herlitz, & Winblad, 1998). In some cases, however, particularly when the attenuating influence of measurement error is controlled, the usually weak negative correlation between Positive Affect and Negative Affect scores is strengthened (Crawford & Henry, 2004; Green et al., 1993; Schmukle, Egloff, & Burns, 2002).

Two important limitations of the Positive and Negative Affect Schedule should concern researchers. First, the items of the Positive and Negative Affect Schedule appear to represent a mixture of what was defined here as emotions, moods, and core affect. For example, the items *proud*, *guilty*, and *ashamed* are commonly considered emotions (e.g., Lazarus, 1991a), the items *irritable*, *upset*, and *hostile* are typically considered moods, and the items *distressed*, *nervous*, and *jittery* probably fall under the category of core affects (Russell, 2003, 2005). It is debatable whether some of the other items even belong in any of these three categories at all (e.g., *interested*, *strong*, *inspired*, *determined*, *attentive*). At the time the Positive and Negative Affect Schedule was developed, Watson was certainly not the only researcher not overly concerned with such distinctions. The fact that the Positive and Negative Affect Schedule was described as a measure of *mood* and yet it was named a measure of (positive and negative) *affect* implies that its developers at that time did not recognize a difference between the constructs described by these two terms. Likewise, as noted in an excerpt cited in Chapter 2, Watson believed that the concept of *mood* subsumes the concept of *emotion* (see "the concept of *mood* subsumes all subjective feeling states, not simply those experiences that accompany classical, prototypical emotions such as fear and anger" in Watson & Vaidya, 2003, p. 351). However, the years since the development of the Positive and Negative Affect Schedule have brought significant progress in delineating and respecting some terminological boundaries (Batson et al., 1992; Russell, 2003; Russell & Feldman Barrett, 1999), as summarized in Chapter 2. As a result, for researchers wishing to adopt the emerging consensus regarding these distinctions, the fuzzy limits of the content domain of the Positive and Negative Affect Schedule are beginning to pose a problem. For example, in recent years, the Positive and Negative Affect Schedule has been variably described in the health-behavioral literature as a measure of affect (e.g., Robinson, Lam, Carter, Wetter, & Cinciripini, 2012), mood (e.g., Parrott et al., 2011), affect or mood (e.g., Stroth, Hille, Spitzer, & Reinhardt, 2009), emotions (e.g., Moon & Lee, 2011), emotional state (e.g., Rousseau, Irons, & Correia, 2011), and emotional experience (e.g., Vandekerckhove, Weiss, Schotte, Exadaktylos, Haex, Verbraecken, & Cluydts, 2011).

Second, several authors have criticized the Positive and Negative Affect Schedule for an apparent inconsistency between the conceptual model that formed its basis (i.e., Watson & Tellegen, 1985; Zevon & Tellegen, 1982) and its eventual content and structure. Specifically, as described in Chapter 3, the dimension of Positive Affect that emerged from the analyses of Zevon and Tellegen (1982) and Watson and Tellegen (1985) extended from high-activation pleasant affect (e.g., *elated, enthusiastic, excited*) to low-activation unpleasant affect (e.g., *drowsy, dull, sluggish*). The Negative Affect dimension extended from high-activation unpleasant affect (e.g., *distressed, jittery, nervous*) to low-activation pleasant affect (e.g., *calm, placid, relaxed*). These empirical results were clear and fully consistent with other two-dimensional models of affect (e.g., Russell, 1980; Thayer, 1986, 1989).

The interpretation that was offered, however, by Zevon and Tellegen (1982) and later by Watson and Tellegen (1985) is rather controversial. Because current and prospective users of the Positive and Negative Affect Schedule, in essence, also choose to adopt its theoretical basis, they should take a clear position on why they have opted to accept this interpretation. Specifically, Zevon and Tellegen (1982) argued that, although the dimensions are *"descriptively bipolar,"* they should be viewed as *"affectively unipolar"* because low-activation states represent "the absence of affect," whereas "emotions are usually conceived of as almost inevitably associated with some degree of arousal" (p. 112). Accordingly, the items for the Positive Affect and Negative Affect scales of the Positive and Negative Affect Schedule were selected to represent only the high-activation poles of the *"descriptively bipolar"* Positive Affect and Negative Affect dimensions. As a result, the scales of the Positive and Negative Affect Schedule "include no terms assessing fatigue and serenity" (Watson & Clark, 1997, p. 276), which are low-activation states.

As has been discussed by several authors (Egloff, 1998; Feldman Barrett & Russell, 1998; Larsen & Diener, 1992; Mossholder et al., 1994), on the basis of this controversial position, Watson, Clark, and Tellegen (1988) cut the domain of content represented in the Positive and Negative Affect Schedule to half compared to what had emerged from their own analyses. This problem may actually be worse than it seems in light of the fact that, as explained earlier, items tapping one pole of a truly bipolar dimension, when accompanied by a unipolar response scale (as in the case of the Positive and Negative Affect Schedule), cannot provide fully redundant information compared to items tapping the opposite pole (Russell & Carroll, 1999a). In practical terms, this means that it cannot be assumed that a decrease in (for example) *tension* corresponds to an equal increase in *calmness*.

Interesting, in recent years, Watson's response on this subject has not been based on a defense of the notion of "*descriptively bipolar*" but "*affectively unipolar*" dimensions on theoretical grounds but rather on a practical point. Specifically, he has argued that items from the low-activation poles tend to be "factorially complex" (i.e., exhibiting cross-loadings on the other factor) and thus reduce the validity and reliability of the Positive and Negative Affect Schedule (Watson & Clark, 1997; Watson & Vaidya, 2003). This argument, however, seems debatable. Although the high-activation items were selected among dozens of others to be "factorially simple" (i.e., load on only one of the two factors), the low-activation items used to provide an empirical illustration of this point were selected on an ad hoc basis. Furthermore, while the high-activation poles were each represented by ten items, the low-Positive Affect pole (i.e., *fatigue*) was represented by only four items and the low-Negative Affect pole (i.e., *serenity*) was represented by only three.

The Positive and Negative Affect Schedule has been enormously popular in health-behavioral research. However, as is also the case with the Profile of Mood States, the selection of the Positive and Negative Affect Schedule cannot be based solely on its overwhelming popularity. The points its critics have raised are substantive and require an acknowledgment and an articulate response by researchers who choose to use the Positive and Negative Affect Schedule in their studies.

The Activation Deactivation Adjective Check List

The developmental history of the Activation Deactivation Adjective Check List (Thayer, 1986, 1989) and the evolution of its theoretical basis from postulating four points along an arousal continuum to two bipolar and oppositely valenced dimensions were described in some detail in an earlier section (Chapter 3). In its present form, the Activation Deactivation Adjective Check List taps two bipolar dimensions. One is termed Energetic Arousal and extends from high-activation pleasant affect (labeled *Energy*, with five items such as *energetic*, *vigorous*, and *lively*) to low-activation unpleasant affect (labeled *Tiredness*, with five items such as *sleepy*, *tired*, and *drowsy*). The other is termed Tense Arousal and extends from high-activation unpleasant affect (labeled *Tension*, with five items such as *jittery*, *clutched up*, and *tense*) to low-activation pleasant affect (labeled *Calmness*, with five items such as *placid*, *calm*, and *at rest*). Each of the 20 items is accompanied by a four-point response scale, with "vv" indicating "definitely feel," "v" indicating "feel slightly," "?" indicating "cannot decide," and "no" indicating "definitely do not feel." The Activation Deactivation Adjective Check List can be scored either in terms of the two bipolar dimensions (Energetic Arousal, Tense Arousal) or in terms of four unipolar scales (Energy, Tiredness, Tension, Calmness).

Although the Activation Deactivation Adjective Check List was developed independently of the Positive and Negative Affect Schedule, it became evident to both Watson and Tellegen (1985) and to Thayer (1989) that Energetic Arousal represents a full bipolar operationalization of the Positive Affect dimension and Tense Arousal a full bipolar operationalization of the Negative Affect dimension. Since, as explained in the section on the Positive and Negative Affect Schedule, the Positive Affect and Negative Affect scales of that instrument only tap the high-activation poles of the respective dimensions, Nemanick and Munz (1994) have suggested that the Activation Deactivation Adjective Check List represents a more complete operationalization of the theoretical space defined by Positive Affect and Negative Affect compared to the Positive and Negative Affect Schedule (see Figure 7.2). Yik et al. (1999) have offered some support for the empirical correspondence between Energetic Arousal-Positive Affect and between Tense Arousal-Negative Affect. Although not positioned at identical locations in circumplex space, these scales occupied the same quadrants. Perhaps not unexpectedly given the developmental histories of the Activation Deactivation Adjective Check List and the Positive and Negative Affect Schedule, the scales of the former appeared slightly more saturated by activation, while the scales of the latter appeared slightly more saturated by pleasure-displeasure. Ekkekakis et al. (2005) examined whether the 20 items of the Activation Deactivation Adjective Check List conform to a circumplex before and after a walk. Using stochastic process modeling (the only confirmatory technique currently available to test for circumplex structure), they showed that the fit to a circumplex was satisfactory at both time points. Importantly, items theorized to belong to different sectors of circumplex space did not cross over into adjacent sectors, thus providing evidence for discriminant validity.

Current and prospective users of the Activation Deactivation Adjective Check List should take certain limitations into account. First, Meddis (1972) and Cruickshank (1984) questioned whether the response scale maintains even ordinal properties (let alone equal interval properties, an assumption that should be met before performing statistical analyses). This is because some respondents might endorse "?" not to indicate strength of experience between "feel slightly" and "definitely do

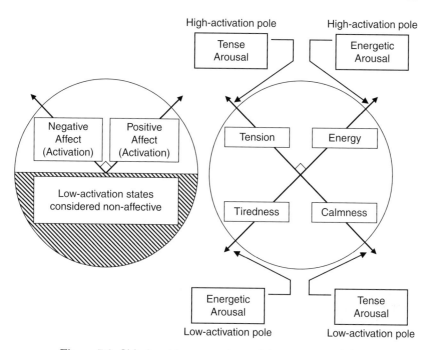

Figure 7.2. Side-by-side comparison of the coverage of the two-dimensional affective space by the Positive Affect/Activation and Negative Affect/Activation dimensions of the Positive and Negative Affect Schedule (Watson, Clark, & Tellegen, 1988) on the left, and the Energetic Arousal and Tense Arousal dimensions of the Activation Deactivation Adjective Check List (Thayer, 1989) on the right. Because the Positive and Negative Affect Schedule taps only the high-activation half of this space, authors have argued that the Activation Deactivation Adjective Check List, which also taps the low-activation half, offers fuller coverage of this space.

not feel" but rather their lack of understanding of the meaning of a particular word or the irrelevance of an item to their present affective state. Responding to this concern, Thayer (1986) performed a series of exploratory factor analyses of the Activation Deactivation Adjective Check List using three different types of response scales, including the original and two others that did not include the "cannot decide" category, showing that the type of response scale did not influence the factor structure in any substantive way.

Second, some problems associated with floor effects and violation of the assumption of normal distributions have been reported in studies with healthy and active college samples (e.g., Ekkekakis et al., 2005; Jerome et al., 2002). These problems pertain to the Tense Arousal scale, more specifically to the Tension pole, and stem from the low mean and variance of items such as *fearful* and perhaps the ambiguous nature of items such as *intense*. As a result, low indices of internal consistency may occur.

Third, for researchers interested in measuring the global affective space from a dimensional perspective, the Activation Deactivation Adjective Check List may indeed provide more complete coverage than the Positive and Negative Affect Schedule (Nemanick & Munz, 1994). However, it has been characterized as a "satisfactory, albeit imperfect, solution" for assessing affect from a circumplex perspective (Ekkekakis et al., 2005, p. 96). The reason is that, although the Activation Deactivation Adjective Check List was found to conform to a circumplex (Ekkekakis et al., 2005; Yik et al., 1999), it was not developed as a measure based a priori on the circumplex model. If it were, it is possible that the items or their intercorrelations might have been a little different. In the item-level analysis performed by Ekkekakis et al. (2005), it was clear that the Activation Deactivation Adjective Check List leaves relatively broad segments of circumplex space without coverage. Authors have argued that a more comprehensive and refined measurement approach should provide coverage over eight (Larsen & Diener, 1992) or even twelve sectors (Yik, Russell, & Steiger, 2011).

Adaptations of the Activation Deactivation Adjective Check List for non-American respondents have been proposed. In these versions, some of the terms respondents may find unusual (e.g., *peppy, full of pep, clutched up, blue*) have been replaced. Two such adaptations are more widely known, namely the Stress and Arousal Check List (Cox & Mackay, 1985; Cruickshank, 1984; Fischer & Donatelli, 1987; Fischer, Hansen, & Zemore, 1988; King, Burrows, & Stanley, 1983; Mackay, Cox, Burrows, & Lazzerini, 1978; McCormick, Walkey, & Taylor, 1985) and the University of Wales Institute of Science and Technology Mood Adjective Check List (Matthews et al., 1990).

Finally, the state version of the 4-Dimension Mood Scale (Huelsman, Furr, & Nemanick, 2003; Huelsman, Nemanick, & Munz, 1998), tested by Gregg and Shepherd (2009), has similar content and structure to that of the Activation Deactivation Adjective Check List (comprising Positive Energy, Tiredness, Negative Arousal, and Relaxation scales), with one exception. Although the Tiredness scale of the Activation Deactivation Adjective Check List includes items that refer mainly to sleepiness-wakefulness (i.e., *sleepy, drowsy, wide awake, wakeful*), the Tiredness scale of the 4-Dimension Mood Scale includes items that refer more directly to tiredness and fatigue (i.e., *exhausted*, *fatigued*, *tired*, *weary*, *worn out*). Because of this difference, Gregg and Shepherd (2009) speculated that "the [Activation Deactivation Adjective Check List] might well be the more sensitive to the effects of monotonous tasks or to diurnal variation" but the 4-Dimension Mood Scale "could be the more sensitive to the effects of physical exercise" (p. 153).

8   Domain-specific measurement: challenges and solutions

As discussed in Chapter 1, the measurement of affect, mood, and emotion in many areas of health-behavioral research suffers from a number of limitations. Primary among them is a generally unprincipled approach to measurement decisions, leading to such phenomena as the selection of measures without any supporting rationale and the unwarranted interchange of terms and constructs. The consequence of this ongoing problem is the inability to integrate information across studies and, in effect, a slower rate of progress than what might have been possible under different circumstances. Approximately a quarter century ago, Russell (1989) wrote that, given the extent of measurement problems, "it is not surprising that despite years of research, the mood-altering effects of even alcohol cannot be clearly stated" (p. 100). Unfortunately, it would be hard to argue that the situation has improved much since then.

With time, each of the many fields that fall under the broad rubric of health-behavioral research seems to have developed its own unique "quasi-paradigm" with regard to the measurement of affect, mood, and emotion. Although no de facto measurement standards have emerged and diversity of measurement choices remains the norm, there is a discernible tendency in some fields to use certain measures more frequently than others. This is probably an indication that specialized fields of applied research gradually loosen their connection to and lessen their input from affective psychology. Instead, they tend to reproduce arguments, concepts, practices, and measurement decisions that have appeared at least once within those same specialized fields.

These "idiosyncrasies" are manifested, for example, in such phenomena as the repeated use of ad hoc item lists and visual analogue scales (usually on the basis of the argument that these "have been used before" or "have been shown to be sensitive" to a certain treatment) and even the *de novo* development of domain-specific measures. When judged from a critical conceptual and methodological standpoint, however, many of these field-specific idiosyncrasies and domain-specific measures can be shown to have problems. For example, commenting on the Global Mood Scale, a measure of mood developed specifically for cardiac patients (Denollet, 1993), Stone (1997) wrote:

> I do not believe that the rationale was particularity sound: What was the evidence that the items on extant mood scales were not "relevant" to cardiac patients? And should we think of a mood scale as being poor if it does not show the effects of a treatment? This seems to me to be a step backwards, defeating the work to establish valid mood scales and diminishing the possibility of comparing results across studies ... I think that new scales developed without a strong rationale should be accepted with much caution. (pp. 165–166)

This chapter addresses some of these issues. Reviewing and critiquing each and every domain-specific measure proposed in the health behavior literature would be unrealistic, especially if one also includes the various item lists and assortments of visual analogue scales that are commonly used in several fields. However, this may not really be necessary because the errors and misunderstandings that characterize many of the domain-specific measures are strikingly similar. They mainly seem to relate to four basic themes (also see Chapter 1, "Domain specificity as panacea").

Lack of theoretical basis

The first notable limitation of most domain-specific measures is the absence of a theoretical basis (which occasionally also manifests itself as the use of incomplete or inaccurate interpretations of theories). For example, Leathwood and Pollet (1982/1983) wanted to study "whether normal people could detect *any* effects" (p. 147, italics added) on their mood after receiving various dietary interventions (caffeine, tryptophan, tyrosine, placebo). To capture the global domain of mood, these researchers developed a self-report measure targeting the following specific states: sleepiness/wakefulness, lethargy/vigor, and "affective state" (which was not defined). No theory was cited as the basis for operationalizing the domain of mood in terms of these particular constructs or for selecting a semantic-differential item format. Instead, the only explicitly identified aim was to develop "a short questionnaire [that would] not take too much time to fill in, because it was to be used by working people" (p. 148). The absence of a theoretical framework, which directly impinges on the measure's ability to capture "any effects" on mood, is not mentioned in the several studies in which this measure was subsequently used.

In other cases, researchers may develop new measures for a particular purpose without citing a theoretical basis, even though measures based on established theories already exist. For example, Martin, Earleywine, Musty, Perrine, and Swift (1993) developed the Biphasic Alcohol Effects Scale with the goal of capturing the stimulant and sedative effects of alcohol. Even though theoretical frameworks that are directly relevant to states of stimulation and sedation, such as those discussed in Chapter 3, do exist, those were not cited as the basis for developing this measure. Furthermore, preexisting measures based on these theoretical frameworks, which might have been appropriate for capturing the intended domain of content, were not cited. Instead, the only measures criticized as inadequate included previous measures of intoxication and addiction and the Profile of Mood States (McNair et al., 1971).

In another variant of this problem, in some cases, researchers may cite a particular theory but their interpretation of the theory is erroneous and, consequently, the structure of the newly developed measure is inconsistent with the theory. For example, Denollet (1993), based on the perceived dearth of measures of "emotional distress and fatigue" that seemed appropriate for heart disease patients, developed the Global Mood Scale. Although Denollet did not specifically identify any previous measures, he claimed that "since most cardiac patients are not psychiatric patients, traditional psychometric scales may be burdensome for [coronary heart disease] patients to complete" (p. 112). Therefore, the Global Mood Scale included "common mood terms" that "may be perceived as being relevant to patients" with heart disease (p. 112). Interesting, Denollet (1993) cited a specific theory as providing the basis for the Global Mood Scale: "Emotional experience is characterized by two dominant dimensions: negative and positive affect (Watson & Tellegen, 1985). Although the terms negative and positive might suggest that these emotional factors are opposites, they are in fact largely independent dimensions" (p. 112).

After this statement, however, Denollet wrote that many patients with heart disease complain about feelings of *fatigue*. Consequently, most of the items comprising the so-called Negative Affect factor of the Global Mood Scale reflected fatigue and, more broadly, low-activation unpleasant affective states (e.g., *weakened, tired, fatigued, physically weak, feeble, wearied, worn out*). Besides the significant problem of interchanging the terms *affect, mood,* and *emotion,* it should be clear that Watson and Tellegen's (1985) theoretical model was misinterpreted. The defining element of Negative Affect according to Watson and Tellegen is unpleasant high activation, whereas *fatigue* is an unpleasant low-activation state. Consequently, the Positive Affect and Negative Affect factors of the Global Mood Scale could not have reflected "largely independent dimensions" as theorized. Indeed their empirical intercorrelation was far from zero ($r = -0.39$). Nevertheless, Denollet (1993) asserted that the Global Mood Scale "was devised on the basis of the two-factor model of mood (Watson & Tellegen, 1985)" (p. 118) and concluded that "this study demonstrates that the model of negative and positive affect that was primarily observed in USA college students (Watson & Tellegen, 1985) is equally applicable to Belgian men with [coronary heart disease]" (p. 116).

This problem surfaced again later in a joint factor analysis of all the items from the Positive and Negative Affect Schedule and the Global Mood Scale (Denollet & De Vries, 2006). In that analysis, most of the items in the Negative Affect scale of the Positive and Negative Affect Schedule loaded on one factor and most of the items in the Negative Affect scale of the Global Mood Scale loaded on another. Denollet and De Vries (2006) noted that "the negative mood terms from the [Global Mood Scale] and [Positive and Negative Affect Schedule] may be separated in two affect dimensions reflecting emotional exhaustion (deactivation) and anxious apprehension (activation) as different affective components of the stress process" (p. 177). Nevertheless, they insisted that the factor analysis provided "new evidence for the notion that the [Global Mood Scale] is a good measure of positive and negative affect" (p. 178).

It is important to underscore that the development of a new measure is far from easy; it is a multistep and extremely labor-intensive process. Specifying the theoretical basis of the measure should always be the first step (DeVellis, 2012). When developing a new theoretical framework to serve as the foundation of the new measure, it is crucial to first have a good grasp of previous relevant theories. In most cases, developing a thorough and accurate understanding of previous theories will cause the idea that a new theory is needed to evaporate; the aspiring theorist will soon realize that the plan amounts to nothing more than a laborious attempt to rediscover the proverbial wheel. If, even after studying the previous theories, one remains convinced that a new theory is necessary, having a good grasp of previous theories will enable the developer of the new measure to present an articulate argument for the need for the new measure, as well as to specify how the new theory complements or extends existing theories. When using an existing theory, it is essential to (a) have in-depth and accurate knowledge and understanding of that theory and (b) use the theory as an a priori basis that guides every step of the measure-development process (as opposed to attempting to retrofit the measure to the theory or, even worse, the theory to the measure).

Domain underrepresentation

Arguments for the necessity of domain-specific measures are often based on claims that existing measures do not capture aspects of affect, mood, or emotion that authors consider relevant within a given domain and, conversely, that existing measures tap aspects that are not relevant. So new measures are developed with the promise of zeroing in on those elements of affect, mood, or emotion that really matter within a given domain. More often than not, new measures, either knowingly and intentionally or unknowingly and inadvertently, tend to follow the distinct-states approach, comprising an assortment of discrete states that their developers deem relevant.

When researchers offer to the scientific community a measure of (for example) affective responses to cocaine inhalation, mood predictors of disturbed sleep, or emotions that raise the propensity for alcohol overconsumption, they are essentially promising that the measure captures the totality (or at least a reasonably close approximation) of that domain of content; that is, the entire universe of affective responses to cocaine, the entire universe of mood predictors of disturbed sleep, and the entire universe of emotions that raise the propensity for alcohol overconsumption. According to the Standards for Educational and Psychological Testing of the American Educational Research Association, the American Psychological Association, and the National Council on Measurement in Education (1999), test developers should give careful consideration to whether "a test measures less or more than its proposed construct" (p. 10).

In particular, "construct underrepresentation refers to the degree to which a test fails to capture important aspects of the construct" (p. 10). Unless developers can actually deliver a measure that captures the entire universe of content that they originally targeted, domain-specific measures would be of little use; in essence, it would behove all subsequent investigators to initiate their own, onerous and inefficient, reexploration of that content domain from the ground up.

Once this point is appreciated, the enormity and complexity of the undertaking of developing a domain-specific measure becomes apparent. The nature, the limits, and the structure of the domain of content must be fully and thoroughly explored before researchers can begin to plan a new measure. It is simply impossible to develop an effective measure before one has a crystalized view of the domain of content one wishes to capture. Not surprising, however, many domain-specific measures fall short of this stringent requirement. The exploration of the nature, the limits, and the structure of the intended content domain typically ranges from nonexistent (when a measure is constructed based entirely on the developers' own subjective opinion of which "relevant" states comprise the universe of content) to inadequate (when an empirical exploration of the content domain is undertaken but it is limited and unlikely to capture the entire universe of relevant content).

As one example, Ryan-Harshman, Leiter, and Anderson (1987) studied the effects of four dosages of phenylalanine and two dosages of aspartame on arousal (*alert, mentally slow*) and "mood" (*drowsy, weak, nervous, tense, drugged, depressed*) using a series of visual analogue scales. They found that "mood and arousal were unaffected by these doses" (p. 250). Since no argument, either theoretical or empirical, was put forth to support the decision to limit the operationalization of "mood" to these particular seven states, this approach leaves open the possibility that, contrary to what was concluded, phenylalanine or aspartame did influence some other sector or sectors of the domain of "mood" beyond those seven.

In another example, Arnow, Kenardy, and Agras (1995) questioned the notion that "all varieties of negative mood precipitate disinhibited eating in the same way" and criticized "the common practice of referring generically to 'negative mood' and its relation to overeating" (p. 81). So they set out to develop a measure that would "permit a more detailed analysis of the relationship between negative mood and disordered eating" (p. 81). This measure was named the Emotional Eating Scale and contained three subscales: anger / frustration, anxiety, and depression. The focus on these three negative "moods" was based on the findings of a previous qualitative study of 19 obese women who self-identified as binge eaters (Arnow, Kenardy, & Agras, 1992). That study showed the mood states that were more prevalent prior to binging were anger/ frustration (42 percent), anxiety/agitation (37 percent), sadness/depression (16 percent), and regret (5 percent). Based on this finding, Arnow et al. (1995) justified the focus on the three states by arguing that "feelings of anger/frustration, anxiety, and sadness/depression accounted for 95% of the antecedent moods reported by respondents" (p. 82). In this case, the very limited size and the specific characteristics of the sample involved in the preliminary qualitative investigation (Arnow et al., 1992) raise concerns about the extent to which their responses could offer an encompassing representation of the intended universe of content (i.e., *all* the specific varieties of "negative mood" that may be associated with "disordered eating"). Although the three-factor structure of the Emotional Eating Scale has gone unquestioned by the numerous researchers who have since adopted this questionnaire, subsequent investigations have yielded credible evidence not only of additional relevant negative states such as loneliness (Masheb & Grilo, 2006) and boredom (Koball, Meers, Storfer-Isser, Domoff, & Musher-Eizenman, 2012), but also of relevant positive states such as joy (Macht, 1999). Therefore, as in the previous example, a failure to discover a relation between "mood" and "disordered eating" based on the Emotional Eating Scale would still leave open the possibility that a mood state other than the ones tapped by this measure may be associated with "disordered eating." Therefore, any generalizations to the global domain of "mood" or "negative mood" or even "negative mood states that predict disordered eating" would be inappropriate since all of these content domains are likely underrepresented by the Emotional Eating Scale.

The troubled notion of domain specificity

The development of domain-specific measures of affect, mood, and emotion is often based on a unitary notion of the domain in question, as if, for example, there were only one universal or archetype form of "eating" or "smoking" or "drinking." Clearly, however, this is an oversimplification. The experience of each episode of a health behavior is jointly determined by a multitude of interacting factors, including the (diverse) biological and psychological characteristics of the individuals involved; the (diverse) social, economic, political, cultural, and physical conditions; and the (diverse) forms or expressions of the health behavior itself. It is, therefore, very likely that an affect, mood, or emotion deemed "relevant" under one particular combination of experimental conditions would be rendered "irrelevant" under another and vice versa. This raises the crucial question of how a behavioral domain is delimited and the extent to which it can be expanded or modified before one must acknowledge that a measure developed to be specific to that domain is rendered no longer relevant.

For example, Herbert, Johns, and Doré (1976) factor analyzed a pool of 18 visual analogue "mood" scales from a series of experiments examining the effects of undisturbed and disturbed sleep (due to noise, heat, or interruptions). Their factor analyses, based on responses collected before and after sleep, revealed two consistent factors, labeled "alertness" and "tranquility." Earlier, Bond and Lader (1974) had factor analyzed 16 of these 18 visual analogue scales based on responses obtained only during neutral conditions and had shown a partially different, three-factor structure. They labeled their factors "alertness," "contentedness," and "calmness." So it seems possible that the context in which the data were collected could have influenced the structure of the item pool. It is, therefore, worth wondering: when McKinney and

Coyle (2006) used the 18 scales of Herbert et al. (1976) in a different context (to investigate the "hangover" effects after a night of drinking alcohol), were they justified in assuming that the item pool would maintain the same structure that the original analysis by Herbert et al. had revealed?

Similarly, it is worth contemplating the meaningfulness of comparisons between two experimental conditions, one involving the same domain whose effects the measure was specifically engineered to detect and another, irrelevant or incompatible one. For example, Leathwood and Pollet (1982/1983) developed a measured they presumed to specifically reflect the effects of dietary interventions, including the ingestion of caffeine. So Peeling and Dawson (2007) used this measure to compare the effects of caffeine ingestion and placebo following a university lecture. If the measure is specifically engineered to detect the effects of caffeine but not the effects of the comparison condition (in this case, the placebo), then what are we actually learning from this experiment? Can the experiment be considered unbiased or are the cards already stacked up in favor of one experimental condition and against the other?

The same criticism applies when comparisons are made against a neutral baseline condition in within-subject analyses. For example, Martin et al. (1993) selected items for the Biphasic Alcohol Effects Scale by asking five men and two women who were frequent drinkers to describe how they felt as they drank a moderate amount of alcohol and for some time afterward (i.e., during the rising and falling limbs of their blood alcohol curves). However, investigators (e.g., King et al., 2011) have also administered the Biphasic Alcohol Effects Scale during the "predrink baseline" by simply modifying the instructions. The meaningfulness of such comparisons can again be questioned, since the measure was specifically engineered to reflect the content domain of experiences "during" and "after" alcohol consumption but not "before."

It is also worth noting that, if a domain-specific measure is engineered in such a way that its content is somehow made entirely irrelevant to neutral baseline conditions, then a host of other problems may arise. For example, by asking respondents to "rate the extent to which drinking alcohol has produced these feelings in you at the present time," Martin et al. (1993) ensured that, under "predrink baseline" conditions, "ratings were at 0 for all items for all subjects" (p. 143). Zeros for all items, however, means zero variance, which, in turn, means zero covariance between items, zero internal consistency, and a collapse of the factor structure of the measure under such conditions. Even if the situation is not as extreme as "all zeroes," but baseline responses exhibit symptoms of floor effects (i.e., close to all zeroes), similar problems may result, making both the psychometric evaluations and any statistical comparisons difficult or impossible.

As one can imagine, the notion of domain specificity can quickly deteriorate into a constant source of concerns, depending on how critical one wants to be. For example, can "items selected to tap ... emotional reactions that are relevant to the daily lives of adolescents" (Whalen, Jamner, Henker, & Delfino, 2001, p. 101) be assumed to remain equally relevant to the daily lives of adolescents scoring near the top of the range in Attention Deficit and Hyperactivity Disorder (ADHD) symptoms (Whalen, Jamner, Henker, Delfino, & Lozano, 2002)? Adolescents in the high-ADHD group report "more negative affectivity, as seen in elevated rates of anger, anxiety, stress, and sadness, along with lower rates of happiness and well-being" (Whalen et al., 2002, p. 220). How can one be certain, however, that the differences are only quantitative and not differences in the content and structure of the domain of interest (i.e., the universe of "emotional reactions that are relevant to the daily lives" of this group of adolescents)?

Likewise, one may argue that the process followed by Martin et al. (1993) in selecting items for the Biphasic Alcohol Effects Scale was a reasonable one (i.e., asking drinkers how they felt as they drank). However, can the universe of content likely to emerge from this procedure be assumed to remain invariant when the amount of alcohol consumed is doubled or tripled? Or when the individuals being tested are occasional drinkers as opposed to regular drinkers? Or when alcohol is administered in conjunction with another substance, such as nicotine, as opposed to independently (e.g., Ralevski et al., 2012)? It is very important to emphasize that these questions are separate from whether the factor structure of the measure remains invariant across categories of respondents or across different experimental conditions (Earleywine & Erblich, 1996; Rueger, McNamara, & King, 2009). The question is whether the nature, the limits, and the structure of the *domain of content* the measure was intended to represent can remain constant.

In sum, even though the notion of domain specificity is usually accepted as something positive and domain-specific measures typically garner considerable popularity within their respective domains, the idea is in fact fraught with complications that may not be immediately apparent. Much like generalizing the findings of a study to a population with characteristics beyond those of the sample actually tested, the universe of content tapped by a measure should not be assumed to remain relevant to stimuli, contexts, or populations of respondents beyond those tested during the item selection and content validation phase of the measure-development process.

The "sensitivity" slippery slope

The only "sensitivity" that can be found in the indices of psychometric texts refers to the ability of a measure to classify cases accurately (i.e., classify a respondent as having a disorder when the disorder is in fact present). However, in many domains of health-behavioral research it is common to encounter a different use of the term "sensitivity." Arguments for the relevance or specificity of a new measure to a given domain are typically accompanied by claims that the new measure is "sensitive" enough to detect differences between groups presumed to be different, benefits of a certain intervention presumed to be inherently effective, or changes in response to a treatment presumed to invariably bring about a certain effect. As one example, the support expressed by Rueger et al. (2009) for the Biphasic Alcohol Effects Scale (BAES) was based in part on the claim that the "adjective items comprising the BAES are sensitive to the stimulant- and sedative-like effects of alcohol" (p. 918). However, although this type of "sensitivity" is instinctively perceived as a positive property, once again, significant complications may lurk beneath the surface.

For example, how is the perceived "sensitivity to change" judged? Oftentimes, a researcher may already believe that a treatment leads to a certain outcome (e.g., reduces something bad and/or promotes something good). In such cases, "sensitivity to change" may be judged by the extent to which the measure yields the anticipated outcome (i.e., confirms a foredrawn conclusion). In such instances, the possibility of bias should be apparent (see Chapter 1, "Domain specificity as panacea"). The desire to produce a measure that finds what the developer wants it to find may lead, for example, to such phenomena as turning a blind eye to construct underrepresentation (i.e., underemphasizing or eliminating undesirable outcomes) or inflating construct-irrelevant variance, defined in the Standards for Educational and Psychological Testing of the American Educational Research Association, the American Psychological Association, and the National Council on Measurement in Education (1999) as "the degree to which test scores are affected by processes that are extraneous to its intended construct" (p. 10).

As an example, while establishing the need for the Global Mood Scale, Denollet (1993) bemoaned the fact that "research [had] largely failed to document a psychological effect of [cardiac rehabilitation programs]" (p. 112). This was characterized as "an unexpected finding because rehabilitation enhances the patient's perceived control ... which is closely related to his or her emotional status" (Denollet, 1993, p. 112). So the items of the Global Mood Scale were selected with the express purpose of compiling a measure that "had to be sensitive to changes in emotional distress as a function of intervention" (p. 112). In his critique of the Global Mood Scale cited earlier in this chapter, Stone (1997) asked "should we think of a mood scale as being poor if it does not show the effect of a treatment?" (p. 166). In Stone's view, the answer to this rhetorical question should be obvious. However, it is not clear that the significance of this point is fully appreciated in all areas of health-behavioral research. Both rejecting a measure because it does not show what a researcher believes to be axiomatic (i.e., a self-evident truth) and engineering a measure to ensure that it does represent highly perilous paths. Researchers concerned with minimizing bias should approach this type of "sensitivity" with the healthy level of skepticism it warrants.

Before criticizing a measure for not being "sensitive," researchers should consider whether they can reframe their criticism as pertaining to validity. A valid measure should reflect the construct it was developed to tap, nothing more and nothing less. If the construct changes but the measure does not reflect this change, then the measure should be deemed invalid, not insensitive. However, to build a case for the invalidity of a measure, a researcher should have other, external and irrefutable, evidence that the construct did change. A belief that it "must have changed because we generally know that it does" cannot be considered compelling. Similarly, when developing a new measure, one should not be concerned with demonstrating "sensitivity" but rather with establishing validity through proper theoretical arguments and multiple sources of empirical evidence. A valid measure of the intended content domain (one that does not underrepresent it and does not introduce construct-irrelevant variance) will inevitably show when the construct changes and the extent to which it does. The notion of "sensitivity" need not be invoked.

If not domain specificity, then what?

The perspective outlined in the previous sections, which deviates from the overwhelming support for domain-specific measures in health-behavioral research, may cause researchers who feel dissatisfied with domain-general measures of affect, mood, and emotion to wonder what a better alternative might be. Two specific recommendations can be offered.

First, it should be clear that domain-specific measures are neither unwarranted nor impossible to develop. They do, however, represent a much larger challenge, both theoretically and methodologically, than the current literature suggests. The case for the need for a new measure should be built on arguments that go well beyond the claim that existing domain-general measures are de facto "irrelevant" or that a domain-specific measure would be more "sensitive" to the effects of a given treatment. If an existing theory is used as the basis, the theory must be fully understood and properly reflected in the content and structure of the measure. If a new theory is developed, its relation to existing theories should be specified. Proper representation of the intended content domain is paramount. Just as important, the developer of the new measure should issue specific directions to prospective users regarding the "domain" (i.e., target population of respondents, experimental contexts, interventions or stimuli) within which the measure can be deemed relevant based on its developmental procedures (i.e., original specification of the domain of content, item selection, content validation).

Measure developers and users should heed the recommendations in the Standards for Educational and Psychological Testing (American Educational Research Association, American Psychological Association, and National Council on Measurement in Education, 1999):

- **Standard 6.3** (p. 68): The rationale for the test, recommended uses of the test, support for such uses, and information that assists in score interpretation should be documented. Where particular misuses of a test can be reasonably anticipated, caution against such misuses should be specified.
- **Standard 6.4** (p. 69): The population for whom the test is intended and the test specifications should be documented. If applicable, the item pool and scale development procedures should be described in the relevant test manuals.

Furthermore, researchers who plan to use a domain-specific measure should keep in mind that "validation is the joint responsibility of the test developer and the test user." In particular, "the test user is ultimately responsible for evaluating the evidence in the particular setting in which the test is to be used. When the use of a test differs from that supported by the test developer, the test user bears special responsibility for validation" (p. 11).

Second, researchers should critically reconsider the arguments for the necessity of a domain-specific measure. As noted in this section, the problems with the concept of domain specificity are many and not necessarily immediately apparent (including the extremely laborious process of investigating the nature, limits, and structure of the content domain, ensuring that the item pool provides adequate representation of the targeted domain of content without introducing extraneous variance, and the inappropriateness of generalizing to populations and contexts beyond those studied during the development of the measure).

On the other hand, the arguments in favor of domain-specific measures are usually the following two, both of which, if deconstructed, seem considerably less compelling: (a) a domain-specific measure would be more "sensitive" than a domain-general one and (b) existing measures contain irrelevant items. As noted in the previous section, if the former argument cannot be reframed in terms of validity (i.e., if a general measure cannot be shown to be *invalid* within a particular context), the "sensitivity" argument should probably be abandoned. If a measure is valid across the full range of the construct, then it will be sensitive.

The problem of "irrelevant" items is perhaps more complex. As noted in Chapters 6 and 7, researchers have raised legitimate concerns regarding the item pools of several popular questionnaires. However, the real problem is usually not that particular items lack relevance to a given context (e.g., drinking caffeine or binge eating) but rather that the content domain of the measure itself was improperly specified, thus introducing construct-irrelevant variance. For example, the inclusion of the Confusion scale in the Profile of Mood States (with such items as *confused, unable to concentrate,* and *forgetful*) is justly seen as problematic by many because confusion does not fit the definition of mood. As explained in Chapter 6, the Confusion scale was added to the Profile of Mood States (McNair et al., 1971) because confusion is a common side effect of psychiatric medication. Contrary to what the newer label "Profile of Mood States" suggests, the original domain of content of this questionnaire (under the label Psychiatric Outpatient Mood Scale) included the universe of subjective responses of psychiatric patients to psychoactive drugs, including moods (such as Depression), emotions (such as Anger), affect (such as Fatigue), and cognitive impairment (such as Confusion).

Similarly, as discussed in Chapter 7, the apparent irrelevance of some of the items of the Positive and Negative Affect Schedule (Watson, Clark, & Tellegen, 1988) to some contexts probably stems from the fact that the domain of content of this questionnaire was not properly delimited during the planning stage. As a result, the Positive and Negative Affect Schedule does not only include items that tap affect and mood but also includes items indicative of specific emotions (e.g., *proud, guilty, ashamed*), as well as items of ambiguous content (e.g., *interested, strong, inspired, determined, attentive*).

Thus, the reason why certain items may seem irrelevant in a given context is because experiencing a specific emotion (such as feeling *proud*, *guilty*, or *ashamed*) presupposes a possible eliciting stimulus and an antecedent cognitive appraisal that is congruent with that emotion. Emotions do not simply emerge out of a vacuum (are not free-floating or constant background feelings) but rather follow the cognitive appraisals of specific environmental stimuli. So, for example, unless a relevant stimulus occurred that happened to be appraised in a specific manner, an individual is unlikely to feel *proud*, *guilty*, or *ashamed* (see Lazarus, 1991a, pp. 271–274 and 240–247 for the patterns of cognitive appraisals underlying pride and guilt/shame, respectively). Thus, although these items are not always or de facto irrelevant to a given context (conceivably, one could feel *proud*, *guilty*, or *ashamed* in the context of drinking caffeine or binge eating), there is a good chance that, statistically speaking, respondents will not find them relevant to their current state.

Such problems are pervasive. For example, as discussed in Chapter 7, the Activation Deactivation Adjective Check List (Thayer, 1989) contains the item *fearful*, which is not an index of core affect or mood but rather an index of a specific emotion that depends on a specific appraisal (see Lazarus, 1991a, pp. 234–240). Unless the appraisal underlying the emotion of fear is experimentally induced, respondents typically do not feel *fearful*, thus finding this item irrelevant, leading to floor effects. Essentially the same problem also plagues measures of emotion. For example, as noted in Chapter 6, the State-Trait Anxiety Inventory (Spielberger, 1983; Spielberger et al., 1970) exhibits a high overlap with measures of depression, which could be attributed to the presence of some items that may be better indicators of depression than anxiety (e.g., "I wish I could be as happy as others seem to be," "I feel like a failure"). A respondent who is anxious but not depressed (i.e., appraises threat but not helplessness) could find such items irrelevant. However, as in the examples in the previous paragraphs, this irrelevance mainly reflects irrelevance of the items to the construct being measured rather than to the context (or "domain") in which the measurement takes place.

So, upon closer inspection, what may initially seem a problem of domain irrelevance is actually a problem of poor content representation or, more accurately, a problem of construct-irrelevant variance. In other words, the problem is that some general measures of affect, mood, and emotion, even very popular ones, are not good measures of their respective content domains. The solution in such cases is not to develop a domain-specific measure but rather to look for a better measure of affect, mood, or emotion.

A reasonable approach would be to follow a systematic progression from targeting the broadest construct in the affective hierarchy (i.e., core affect) and the most encompassing conceptual model of that construct (i.e., a dimensional model, such as the circumplex) to the elaboration offered by the distinct-state or categorical approach to the measurement of moods and emotions (Ekkekakis & Petruzzello, 2002). This approach stems directly from the notion of the hierarchical structure of the affective domain (see Chapter 3, section entitled "The hierarchical structure of the affective domain: an integrative framework").

As explained in Chapter 2, core affect can be found in free-floating form and is "always available to consciousness" (Russell & Feldman Barrett, 2009, p. 104). Its presence does not presuppose an eliciting stimulus or an antecedent appraisal and, therefore, items that tap core affect (e.g., pleasure-displeasure, tension-calmness, energy-tiredness) generally do not give the impression that they are "irrelevant" in any situation. Using a dimensional model, such as the circumplex, to operationalize the domain of core affect offers the benefit of a broad and balanced investigative scope, theoretically extending over the entire universe of core affect. Of course, this breadth of scope comes at a cost, namely the loss of some degree of detail (e.g., one can tell that the respondent's current state is characterized by pleasant low activation but cannot distinguish whether that state is closer to calmness or to relaxation). Using appropriate measures, such as straightforward and content-valid rating scales of pleasure-displeasure and low-high activation, one can track the changes that occur over time (e.g., in response to a drug or a behavior) within this core affective space (for an example, see Figure 8.1; Backhouse et al., 2011; Ekkekakis, Backhouse, Gray, & Lind, 2008; Ekkekakis et al., 2000; Taylor, Katomeri, & Ussher, 2006).

The main benefit of a measurement approach with a wide scope is that it does not leave out any major variants of affect in which changes may occur and it does not place any heavier emphasis on one versus another segment of affective space (Ekkekakis & Petruzzello, 2002; Stritzke, Lang, & Patrick, 1996; Wiers, 2008). A dimensional measure of core affect should be equally apt to capture a neutral baseline state as it would be to capture a state that resulted from an intervention (e.g., just as much the predrink baseline as the stimulant and sedative effects of alcohol consumption). Furthermore, a dimensional model of core affect is essentially a universal and invariant map or template of core affect. As such, it represents the best available option for facilitating the integration of information from different studies onto a common platform (e.g., different doses, behaviors, stimuli, or contexts; see Ekkekakis,

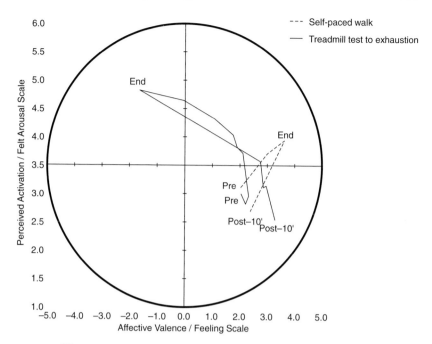

Figure 8.1. An example of tracking affective changes in circumplex affective space, using the Feeling Scale (Hardy & Rejeski, 1989) as a measure of valence and the Felt Arousal Scale (Svebak & Murgatroyd, 1985) as a measure of activation. The two conditions were (a) a 15-min treadmill walk at a self-chosen pace, resulting in a pleasant high-activation state during and a pleasant low-activation state following a 10-min seated recovery period, and (b) a treadmill test (lasting on average 11.3 min), during which the speed and grade are gradually increased until the point of volitional exhaustion, resulting in an unpleasant high-activation state during and a return to a pleasant low-activation state after a short cool-down and a 10-min seated recovery period. "Pre" indicates the beginning of each activity, "End" indicates its end and "Post-10'" indicates a time point 10 min after the end. Plotted with data from Ekkekakis et al. (2000) and Hall, Ekkekakis, and Petruzzello (2002).

Hall, & Petruzzello, 2008; Taylor & Oliver, 2009). This type of synthesis could greatly accelerate the accumulation of knowledge since each new study would build upon a common foundation.

Once the main affective features of an experimental stimulus have been explored, the path would be paved for follow-up investigations focusing on specific moods or emotions. For example, if researchers discover that high-activation unpleasant states tend to predispose individuals to smoke, a reasonable next step would be to examine whether anxiety or anger provides a more potent stimulus.

An important advantage of starting out with a broad perspective (i.e., on core affect) and gradually zeroing in on specific mood and emotional states shown to be of particular interest in a given domain is that the decision to focus on a set of specific states is supported by prior empirical evidence instead of depending solely on arguments about what seems intuitive. Compared to the limitations associated with the now prevalent practice of using lists of affect, mood, or emotion-related terms, this represents a crucial advance. Lists of items, as reasonable as they may seem on the surface, usually only offer partial coverage of the global domain of interest (affect, mood, or emotion), possibly leaving important parts of that domain untapped (i.e., the problem referred to in this chapter as "underrepresentation").

As always, however, the quality of the measures used to operationalize the core affective dimensions that are chosen does matter. This is important to emphasize because, perhaps in an effort to associate their measures with a theoretical model, researchers have used item lists *derived from* or *based on* dimensional models of core affect, such as the circumplex (e.g., Greeno, Wing, & Shiffman, 2000; Magid, Colder, Stroud, Nichter, & Nichter, 2009; Mohr, Brannan, Mohr, Armeli, & Tennen, 2008; Shiffman & Gwaltney, 2008; Simons, Dvorak, Batien, & Wray, 2010). Much like item lists not claiming an association to a theoretical model, however, the selective extraction of items from a model does not entail comprehensive coverage of the space the model was developed to represent; the possibility of sectors of the models remaining untapped still remains. Sampling sectors from a dimensional model, such as the circumplex, is no different than sampling items from the entire affective lexicon since, theoretically, dimensional models were developed to represent the entire universe of affective states. It is, therefore, preferable to use measures that directly assess the main affective dimensions, such as valence and activation (e.g., Backhouse et al., 2011; Ekkekakis et al., 2000; Taylor et al., 2006).

9 Problems of domain specificity: examples from exercise

The challenges identified in Chapter 8 are common to many domain-specific measures. Since commenting on every single domain-specific measure that has appeared in the health-behavior literature would be impossible, this chapter focuses on three measures specifically developed to assess affective responses to exercise. Exercise represents an interesting example because this area has sparked the development of more domain-specific measures than perhaps any other health behavior. With more measures came more debate, more controversy, and more measurement-associated claims that can serve as the basis for illustrating some of the points made in Chapter 8. The problems identified, including the consequences of lacking a theoretical basis, the risks associated with construct underrepresentation, and the possible fallacies emanating from the notion of "sensitivity to change" are all highlighted in the critiques that follow. In turn, these critiques can serve as blueprints for evaluating most other domain-specific measures being used in health-behavioral research.

The Exercise-induced Feeling Inventory

The Exercise-induced Feeling Inventory (Gauvin & Rejeski, 1993) was developed on the basis of the fundamental assumption that "the stimulus properties of physical activity are capable of producing several distinct feelings states" (p. 404). The exploration of the domain of "distinct feeling states" associated with the "stimulus properties of physical activity" was motivated by the belief that commonly used measures, such as the Profile of Mood States, the Positive and Negative Affect Schedule, and the State-Trait Anxiety Inventory, "may have questionable content and construct validity in exercise research" (p. 404). The great challenge in developing the Exercise-induced Feeling Inventory was to delineate the nature, the limits, and the structure of its novel content domain. Which are the "distinct feeling states" that characterize the exercise experience? Arguably, this is an unanswerable question or at least a question that is extremely difficult to answer. The reason is that there is no archetype "exercise," no archetype "exerciser," and no archetype physical and psychological context in which the exercise takes place (Ekkekakis & Petruzzello, 2001b). The combination of people, exercise stimuli, and exercise contexts creates the possibility of an endless (or at least unmanageably large) repertoire of "feeling states." So a related and equally important challenge would be to decide how far to extend the domain of content. In particular, a significant risk is to have a measure that suffers from domain underrepresentation. Practically, this means having a measure that covers some of the "feeling states" likely to emerge from exercise participation but omits others (e.g., covers those feeling states commonly experienced by young, healthy, and physically active people but omits those experienced by middle-aged or older individuals who are in less than perfect health and have led sedentary lives). If the measure underrepresents the domain of content it is supposed to tap, this raises the risk of making baseless and misleading generalizations (e.g., concluding that an exercise bout had no effects on "feeling states" in general when it might have had significant effects in states other than those tapped by the measure).

Gauvin and Rejeski (2001) noted that they entered the process of exploring their target domain of content without having preconceived notions (i.e., an a priori theoretical basis) about its nature and structure. In particular, although Gauvin and Rejeski (1993) had alluded to an "*a priori* structure" (p. 409), an "*a priori* framework" (p. 410), an "*a priori* conceptual framework" (p. 411), and an "*a priori* model" (p. 414), they later acknowledged that they did not identify and label the states assessed by the Exercise-induced Feeling Inventory "until after the data had been collected ... commensurate with the 'inductive' approach" (Gauvin & Rejeski, 2001, p. 77). They also stated that they "had not initially opted for a dimensional or a categorical approach" (p. 77) but eventually arrived at the conclusion that the domain of content was best represented as "categorical," consisting of distinct states. This lack of an a priori theoretical basis and the eventual decision to follow a categorical, as opposed to a dimensional, approach contrasts sharply with an eloquent conceptual case made in the same year by Gauvin and Brawley (1993) in favor of dimensional models:

[The dimensional] approach seems better suited to the understanding of exercise and affect because the models stemming from it are intended to be broad, encompassing conceptualizations of affective experience. Because the affective experience that accompanies exercise has not been thoroughly described, a model of affect that has a wider breadth is more likely to capture the essence of exercise-induced affect than a model that, at the outset, limits the focus of investigation to specific emotions. (p. 152)

Despite the position in favor of dimensional models, the Exercise-induced Feeling Inventory was developed as a categorical instrument tapping the specific states of positive engagement, revitalization, physical exhaustion, and tranquility. It was argued that these four states capture "the phenomenology of people involved in exercise in the real world" (Gauvin & Rejeski, 1993, p. 408), are "consistent with the phenomenology of men and women who exercise with some regularity" (Gauvin & Rejeski, 1993, p. 419), and "appear to be the primary forms of affect that are directly influenced by physical activity" (Rejeski et al., 1999, p. 98).

These statements seem to imply that researchers would be justified in generalizing, on the basis of data obtained with the Exercise-induced Feeling Inventory, to the domain of "exercise-induced feeling states" in general. It is, therefore, important to consider the methods by which Gauvin and Rejeski (1993) arrived at these four states. In particular, it is critical for researchers to evaluate (a) whether the four-state domain of content was derived from open-ended surveys of exercise experiences across diverse and representative samples of participants and (b) whether the process of reducing these phenomenological accounts to a manageable set of scales permitted the faithful and comprehensive representation of the richness of the raw material. To arrive at the four states eventually included in the Exercise-induced Feeling Inventory, Gauvin and Rejeski (1993) started with over 500 adjectives. To reduce this large item pool, they then had three experts in exercise psychology evaluate the relevance of each of these items to exercise. This process resulted in 145 remaining items. These 145 items were then submitted to a sample of college students who agreed that all 145 items were potentially relevant to exercise. Gauvin and Rejeski then categorized these 145 items into 15 clusters on the basis of subjective similarity judgments. Finally, they progressively eliminated 11 of the 15 clusters, which left the 4 that now comprise the Exercise-induced Feeling Inventory, namely positive engagement, revitalization, physical exhaustion, and tranquility.

A thorough critique of the criteria cited for eliminating the 11 clusters is well beyond the scope of this review. However, it is fair to say that they were somewhat controversial. For example, it was stated that states pertaining to physical symptoms were dropped because such symptoms are "highly variable" across participants or that states such as confusion, anxiety, and depression were dropped because they can be measured by other questionnaires such as the Profile of Mood States. Arguably, items or clusters of items should only be dropped if they are deemed outside the previously specified and delimited domain of content, regardless of whether they exhibit variability or they can also be measured by other available instruments. So researchers must decide whether or not these reasons are compelling. However, in making a case for selecting the Exercise-induced Feeling Inventory, avoiding to take a position on this issue should not be seen as optional.

Recall that, in choosing a measure, one also accepts and adopts the conceptual model upon which the measure was built. Therefore, by selecting the Exercise-induced Feeling Inventory, a researcher essentially takes the conceptual position that the entire universe of content of "exercise-induced feeling states" can be reduced to (a) positive engagement, (b) revitalization, (c) physical exhaustion, and (d) tranquility. By implication, this also means that the researcher agrees with the methods and the arguments used in reducing the item pool to these four states. If a researcher is going to draw conclusions from data collected with the Exercise-induced Feeling Inventory about the entire domain of "exercise-induced feeling states," he or she would only be justified to do so after building a convincing case that these four states fully encompass the domain of content and, consequently, that domain underrepresentation does not pose a threat. In particular, researchers should note that the Exercise-induced Feeling Inventory does not include items describing moderate-activation unpleasant states (e.g., *unhappy, sad*) or high-activation unpleasant states (e.g., *tense, distressed*).

Until now, no such arguments have been presented by authors in exercise psychology, despite the fact that some express the view that the four states are "the most sensitive to the stimulus properties of exercise" (Annesi, 2006, p. 777). Moreover, the Exercise-induced Feeling Inventory appears to be frequently misused. For example, although Gauvin and Rejeski (1993) had specified that the content represented by the Exercise-induced Feeling Inventory is consistent with the phenomenology of "men and women *who exercise with some regularity*" (Gauvin & Rejeski, 1993, p. 419, emphasis added), the Exercise-induced Feeling Inventory has been used with children (Vlachopoulos et al., 1996), sedentary young adults (Focht & Hausenblas, 2006; Martin Ginis et al., 2003, 2007; Treasure & Newbery, 1998), sedentary middle-aged adults (Gauvin et al., 1997), sedentary older adults (Focht, Knapp, Gavin, Raedeke, & Hickner, 2007), and obese older adults with knee osteoarthritis (Focht et al., 2004). Nowhere in these studies is there any mention of the interpretational problems likely to emerge from the incompatibility between the personal characteristics and exercise experiences of the development samples and those of the samples being studied. Since what is being measured with the Exercise-induced Feeling Inventory was based on the experiences of physically active individuals, for example, would the absence of significant changes in some or all four of the scales imply that exercise did not induce changes in the domain of "exercise-induced feeling states" or would it imply that changes might have occurred in other, untapped states? Similar issues should be of concern for users of the short version of the Exercise-induced Feeling Inventory (Annesi, 2006) and the version intended for use in chronic exercise intervention studies (Rejeski et al., 1999).

Importantly, researchers should be aware that "reductions in pleasant feeling states" (Focht et al., 2007, p. 132), such as Positive Engagement, Revitalization, and Tranquility, do not entail and should not be interpreted as equal but opposite changes (i.e., increases) in (untapped) negative states (i.e., as "negative affective responses," Focht et al., 2007, p. 133). As explained earlier and illustrated by Russell and Carroll (1999a, 1999b), scales theorized to represent two opposite poles of a bipolar continuum (e.g., pleasant-unpleasant or positive-negative), if they are assessed using unipolar response formats (such as the one used in the Exercise-induced Feeling Inventory, which ranges from 0: Do not feel to 4: Feel very strongly), cannot provide fully redundant information and thus cannot have a perfect −1.00 correlation. In other words, a researcher would not be justified in extrapolating from changes in one pole to possible changes in the other.

The Subjective Exercise Experiences Scale

Like the Exercise-induced Feeling Inventory, the Subjective Exercise Experiences Scale (McAuley & Courneya, 1994) was developed out of a desire to provide a domain-specific measure for exercise. The development of the Subjective Exercise Experiences Scale was also motivated by the fundamental belief that participation in exercise can elicit responses that form a distinct domain of content, which domain-general measures cannot fully capture. According to McAuley and Courneya (1994), there are "subjective experiences that are *unique* to the exercise domain" (p. 165, italics added). However, the Subjective Exercise Experiences Scale also differs from the Exercise-induced Feeling Inventory in several important respects.

Primary among the differences is that the Subjective Exercise Experiences Scale appears to have been based on a tentative theoretical framework: "From a conceptual perspective, we concur with the broader social psychological literature that suggests emotional or affective responses vary along two (positive and negative) and possibly more dimensions" (McAuley & Courneya, 1994, p. 165). It also seems that the intention was to develop a dimensional measure. Although McAuley and Courneya (1994) did not directly address the issue of dimensional versus categorical (or distinct states) models, their views on this subject could be gleaned from their comparisons between the Subjective Exercise Experiences Scale and the Exercise-induced Feeling Inventory. Specifically, they referred to a "hierarchy of psychological responses to exercise participation" (p. 173), a reference reminiscent of the hierarchical models of the affective domain described in Chapter 3. They characterized the Subjective Exercise Experiences Scale as a measure of "general psychological responses" (p. 173) designed to assess responses on a "global level" (p. 173), and the Exercise-induced Feeling Inventory as a measure which may "represent further under-lying structural aspects" (p. 173) of these responses. From these descriptions, it appears that the intent was to develop a measure comprising a "positive" and a "negative" dimension but one which, unlike the Positive and Negative Affect Schedule, would not contain items "of questionable relevance to the stimulus properties of exercise" (McAuley & Courneya, 1994, p. 165). Based on the results of factor analyses, in addition to a positive dimension (labeled Positive Well-being) and a negative dimension (labeled Psychological Distress), a third dimension, namely Fatigue, also emerged.

In a sense, although it may appear that, by postulating that "subjective exercise experiences" form a dimensional domain of content instead of a few distinct states, the Subjective Exercise Experiences Scale avoided some of the problems of the Exercise-induced Feeling Inventory, it still ran into some of the same problems by resting on the assumption that some items could be deemed as de facto "relevant" or de facto "irrelevant" to exercise. When such determinations have to be made, the question that inevitably arises is: "relevant" or "irrelevant" for whom and under what conditions? For example, consider the anecdote recounted by McAuley and Rudolph (1995) to illustrate the perceived irrelevance to exercise of some of the items in the Positive and Negative Affect Schedule (PANAS; Watson, Clark, & Tellegen, 1988):

In a recent laboratory study, our research group assessed responses on the PANAS during activity; responses to such items (especially "guilty") resulted in very negative emotional responsivity. Individuals were clearly frustrated at having to respond to what they perceived as a nonrelevant emotion. (p. 90)

Although it is probably unsurprising that some individuals found the item "guilty" irrelevant, there is no basis for judging "guilty" to be de facto irrelevant for all participants under all possible circumstances. A cardiac rehabilitation patient who did not adhere to his or her exercise prescription (only did 15 min instead of the prescribed 45) might feel "guilty." A mother who left her children at home with a nanny to exercise for an hour might feel "guilty." A college student with anorexia who has been instructed by her physician to moderate her exercise might feel "guilty" after working out incessantly for two hours. As noted in Chapter 8, the problem with items such as "guilty" is not their inherent irrelevance to the context of exercise but rather the fact that they reflect neither core affect nor mood; guilt is an emotion, the emergence of which depends on a very specific antecedent appraisal.

Furthermore, a weakness of the Subjective Exercise Experiences Scale stems from a conceptual ambiguity regarding the relationship between the positive and negative affective experiences. As explained in Chapter 3, considerable controversy surrounds the issue of the independence versus bipolarity of positive and negative affect. McAuley and Courneya (1994) did not clarify their position in this debate and, consequently, did not follow specific methodological steps to ensure that the positive and negative components of their measure would assume either a relation of independence or one of bipolarity. As it turned out, the relation of the Positive Well-being and Psychological Distress factors of the Subjective Exercise Experiences Scale falls somewhere in between independence versus bipolarity (see Ekkekakis & Petruzzello, 2001b for more on this topic).

The item selection process was similar to that followed in the development of the Exercise-induced Feeling Inventory and thus shares some of the same limitations. Specifically, an initial pool of 367 items was reduced to 46 by having judges evaluate the perceived relevance of each item to exercise. Arguably, resting solely on the opinions of three judges might have had a damaging effect on the representativeness of the domain of content reflected in the item pool. Although a subsequent exploratory factor analysis was conducted with a student sample and a confirmatory factor analysis was conducted with middle-aged adults, these procedures could not have corrected this problem. McAuley and Courneya (1994) stated that by conducting the confirmatory factor analysis with a middle-aged sample, they could examine whether "the hypothesized factor structure is generalizable to other samples" (p. 168). However, this should not be taken to mean that the middle-aged sample would not have found different items "relevant" or "irrelevant" to their exercise experiences if they were given a chance. Factor analysis performed on a given pool of items cannot uncover the content, structure, or limits of the intended domain of content. Factor analysis only investigates patterns of intercorrelations among those variables entered into the analysis.

The Subjective Exercise Experiences Scale has been quite popular in exercise psychology, having been used with diverse samples, including British children in physical education classes (Markland et al., 1997), pregnant women doing aquatic exercise (Lox & Treasure, 2000), sedentary older adults (McAuley et al., 2000), and patients with major depressive disorder (Bartholomew et al., 2005). Prospective users should evaluate whether the content of the Subjective Exercise Experiences Scale truly captures the full spectrum of affective experiences likely to be elicited among diverse samples of participants in the context of exercise and whether the three-factor structure offers sufficient information. For example, the Positive Well-being scale does not distinguish between pleasant states characterized by high activation (excitement, energy), moderate activation (e.g., happiness, gladness), and low arousal (e.g., calmness, relaxation). Although the presence of the Fatigue scale does provide information about this low-activation unpleasant state, the Psychological Distress scale similarly does not distinguish between different types of negative affect. Ultimately, one must ask whether the Subjective Exercise Experiences Scale, despite the presumed relevance of its items to the context of exercise, can offer an encompassing enough and differentiated enough perspective in a way that it could really help researchers gain insight into those "subjective experiences that are unique to the exercise domain" (McAuley & Courneya, 1994, p. 165).

The Physical Activity Affect Scale

The Physical Activity Affect Scale (Lox et al., 2000) is a rare case in the measurement literature in that it is a hybrid questionnaire that emerged from the merger of the Exercise-induced Feeling Inventory and the Subjective Exercise Experiences Scale. Lox et al. (2000) argued that "both instruments are ... incomplete" because "the [Exercise-induced Feeling Inventory] lacks a subscale that assesses negative feeling states, whereas the [Subjective Exercise Experiences Scale] fails to include measures of tranquility and revitalization" (p. 82). Furthermore, they observed that, contrary to the argument that the scales of the two questionnaires assess constructs from different levels of the affective hierarchy, the high intercorrelations between their scales points instead to a redundancy. Thus, Lox et al. (2000) combined the Psychological Distress scale of the Subjective Exercise Experiences Scale with the four scales of the Exercise-induced

Feeling Inventory. A subsequent factor analysis showed that the items from the Revitalization and Positive Engagement scales of the Exercise-induced Feeling Inventory clustered together forming a single factor. The three highest loading items from each of the four remaining factors were retained, forming a four-factor, 12-item questionnaire. The four factors were labeled Positive Affect (containing the items *enthusiastic* and *upbeat* from the Positive Engagement scale of the Exercise-induced Feeling Inventory and *energetic* from the Revitalization scale), Negative Affect (containing the items *discouraged, crummy,* and *miserable* from the Psychological Distress scale of the Subjective Exercise Experiences Scale), Fatigue (containing the items *tired, fatigued,* and *worn out* from the Physical Exhaustion scale of the Exercise-induced Feeling Inventory), and Tranquility (containing the items *calm, peaceful,* and *relaxed* from the Tranquility scale of the Exercise-induced Feeling Inventory). Lox et al. (2000) concluded that "the factor structure of the [Physical Activity Affect Scale] is ... well supported, theoretically, by the four quadrants of the circumplex model of affect proposed by Russell (1980)" (p. 92). Specifically, they speculated that the items of the Positive Affect scale would fall "within the positive-high activation quadrant," the items of the Negative Affect scale "within the negative-high activation quadrant," the items of the Fatigue scale would be "contained within the negative-low activation quadrant," and the items of the Tranquility scale would "fall within the positive-low activation quadrant" (p. 92).

Being a hybrid measure, the Physical Activity Affect Scale inherited some of the weaknesses of its progenitors. First, Lox et al. (2000) fully endorsed the idea of exercise-specific affect. For example, they expressed the hope that, in testing hypotheses derived from social-cognitive theory, "exercise-specific self-efficacy may be a better predictor of affective states known to be influenced by exercise than more general affective states assessed by instruments such as the [Positive and Negative Affect Schedule], [Profile of Mood States], or [State-Trait Anxiety Inventory]" (p. 92). However, the contradistinction between "states known to be influenced by exercise" versus "more general affective states" appears to be more assumed than real. After all, half of the items of the Physical Activity Affect Scale have come from the Profile of Mood States (*fatigued, worn out, energetic, relaxed, discouraged, miserable*), two from the State-Trait Anxiety Inventory (*calm, relaxed*), and one from the Positive and Negative Affect Schedule (*enthusiastic*). Therefore, whether there is truly a section of affective space defined by "exercise-specific" affective states and whether the "exercise-specific" measures are uniquely capable of capturing these states has yet to be firmly established.

For example, Lox et al. (2000) considered as the "unique stimulus properties of exercise" those states related to "physical work, bodily movements, and perceptions" (p. 81). However, expressing a different point of view, Gauvin and Rejeski (1993) stated that "physical symptoms are directly tied to the physiological changes that accompany activity" (p. 407), so states tied to such "physical symptoms" were specifically excluded from the Exercise-induced Feeling Inventory. Likewise, according to McAuley and Courneya (1994), "individuals' perceptions of somatic states (fatigue, pain)," although they may seem as if they could "be classified as affective responses," they are probably more "representative of perceived physiological activation (i.e., nonmental states)" and, consequently, they "may be discarded as affects" (McAuley & Courneya, 1994, p. 165). So, if affective states tied to or emanating from the exercising body were specifically excluded from both the Exercise-induced Feeling Inventory and the Subjective Exercise Experiences Scale, what is the basis for the belief that the items of the Physical Activity Affect Scale (all of which come from the Exercise-induced Feeling Inventory and the Subjective Exercise Experiences Scale) can somehow shed light upon the "unique stimulus properties of exercise" such as "physical work, bodily movements, and perceptions"?

Second, it should be clear that neither the Exercise-induced Feeling Inventory (the source of the majority of the items in the Physical Activity Affect Scale) nor the Subjective Exercise Experiences Scale were developed on the basis of the circumplex model. Certainly no procedure was followed during the item selection and content validation of either instrument to ensure that items would be sampled to represent specific sectors of the circumplex affective space. As a matter of fact, revising an earlier position that, within the circumplex model, "three of the four subscales on the [Exercise-induced Feeling Inventory] capture different octants of pleasant affect, whereas the fourth would be classified as unpleasant affect, namely physical exhaustion" (Rejeski et al., 1999, p. 98), Gauvin and Rejeski (2001) specifically stated that their analyses led them to conclude that "those states that are particularly sensitive to the stimulus properties of physical activity *do not* fall along a circumplex" (p. 77, emphasis added).

Therefore, the claim by Lox et al. (2000) that the Physical Activity Affect Scale is "well supported, theoretically, by the four quadrants of the circumplex model of affect proposed by Russell (1980)" (p. 92) seems questionable. However, subsequent users of the Physical Activity Affect Scale have widely echoed this assertion, stating, for example, that "the [Physical Activity Affect Scale] is theoretically supported by the circumplex model of affect (Russell, 1980)" (Kwan & Bryan, 2010a,

p. 119), that "the [Physical Activity Affect Scale] subscales satisfactorily map onto the four quadrants of the circumplex model of affect" (Kwan & Bryan, 2010b, p. 73), and that "the [Physical Activity Affect Scale] is an exercise-specific measure based on Russell's (1980) circumplex model of affect" (Loughead et al. 2008, p. 57). That these statements are inaccurate can be gleaned from various sources.

As explained in Chapter 1 (see section entitled "Armed with easy to use software but no theory: confirmatory factor analysis misapplied"), to claim a circumplex structure, it is not sufficient for a traditional confirmatory factor analyses to show good fit to a four-factor model. In fact, this is not a requirement for circumplex structure at all. Instead, what is needed is to demonstrate that the variables have a very specific pattern of intercorrelations, such that they can be represented as located along the perimeter of a circle. Assuming such a circular arrangement, their intercorrelations can be modeled as angles of separation (the angle of separation is given by the inverse cosine of the correlation coefficient). For example, two states that have a correlation of 0.00 will be positioned 90° apart on the perimeter of the circle. Thus, in the circumplex, items representing the high-activation pleasant quadrant and those representing the high-activation unpleasant quadrant (such as those in the Positive Affect and Negative Affect scales of the Positive and Negative Affect Schedule, respectively) should be statistically independent (with a correlation close to 0.00) and, thus, separated by a 90° angle. Similarly, states with a correlation approaching −1.00 will be across from each other on the circle (angle of separation approaching 180°).

If the assertions about the fit of the Physical Activity Affect Scale to the circumplex were correct, this would imply that the intercorrelations between the scales would be close to either 0.00 (for the correlations between Positive Affect and Negative Affect, between Negative Affect and Fatigue, between Fatigue and Tranquility, between Tranquility and Positive Affect) or −1.00 (for the correlations between Positive Affect and Fatigue and between Negative Affect and Tranquility). Contrary to claims, however, intercorrelations between the latent factors (theorized to be free of random measurement error), the actual pattern is very different from what would have been predicted on the basis of the circumplex model. Instead of being (close to) 0.00 (90° apart), the correlation between Positive Affect and Negative Affect was −0.46 (117° apart), that between Negative Affect and Fatigue was 0.59 (54° apart), and that between Tranquility and Positive Affect was 0.58 (55° apart). Only the correlation between Fatigue and Tranquility approached zero (−0.18 or 100° apart). Similarly, instead of being (close to) −1.00 (180°

apart), the correlation between Positive Affect and Fatigue was only -0.27 ($106°$), and that between Negative Affect and Tranquility was only -0.40 ($114°$ apart).

Besides this empirical evidence, the poor fit of the Physical Activity Affect Scale factors to the circumplex could have been gleaned by examining the content of the items, particularly those of the Negative Affect scale. Lox et al. (2000) claimed that the items of the Negative Affect scale would fall "within the negative-high activation quadrant" (p. 92). However, the items *discouraged*, *crummy*, and *miserable* all seem closer to the negative low-activation quadrant than the negative high-activation quadrant. For example, in the Profile of Mood States, the items *discouraged* and *miserable* belong to the Depression scale, a low-activation unpleasant state. Therefore, the relatively high ($r = 0.59$), as opposed to near-zero, correlation between the Negative Affect and Fatigue latent factors should not be surprising. Parenthetically, this problem was also identified by Markland et al. (1997), who noted that the Psychological Distress scale of the Subjective Exercise Experiences Scale (the source of the items in the Negative Affect scale of the Physical Activity Affect Scale) and the Fatigue scale of the Subjective Exercise Experiences Scale (which shares two out of three items with the Fatigue scale of the Physical Activity Affect Scale), in some cases, were "in effect perfectly correlated" (p. 424). The latent factors had correlations ranging from 0.54 to 0.98.

Third, Lox et al. (2000) rejected the notion that the scales of the Exercise-induced Feeling Inventory and the Subjective Exercise Experiences Scale represent constructs at different levels of the affective hierarchy (distinct states versus dimensions, respectively). They noted that high intercorrelations between scales of the two questionnaires "refute the proposition that the [Exercise-induced Feeling Inventory] and [Subjective Exercise Experiences Scale] measure different levels of affective response" (p. 86). In particular, they pointed to such correlations as the 0.783 and the 0.810 that the Positive Well-Being scale of the Subjective Exercise Experiences Scale showed with the Positive Engagement and Revitalization scales of the Exercise-induced Feeling Inventory, respectively. However, scales representing constructs at two levels of a hierarchy are expected to have high correlations, even of this magnitude. For example, in support of their hierarchical model, Tellegen et al. (1999a) reported a correlation between happiness (a distinct state) and Positive Affect (a dimension) of 0.83. Similarly, Watson and Clark (1994b) found that the Vigor scale of the Profile of Mood States (theorized to represent a distinct state) correlated 0.86 with the

Positive Affect scale of the Positive and Negative Affect Schedule (theorized to represent a dimension) of 0.86. Yet these results are interpreted as supporting, not refuting, the notion of a hierarchical structure.

To take the argument a step further, assuming that there are *conceptually* valid reasons for differentiating between two constructs, a high intercorrelation between two scales presumed to measure them should be an argument for refining the measures to improve their discriminant validity, not an argument for merging them (thereby obliterating the conceptual distinction between them). To draw an analogy, Gotlib and Meyer (1986) found a correlation of 0.82 between the Depression and Anxiety scales of the Multiple Affect Adjective Check List. Following the logic that a high intercorrelation is an argument for a merger, Gotlib and Meyer (1986) should have argued for merging the two scales into a hybrid assessing, for example, generalized negative affect. Instead, these authors strongly criticized the fact that the Multiple Affect Adjective Check List "at best reflects the degree of general negative affect or dysphoria experienced by the individual" (p. 1163), warned researchers of the poor discriminant validity of the Multiple Affect Adjective Check List, and called for more refined measures. Arguably, a similar line of reasoning should have been pursued upon finding high intercorrelations between the scales of the Exercise-induced Feeling Inventory and the Subjective Exercise Experiences Scale.

Epilogue

When research interest in a new topic or a new approach surges, several accompanying phenomena begin to appear. Some of those are wonderful. New discoveries are made. Previously unknown connections are revealed and those that might have been underappreciated receive the attention they warrant. Creativity is sparked. Science progresses. At the same time, however, with growing enthusiasm comes haste. Researchers rush to become part of the new trend and take advantage of emerging opportunities. Under those circumstances, there is no time for in-depth analysis. By necessity, background study and preparation is limited to the bare essentials. In essence, corners must be cut. As a result, most emerging research fields undergo an "infantile" period characterized by confusion, trial and error, and more cyclical moves than linear forward advances.

Perhaps more interesting, however, is to observe what happens next. There are two possibilities. Research will either grow out of its infancy, having refined its methods and sharpened its concepts, or continue making the same mistakes over and over again until the lack of real progress results in frustration and the eventual abandonment of a direction that once seemed fascinating and full of promise.

There is little doubt that the study of the role played by affective variables in health behaviors is currently seeing a surge of interest. This trend is so robust, consistent, and wide-ranging that it could be characterized as a veritable paradigmatic shift. Naturally, as with any emerging trend, this line of research is experiencing all the positive and negative accompaniments of its infantile period. The question is what will happen next.

The signs so far are somewhat disconcerting. There are no indications that the complexities and challenges of measuring core affect, mood, and emotion are fully appreciated within the context of health-behavioral research. A cynic might argue that the "cavalier treatment" (Pedhazur & Pedhazur Schmelkin, 1991, p. 28) of measurement issues is becoming the norm. Thus, there is a real risk that measurement will prove to be the "Achilles' heel" (Kerlinger, 1979, p. 141) of this nascent research field. All the symptoms are present: "Measures seem to be used because they are 'there,' because someone else has used them, because nothing 'better' is available" (Pedhazur & Pedhazur Schmelkin, 1991, p. 28). The "ignorance and misunderstanding" that Kerlinger (1979, p. 142) cautioned about decades ago reign supreme. Clearly, the safety mechanism of peer review is failing because problematic measurement practices and claims find their way even into the most prestigious and high-impact journals.

As usually happens, once something, no matter how dubious or flawed, is published in the literature, many other researchers will eagerly endorse it, adopt it, and repeat it. Once a critical number of repetitions is reached, any hope of an intervention succeeding in stopping the runaway train is lost. Consider this: if a researcher has built a publication record on what is later shown to be a conceptually or psychometrically flawed measure, what are the chances that the mistake will be acknowledged, any potentially erroneous or unwarranted conclusions will be retracted, and a new direction will be followed? It is almost certain that ego defenses will take over, making any corrective action impossible.

So time is of the essence. If problems are to be fixed, this needs to be done early on, before a research line reaches the point at which taking a few steps backward to correct past mistakes is perceived as costlier than continuing down the wrong path. Today, a growing number of young investigators are becoming interested in the role of affective constructs in the domain of health behaviors. The pressures they are facing in the current academic environment are so intense that the option of delving into the complicated, jargon-filled, and contradictory primary literature on affect, mood, and emotion seems unrealistic and, arguably, unappealing. So, accepting what has been said and emulating what has been done may seem very tempting by comparison.

Hence the challenge – and the *raison d'être* of this guidebook. Reducing more than a century of theorizing and psychometric developments to a few pages is admittedly unrealistic. Arguably, it would not even be desirable as a goal. The complexities and controversies are not to be concealed, dismissed, or avoided. Their instructional value is tremendous because they highlight crucial dilemmas and alternative points of view. So the goal of this book was not to create the false impression that all debates have been resolved, all solutions found, and all paths cleared. Instead, the main goal was to sound an alarm, sensitizing the scientific community to the fact that current measurement practices are less than optimal, and to propose a simple, but potentially powerful, method for returning to a more sound approach.

The bedrock of the three-tiered measure-selection process proposed in this book is the idea that the important differences between the constructs of core affect, mood, and emotion must be appreciated and respected. This point is of fundamental significance because it has a decisive impact on the rest of the measure-selection process. As suggested in Chapter 3, if the object of study is core affect, in most cases a dimensional model would provide an appropriate and adequate investigative perspective. If, on the other hand, the object of study is a mood or an emotion, both of which depend on an antecedent cognitive appraisal, then a distinct-states approach has the potential to offer a fuller understanding.

Before deciding whether a dimensional model or the distinct-states approach is preferable for the purposes of a particular investigation, it is crucial to develop a clear understanding of the benefits and limitations of these two alternative perspectives. The main benefit of dimensional models is the promise that they can represent a global domain of content, such as affect, mood, or emotion. On the other hand, their main limitation is that, because this domain is represented by only a small set of underlying dimensions, much of the variance of the numerous individual states encompassed within this domain of content is missed. A good dimensional model would reflect the majority of this variance but it cannot reflect all of it. However, the variance that is left unaccounted by dimensional models may hold considerable psychological interest.

To capture most of the reliable variance in the domain of core affect, as few as two dimensions may suffice (as in the circumplex model; Russell, 1980). To capture most of the reliable variance in the domain of emotion, it has been argued that twice as many dimensions may be needed (Fontaine et al., 2007). Even then, however, some emotion theorists would argue that the remaining variance cannot be ignored, essentially rejecting the idea that dimensional models can have any real utility in the study of emotion (Clore et al., 1987; Lazarus, 1991a; Smith & Ellsworth, 1985). For any investigation aiming to achieve a high degree of specificity and in-depth analysis (e.g., probe the cognitive antecedents of a specific emotion or distinguish among two related emotions), the distinct-states approach is the only reasonable option. At the same time, as was emphasized throughout this book, attempts to represent a global domain of content, such as affect, mood, or emotion, by assessing a laundry list of distinct states will likely result in construct underrepresentation, with a host of possible adverse consequences for the validity of any conclusions that are drawn. So, ultimately, as is often

said though perhaps not as often explained, it all depends on the objective of the particular study. Investigators must make informed decisions
on this issue and, crucially, present their reasoning, so that readers,
including editors and reviewers, can evaluate it.

If one has chosen to use a dimensional approach, the next challenge
is to select one among the multiple dimensional models in the literature. Often these dimensional models are presented as alternatives by
deemphasizing their (arguably, more fundamental) similarities and
accentuating their (arguably, more superficial) differences. The dizzy-
ing array of inconsistent and often counterintuitive terms that have
been used by different theorists to label the dimensions has contributed to an astounding level of confusion. Primary among the many
misunderstandings that permeate the applied literature is the nature of
the relationship between pleasant and unpleasant affective states (often
termed positive and negative affect). As explained in Chapter 4, if by
"positive affect" one means pleasure (e.g., *happy, pleased*) and by "negative affect" one means displeasure (e.g., *sad, unhappy*), theorists agree
that these represent the two opposite poles of the same bipolar dimension. It is only when by "positive affect" one means states combining
pleasure with high activation (e.g., *excited, enthusiastic*) and by "negative
affect" one means states combining displeasure with high activation
(e.g., *nervous, distressed*) that "positive affect" and "negative affect" are
uncorrelated (i.e., are orthogonal to each other). This crucial point has
now been made so many times, so clearly, and so emphatically in the
affective psychology literature that it should no longer be a source of
confusion in health-behavioral research – and yet it still is.

It should also be clear that, if the space represented by a dimensional
model is cut in half, retaining (for example) only the high-activation
states (e.g., Watson & Clark, 1997) or only the unpleasant states (e.g.,
Magid et al., 2009), then the main advantage of dimensional models,
namely the potential for representing the global domain of content,
evaporates. Likewise, if only select sectors or states of the dimensional
model are assessed (e.g., Simons et al., 2010), measurement essentially
reverts to the distinct-states approach, with all its associated limitations
(i.e., potential for construct underrepresentation).

The method proposed in this guidebook as a possible way to stop the
ongoing crisis is to ask authors to provide a three-tiered justification for
the measures of affect, mood, or emotion that they use. The first step
is to explain which of these three constructs they are targeting in their
study and why. The second step is to explain which conceptual model of
the chosen construct they decided to adopt and why (e.g., distinct-states
or dimensions and, if the latter, bipolarity or orthogonality). The third

and final step is to explain why the measure they chose represents the best available option for operationalizing the components of the chosen conceptual model. At this step, they need to provide information on how validly the scope and structure of the measure represents the postulates of the model (e.g., how adequate construct representation was ensured, how the theorized relation between factors was modeled and confirmed). By encouraging authors to follow this systematic decision-making process, and informing readers of their reasoning, most of the problems identified here can be avoided. On the contrary, as long as measures are presented without a rationale, the choice of measures will likely continue to be characterized by arbitrariness or be driven by non-substantive considerations and, as a result, the quality of measurement of affect, mood, and emotion will continue to be less than optimal.

References

Acevedo, E.O., Dzewaltowski, D.A., Kubitz, K.A., & Kraemer, R.R. (1999). Effects of a proposed challenge on effort sense and cardiorespiratory responses during exercise. *Medicine and Science in Sports and Exercise*, 31, 1460–1465.

Acevedo, E.O., Kraemer, R.R., Haltom, R.W., & Tryniecki, J.L. (2003). Perceptual responses proximal to the onset of blood lactate accumulation. *Journal of Sports Medicine and Physical Fitness*, 43, 267–273.

Acton, G.S., & Revelle, W. (2002). Interpersonal personality measures show circumplex structure based on new psychometric criteria. *Journal of Personality Assessment*, 79, 446–471.

Ajzen, I., & Fishbein, M. (2005). The influence of attitudes on behavior. In D. Albarracín, B.T. Johnson, & M.P. Zanna (Eds.), *The handbook of attitudes* (pp. 173–221). Mahwah, NJ: Lawrence Erlbaum.

Alpert, M., & Rosen, A. (1990). A semantic analysis of the various ways that the terms "affect," "emotion," and "mood" are used. *Journal of Communication Disorders*, 23, 237–246.

American Educational Research Association, American Psychological Association, and National Council on Measurement in Education (1999). *Standards for educational and psychological testing*. Washington, DC: American Educational Research Association.

American Psychiatric Association (2000). *Diagnostic and statistical manual of mental disorders* (4th edn., Text revision). Washington, DC: Author.

Annesi, J.J. (2006). Preliminary testing of a brief inventory for assessing changes in exercise-induced feeling states. *Perceptual and Motor Skills*, 102, 776–780.

Apolzan, J.W., Flynn, M.G., McFarlin, B.K., & Campbell, W.W. (2009). Age and physical activity status effects on appetite and mood state in older humans. *Applied Physiology, Nutrition, and Metabolism*, 34, 203–211.

Arnow, B., Kenardy, J., & Agras, W.S. (1992). Binge eating among the obese: A descriptive study. *Journal of Behavioral Medicine*, 15, 155–170.

(1995). The Emotional Eating Scale: The development of a measure to assess coping with negative affect by eating. *International Journal of Eating Disorders*, 18, 79–90.

Backhouse, S.H., Ali, A., Biddle, S.J.H., & Williams, C. (2007). Carbohydrate ingestion during prolonged high-intensity intermittent exercise: Impact on affect and perceived exertion. *Scandinavian Journal of Medicine and Science in Sports*, 17, 605–610.

Backhouse, S.H., Biddle, S.J.H., Bishop, N.C., & Williams, C. (2011). Caffeine ingestion, affect and perceived exertion during prolonged cycling. *Appetite*, 57, 247–252.

Backhouse, S.H., Bishop, N.C., Biddle, S.J.H., & Williams, C. (2005). Effect of carbohydrate and prolonged exercise on affective states and perceived exertion. *Medicine and Science in Sports and Exercise*, 37, 1768–1773.

Backhouse, S.H., Ekkekakis, P., Biddle, S.J.H., Foskett, A., & Williams, C. (2007). Exercise makes people feel better but people are inactive: Paradox or artifact? *Journal of Sport and Exercise Psychology*, 29, 498–517.

Baker, T.B., Piper, M.E., McCarthy, D.E., Majeskie, M.R., & Fiore, M.C. (2004). Addiction motivation reformulated: An affective processing model of negative reinforcement. *Psychological Review*, 111, 33–51.

Bandura, A. (1977). Self-efficacy: Toward a unifying theory of behavioral change. *Psychological Review*, 84, 191–215.

(1997). *Self-efficacy: The exercise of control*. New York: W.H. Freeman.

(2001). Social cognitive theory: An agentic perspective. *Annual Review of Psychology*, 52, 1–26.

(2006). Guide for constructing self-efficacy scales. In F. Pajares & T. Urdan (Eds.), *Self-efficacy beliefs of adolescents* (pp. 307–337). New York: Information Age Publishing.

Banse, R., & Scherer, K.R. (1996). Acoustic profiles in vocal emotion expression. *Journal of Personality and Social Psychology*, 70, 614–636.

Bartholomew, J.B., & Linder, D.E. (1998). State anxiety following resistance exercise: The role of gender and exercise intensity. *Journal of Behavioral Medicine*, 21, 205–219.

Bartholomew, J.B., & Miller, B.M. (2002). Affective responses to an aerobic dance class: The impact of perceived performance. *Research Quarterly for Exercise and Sport*, 73, 301–309.

Bartholomew, J.B., Morrison, D., & Ciccolo, J.T. (2005). Effects of acute exercise on mood and well-being in patients with major depressive disorder. *Medicine and Science in Sports and Exercise*, 37, 2032–2037.

Batson, C.D., Shaw, L.L., & Oleson, K.C. (1992). Differentiating affect, mood, and emotion: Toward functionally based conceptual distinctions. In M.S. Clark (Ed.), *Review of personality and social psychology* (Vol. 13, pp. 294–326). Newbury Park, CA: Sage.

Bechara, A. (2005). Decision making, impulse control and loss of willpower to resist drugs: A neurocognitive perspective. *Nature Neuroscience*, 8, 1458–1463.

Beck, A.T., & Clark, D.A. (1997). An information processing model of anxiety: Automatic and strategic processes. *Behavior Research and Therapy*, 35, 49–58.

Beedie, C.J., Terry, P.C., & Lane, A.M. (2005). Distinctions between emotion and mood. *Cognition and Emotion*, 19, 847–878.

Bentler, P.M. (1969). Semantic space is (approximately) bipolar. *Journal of Psychology*, 71, 33–40.

Berger, B.G., & Motl, R.W. (2000). Exercise and mood: A selective review and synthesis of research employing the profile of mood states. *Journal of Applied Sport Psychology*, 12, 69–92.

Bernstein, I.H., & Eveland, D.C. (1982). State vs trait anxiety: A case study in confirmatory factor analysis. *Personality and Individual Differences*, 3, 361–372.

Berntson, G.G., & Cacioppo, J.T. (2008). The neuroevolution of motivation. In J.Y. Shah & W.L. Gardner (Eds.), *Handbook of motivation science* (pp. 188–200). New York: Guilford.

Bieling, P.J., Antony, M.M., & Swinson, R.P. (1998). The State-Trait Anxiety Inventory, trait version: Structure and content re-examined. *Behaviour Research and Therapy*, 36, 777–788.

Blanchard, C.M., Rodgers, W.M., Bell, G., Wilson, P.M., & Gesell, J. (2002). An empirical test of the interaction model of anxiety in an acute exercise setting. *Personality and Individual Differences*, 32, 329–336.

Blanchard, C.M., Rodgers, W.M., & Gauvin, L. (2004). The influence of exercise duration and cognitions during running on feeling states in an indoor running track environment. *Psychology of Sport and Exercise*, 5, 119–133.

Blanchard, C.M., Rodgers, W.M., Spence, J.C., & Courneya, K.S. (2001). Affective responses to acute exercise of high and low intensity. *Journal of Science and Medicine in Sport*, 4, 30–38.

Bodin, T., & Martinsen, E.W. (2004). Mood and self-efficacy during acute exercise in clinical depression: A randomized, controlled study. *Journal of Sport and Exercise Psychology*, 26, 623–633.

Bond, A., & Lader, M. (1974). The use of analogue scales in rating subjective feelings. *British Journal of Medical Psychology*, 47, 211–218.

Bonke, B., Smorenburg, J.M.J., van der Ent, C.K., & Spielberger, C.D. (1987). Evidence of denial and item-intensity specificity in the State-Trait Anxiety Inventory. *Personality and Individual Differences*, 8, 185–191.

Boutcher, S.H. (1993). Emotion and aerobic exercise. In R.N. Singer, M. Murphey, & L.K. Tennant (Eds.), *Handbook of research on sport psychology* (pp. 799–814). New York: Macmillan.

Boyle, G.J. (1987). A cross-validation of the factor structure of the Profile of Mood States: Were the factors correctly identified in the first instance? *Psychological Reports*, 60, 343–354.

Bradley, M.M., Greenwald, M.K., & Hamm, A.O. (1993). Affective picture processing. In N. Birbaumer & A. Öhman (Eds.), *The structure of emotion* (pp. 48–65). Seattle, WA: Hogrefe & Huber.

Bradley, M.M., & Lang, P.J. (1994). Measuring emotion: The self-assessment manikin and the semantic differential. *Journal of Behavior Therapy and Experimental Psychiatry*, 25, 49–59.

Brehm, J.W., & Miron, A.M. (2006). Can the simultaneous experience of opposing emotions really occur? *Motivation and Emotion*, 30, 13–30.

Breus, M.J., & O'Connor, P.J. (1998). Exercise-induced anxiolysis: A test of the "time out" hypothesis in high anxious females. *Medicine and Science in Sports and Exercise*, 30, 1107–1112.

Brown, T.A. (2006). *Confirmatory factor analysis for applied research.* New York: Guilford.

Browne, M.W. (1992). Circumplex models for correlation matrices. *Psychometrika*, 57, 469–497.

Bryan, A., Hutchison, K.E., Seals, D.R., & Allen, D.L. (2007). A transdisciplinary model integrating genetic, physiological, and psychological correlates of voluntary exercise. *Health Psychology*, 26, 30–39.

Buck, R. (1990). Mood and emotion: A comparison of five contemporary views. *Psychological Inquiry*, 1, 330–336.

Cabanac, M. (1979). Sensory pleasure. *Quarterly Review of Biology*, 54, 1–29.

Caci, H., Baylé, F.J., Dossios, C., Robert, P., & Boyer, P. (2003). The Spielberger trait anxiety inventory measures more than anxiety. *European Psychiatry*, 18, 394–400.

Cacioppo, J.T., & Berntson, G.G. (1994). Relationship between attitudes and evaluative space: A critical review with emphasis on the separability of positive and negative substrates. *Psychological Bulletin*, 115, 401–423.

Cacioppo, J.T., & Gardner, W.L. (1999). Emotion. *Annual Review of Psychology*, 50, 191–214.

Cacioppo, J.T., Gardner, W.L., & Berntson, G.G. (1997). Beyond bipolar conceptualizations and measures: The case of attitudes and evaluative space. *Personality and Social Psychology Review*, 1, 3–25.

(1999). The affect system has parallel and integrative processing components: Form follows function. *Journal of Personality and Social Psychology*, 76, 839–855.

Carmody, T.P., Vieten, C., & Astin, J.A. (2007). Negative affect, emotional acceptance, and smoking cessation. *Journal of Psychoactive Drugs*, 39, 499–508.

Carpenter, L.C., Tompkins, S.A., Schmiege, S.J., Nilsson, R., & Bryan, A. (2010). Affective response to physical activity: Testing for measurement invariance of the physical activity affect scale across active and non-active individuals. *Measurement in Physical Education and Exercise Science*, 14, 1–14.

Carroll, J.M., Yik, M.S.M., Russell, J.A., & Feldman Barrett, L. (1999). On the psychometric principles of affect. *Review of General Psychology*, 3, 14–22.

Carver, C.S. (2001). Affect and the functional bases of behavior: On the dimensional structure of affective experience. *Personality and Social Psychology Review*, 5, 345–356.

Carver, C.S., & Harmon-Jones, E. (2009a). Anger and approach: Reply to Watson (2009) and to Tomarken and Zald (2009). *Psychological Bulletin*, 135, 215–217.

(2009b). Anger is an approach-related affect: Evidence and implications. *Psychological Bulletin*, 135, 183–204.

Carver, C.S., & Scheier, M.F. (1990). Origins and functions of positive and negative affect: A control-process view. *Psychological Review*, 97, 19–35.

Clark, L.A., & Watson, D. (1991). Tripartite model of anxiety and depression: Psychometric evidence and taxonomic implications. *Journal of Abnormal Psychology*, 100, 316–336.

Clore, G.L., & Ortony, A. (2008). Appraisal theories: How cognition shapes affect into emotion. In M. Lewis, J.M. Haviland-Jones, & L. Feldman Barrett (Eds.), *Handbook of emotions* (3rd edn., pp. 628–642). New York: Guilford.

Clore, G.L., Ortony, A., & Foss, M.A. (1987). The psychological foundations of the affective lexicon. *Journal of Personality and Social Psychology*, 53, 751–766.

Cortina, J.M. (1993). What is coefficient alpha? An examination of theory and applications. *Journal of Applied Psychology*, 78, 98–104.

Cox, T., & Mackay, C. (1985). The measurement of self-reported stress and arousal. *British Journal of Psychology*, 76, 183–186.

Cox, R.H., Thomas, T.R., Hinton, P.S., & Donahue, O.M. (2004). Effects of acute 60 and 80% VO2max bouts of aerobic exercise on state anxiety of women of different age groups across time. *Research Quarterly for Exercise and Sport*, 75, 165–175.

Cramp, A.G., & Bray, S.R. (2010). Postnatal women's feeling state responses to exercise with and without baby. *Maternal and Child Health Journal*, 14, 343–349.

Crawford, J.R., & Henry, J.D. (2004). The Positive and Negative Affect Schedule (PANAS): Construct validity, measurement properties and normative data in a large non-clinical sample. *British Journal of Clinical Psychology*, 43, 245–265.

Crocker, P.R.E. (1997). A confirmatory factor analysis of the positive affect negative affect schedule (PANAS) with a youth sport sample. *Journal of Sport and Exercise Psychology*, 19, 91–97.

Crocker, P.R., & Grozelle, C. (1991). Reducing induced state anxiety: Effects of acute aerobic exercise and autogenic relaxation. *Journal of Sports Medicine and Physical Fitness*, 31, 277–282.

Cronbach, L.J. (1951). Coefficient alpha and the internal structure of tests. *Psychometrika*, 16, 297–334.

Cronbach, L.J., & Shavelson, R.J. (2004). My current thoughts on coefficient alpha and successor procedures. *Educational and Psychological Measurement*, 64, 391–418.

Cruickshank, P.J. (1984). A stress and arousal mood scale for low vocabulary subjects: A reworking of Mackay et al. (1978). *British Journal of Psychology*, 75, 89–94.

Cudeck, R. (1986). A note on structural models for the circumplex. *Psychometrika*, 51, 143–147.

Davidson, R.J. (1992a). Anterior cerebral asymmetry and the nature of emotion. *Brain and Cognition*, 20, 125–151.

(1992b). Emotion and affective style: Hemispheric substrates. *Psychological Science*, 3, 39–43.

(1994). On emotion, mood, and related affective constructs. In P. Ekman & R.J. Davidson (Eds.), *The nature of emotion: Fundamental questions* (pp. 51–55). New York: Oxford University Press.

(1998). Anterior electrophysiological asymmetries, emotion, and depression: Conceptual and methodological conundrums. *Psychophysiology*, 35, 607–614.

(2003). Seven sins in the study of emotion: Correctives from affective neuro-science. *Brain and Cognition*, 52, 129–132.

Denollet, J. (1993). Emotional distress and fatigue in coronary heart disease: The Global Mood Scale (GMS). *Psychological Medicine*, 23, 111–121.

Denollet, J., & De Vries, J. (2006). Positive and negative affect within the realm of depression, stress and fatigue: The two-factor distress model of the Global Mood Scale (GMS). *Journal of Affective Disorders*, 91, 171–180.

DeVellis, R.F. (2012). *Scale development: Theory and applications* (3rd edn.). Los Angeles, CA: Sage.

Diener, E., & Emmons, R.A. (1984). The independence of positive and negative affect. *Journal of Personality and Social Psychology*, 47, 1105–1117.

Diener, E., & Iran-Nejad, A. (1986). The relationship in experience between various types of affect. *Journal of Personality and Social Psychology*, 50, 1031–1038.

DiLorenzo, T.M., Bargman, E.P., Stucky-Ropp, R., Brassington, G.S., Frensch, P.A., & LaFontaine, T. (1999). Long-term effects of aerobic exercise on psychological outcomes. *Preventive Medicine*, 28, 75–85.

Dishman, R.K. (1995). Physical activity and public health: Mental health. *Quest*, 47, 362–385.

Doan, B.-T.T., Plante, T.G., Digregorio, M.P., & Manuel, G.M. (1995). Influence of aerobic exercise activity and relaxation training on coping with test-taking anxiety. *Anxiety, Stress, and Coping*, 8, 101–111.

Driver, S. (2006). Measuring exercise induced affect in adults with brain injuries. *Adapted Physical Activity Quarterly*, 23, 1–13.

Earleywine, M., & Erblich, J. (1996). A confirmed factor structure for the Biphasic Alcohol Effects Scale. *Experimental and Clinical Psychopharmacology*, 4, 107–113.

Egloff, B. (1998). The independence of positive and negative affect depends on the affect measure. *Personality and Individual Differences*, 25, 1101–1109.

Ekkekakis, P. (2008). Affect circumplex redux: The discussion on its utility as a measurement framework in exercise psychology continues. *International Review of Sport and Exercise Psychology*, 1, 139–159.

(2012). Affect, mood, and emotion. In G. Tenenbaum, R.C. Eklund, & A. Kamata (Eds.), *Measurement in sport and exercise psychology* (pp. 321–332). Champaign, IL: Human Kinetics.

Ekkekakis, P., & Backhouse, S.H. (2009). Exercise and psychological well-being. In R. Maughan (Ed.), *Olympic textbook of science in sport* (pp. 251–271). Hoboken, NJ: Wiley-Blackwell.

Ekkekakis, P., Backhouse, S.H., Gray, C., & Lind, E. (2008). Walking is popular among adults but is it pleasant? A framework for clarifying the link between walking and affect as illustrated in two studies. *Psychology of Sport and Exercise*, 9, 246–264.

Ekkekakis, P., Hall, E.E., & Petruzzello, S.J. (1999). Measuring state anxiety in the context of acute exercise using the State Anxiety Inventory: An attempt to resolve the brouhaha. *Journal of Sport and Exercise Psychology*, 21, 205–229.

(2005). Evaluation of the circumplex structure of the Activation Deactivation Adjective Check List before and after a short walk. *Psychology of Sport and Exercise*, 6, 83–101.

(2008). The relationship between exercise intensity and affective responses demystified: To crack the forty-year-old nut, replace the forty-year-old nutcracker! *Annals of Behavioral Medicine*, 35, 136–149.

Ekkekakis, P., Hall, E.E., Van Landuyt, L.M., & Petruzzello, S.J. (2000). Walking in (affective) circles: Can short walks enhance affect? *Journal of Behavioral Medicine*, 23, 245–275.

Ekkekakis, P., Parfitt, G., & Petruzzello, S.J. (2011). The pleasure and displeasure people feel when they exercise at different intensities: Decennial update and progress towards a tripartite rationale for exercise intensity prescription. *Sports Medicine*, 41, 641–671.

Ekkekakis, P., & Petruzzello, S.J. (2001a). Analysis of the affect measurement conundrum in exercise psychology: III. A conceptual and methodological critique of the Subjective Exercise Experiences Scale. *Psychology of Sport and Exercise*, 2, 205–232.

(2001b). Analysis of the affect measurement conundrum in exercise psychology: II. A conceptual and methodological critique of the Exercise-induced Feeling Inventory. *Psychology of Sport and Exercise*, 2, 1–26.

(2002). Analysis of the affect measurement conundrum in exercise psychology: IV. A conceptual case for the affect circumplex. *Psychology of Sport and Exercise*, 3, 35–63.

(2004). Affective, but hardly effective: A response to Gauvin and Rejeski (2001). *Psychology of Sport and Exercise*, 5, 135–152.

Ekman, P. (1992). An argument for basic emotions. *Cognition and Emotion*, 6, 169–200.

(1994). Moods, emotions, and traits. In P. Ekman & R.J. Davidson (Eds.), *The nature of emotion: Fundamental questions* (pp. 56–58). New York: Oxford University Press.

Ekman, P., Sorenson, E.R., & Friesen, W.V. (1969). Pan-cultural elements in facial displays of emotion. *Science*, 164, 86–88.

Ellsworth, P.C. (2009). Functionalist theories of emotion. In D. Sander & K.R. Scherer (Eds.), *The Oxford companion to emotion and the affective sciences* (pp. 188–189). New York: Oxford University Press.

Ellsworth, P.C., & Smith, C.A. (1988a). Shades of joy: Patterns of appraisal differentiating pleasant emotions. *Cognition and Emotion*, 2, 301–331.

(1988b). From appraisal to emotion: Differences among unpleasant feelings. *Motivation and Emotion*, 12, 271–302.

Endler, N.S., Cox, B.J., Parker, J.D.A., & Bagby, R.M. (1992). Self-reports of depression and state-trait anxiety: Evidence for differential assessment. *Journal of Personality and Social Psychology*, 63, 832–838.

Endler, N.S., Edwards, J.M., Vitelli, R., & Parker, J.D.A. (1989). Assessment of state and trait anxiety: Endler Multidimensional Anxiety Scales. *Anxiety Research*, 2, 1–14.

Endler, N.S., Magnusson, D., Ekehammar, B., & Okada, M. (1976). The multidimensionality of state and trait anxiety. *Scandinavian Journal of Psychology*, 17, 81–96.

Endler, N.S., Parker, J.D.A., Bagby, R.M., & Cox, B.J. (1991). Multidimensionality of state and trait anxiety: Factor structure of the Endler Multidimensional Anxiety Scales. *Journal of Personality and Social Psychology*, 60, 919–926.

Evatt, D.P., & Kassel, J.D. (2010). Smoking, arousal, and affect: The role of anxiety sensitivity. *Journal of Anxiety Disorders*, 24, 114–123.

Everson, E.S., Daly, A.J., & Ussher, M. (2008). The effects of moderate and vigorous exercise on desire to smoke, withdrawal symptoms and mood in abstaining young adult smokers. *Mental Health and Physical Activity*, 1, 26–31.

Eysenck, M.W., Derakshan, N., Santos, R., & Calvo, M.G. (2007). Anxiety and cognitive performance: Attentional control theory. *Emotion*, 7, 336–353.

Fabrigar, L.R., Visser, P.S., & Browne, M.W. (1997). Conceptual and methodological issues in testing the circumplex structure of data in personality and social psychology. *Personality and Social Psychology Review*, 1, 184–203.

Feldman Barrett, L., & Russell, J.A. (1998). Independence and bipolarity in the structure of current affect. *Journal of Personality and Social Psychology*, 74, 967–984.

(1999). The structure of current affect: Controversies and emerging consensus. *Current Directions in Psychological Science*, 8, 10–14.

(2009). Circumplex models. In D. Sander & K.R. Scherer (Eds.), *The Oxford companion to emotion and the affective sciences* (pp. 85–88). New York: Oxford University Press.

Fischer, D.G., & Donatelli, M.J. (1987). A measure of stress and arousal: Factor structure of the Stress Adjective Checklist. *Educational and Psychological Measurement*, 47, 425–435.

Fischer, D.G., Hansen, R.J., & Zemore, R.W. (1988). Factor structure of the Stress Adjective Checklist: Replicated. *Educational and Psychological Measurement*, 48, 127–136.

Focht, B.C. (2009). Brief walks in outdoor and laboratory environments: Effects on affective responses, enjoyment, and intentions to walk for exercise. *Research Quarterly for Exercise and Sport*, 80, 611–620.

Focht, B.C., Gauvin, L., & Rejeski, W.J. (2004). The contribution of daily experiences and acute exercise to fluctuations in daily feeling states among older, obese adults with knee osteoarthritis. *Journal of Behavioral Medicine*, 27, 101–121.

Focht, B.C., & Hausenblas, H.A. (2003). State anxiety responses to acute exercise in women with high social physique anxiety. *Journal of Sport and Exercise Psychology*, 25, 123–144.

(2006). Exercising in public and private environments: Effects on feeling states in women with social physique anxiety. *Journal of Applied Biobehavioral Research*, 11, 147–165.

Focht, B.C., Knapp, D.J., Gavin, T.P., Raedeke, T.D., & Hickner, R.C. (2007). Affective and self-efficacy responses to acute aerobic exercise in sedentary older and younger adults. *Journal of Aging and Physical Activity*, 15, 123–138.

Focht, B.C., & Koltyn, K.F. (1999). Influence of resistance exercise of different intensities on state anxiety and blood pressure. *Medicine and Science in Sports and Exercise*, 31, 456–463.

Folkman, S., & Lazarus, R.S. (1985). If it changes it must be a process: Study of emotion and coping during three stages of a college examination. *Journal of Personality and Social Psychology*, 48, 150–170.

Fontaine, J.R.J., Scherer, K.R., Roesch, E.B., & Ellsworth, P.C. (2007). The world of emotions is not two-dimensional. *Psychological Science*, 18, 1050–1057.

Fox, E. (2008). *Emotion science: Cognitive and neuroscientific approaches to understanding human emotions*. New York: Palgrave Macmillan.

Fredrickson, B.L. (2000). Extracting meaning from past affective experiences: The importance of peaks, ends, and specific emotions. *Cognition and Emotion*, 14, 577–606.

(2001). The role of positive emotions in positive psychology: The broaden-and-build theory of positive emotions. *American Psychologist*, 56, 218–226.

Frijda, N.H. (2008). The psychologists' point of view. In M. Lewis, J.M. Haviland-Jones, & L. Feldman Barrett (Eds.), *Handbook of emotions* (3rd edn., pp. 68–87). New York: Guilford.

(2009). Mood. In D. Sander & K.R. Scherer (Eds.), *The Oxford companion to emotion and the affective sciences* (pp. 258–259). New York: Oxford University Press.

Frijda, N.H., & Scherer, K.R. (2009). Emotion definitions (psychological perspectives). In D. Sander & K.R. Scherer (Eds.), *The Oxford companion to emotion and the affective sciences* (pp. 142–144). New York: Oxford University Press.

Gauvin, L., & Brawley, L.R. (1993). Alternative psychological models and methodologies for the study of exercise and affect. In P. Seraganian (Ed.), *Exercise psychology: The influence of physical exercise on psychological processes* (pp. 146–171). New York: John Wiley & Sons.

Gauvin, L., & Rejeski, W.J. (1993). The Exercise-induced Feeling Inventory: Development and initial validation. *Journal of Sport and Exercise Psychology*, 15, 403–423.

(2001). Disentangling substance from rhetoric: A rebuttal to Ekkekakis & Petruzzello (2001). *Psychology of Sport and Exercise*, 2, 73–88.

Gauvin, L., Rejeski, W.J., Norris, J.L., & Lutes, L. (1997). The curse of inactivity: Failure of acute exercise to enhance feeling states in a community sample of sedentary adults. *Journal of Health Psychology*, 2, 509–523.

Gauvin, L., & Russell, S.J. (1993). Sport-specific and culturally adapted measures in sport and exercise psychology research: Issues and strategies. In R.N. Singer, M. Murphey, & L.K. Tennant (Eds.), *Handbook of research on sport psychology* (pp. 891–900). New York: Macmillan.

Gill, D.L. (1997). Measurement, statistics, and research design issues in sport and exercise psychology. *Measurement in Physical Education and Exercise Science*, 1, 39–53.

Gilman, J.M., Ramchandani, V.A., Davis, M.B., Bjork, J.M., & Hommer, D.W. (2008). Why we like to drink: A functional magnetic resonance imaging study of the rewarding and anxiolytic effects of alcohol. *Journal of Neuroscience*, 28, 4583–4591.

Goldstein, M.D., & Strube, M.J. (1994). Independence revisited: The relation between positive and negative affect in a naturalistic setting. *Personality and Social Psychology Bulletin*, 20, 57–64.

Gotlib, I.H. (1984). Depression and general psychopathology in university students. *Journal of Abnormal Psychology*, 93, 19–30.

Gotlib, I.H., & Meyer, J.P. (1986). Factor analysis of the Multiple Affect Adjective Check List: A separation of positive and negative affect. *Journal of Personality and Social Psychology*, 50, 1161–1165.

Gray, E.K., & Watson, D. (2007). Assessing positive and negative affect via self-report. In J.A. Coan & J.J.B. Allen (Eds.), *Handbook of emotion elicitation and assessment* (pp. 171–183). New York: Oxford University Press.

Green, D.P., Goldman, S.L., & Salovey, P. (1993). Measurement error masks bipolarity in affect ratings. *Journal of Personality and Social Psychology*, 64, 1029–1041.

Green, D.P., & Salovey, P. (1999). In what sense are positive and negative affect independent? A Reply to Tellegen, Watson, and Clark. *Psychological Science*, 10, 304–306.

Green, D.P., Salovey, P., & Truax, K.M. (1999). Static, dynamic, and causative bipolarity of affect. *Journal of Personality and Social Psychology*, 76, 856–867.

Green, R.F., & Nowlis, V. (1957). A factor analytic study of the domain of mood with independent experimental validation of the factors [abstract]. *American Psychologist*, 12, 438.

Green, S.B., Lissitz, R.W., & Mulaik, S.A. (1977). Limitations of coefficient alpha as an index of test unidimensionality. *Educational and Psychological Measurement*, 37, 827–838.

Greenfield, S.A. (1995). *Journey to the centers of the mind: Toward a science of consciousness*. New York: Freeman.

Greeno, C.G., Wing, R.R., & Shiffman, S. (2000). Binge antecedents in obese women with and without binge eating disorder. *Journal of Consulting and Clinical Psychology*, 68, 95–102.

Gregg, V.H., & Shepherd, A.J. (2009). Factor structure of scores on the state version of the Four Dimension Mood Scale. *Educational and Psychological Measurement*, 69, 146–156.

Gross, J.J. (1998). The emerging field of emotion regulation: An integrative review. *Review of General Psychology* 2, 271–299.

Grös, D.F., Antony, M.M., Simms, L.J., & McCabe, R.E. (2007). Psychometric properties of the State-Trait Inventory for Cognitive and Somatic Anxiety (STICSA): Comparison to the State-Trait Anxiety Inventory (STAI). *Psychological Assessment*, 19, 369–381.

Guadagnoli, E., & Mor, V. (1989). Measuring cancer patients' affect: Revision and psychometric properties of the Profile of Mood States (POMS). *Psychological Assessment*, 1, 150–154.

Gurtman, M.B., & Pincus, A.L. (2000). Interpersonal adjective scales: Confirmation of circumplex structure from multiple perspectives. *Personality and Social Psychology Bulletin*, 26, 374–384.

(2003). The circumplex model: Methods and research applications. In I.B. Weiner (Series Ed.), *Handbook of psychology* (Vol. 2, pp. 407–428). Hoboken, NJ: John Wiley & Sons.

Hagemann, D., Naumann, E., Becker, G., Maier, S., & Bartussek, D. (1998). Frontal brain asymmetry and affective style: A conceptual replication. *Psychophysiology*, 35, 372–388.

Hagemann, D., Naumann, E., Lürken, A., Becker, G., Maier, S., & Bartussek, D. (1999). EEG asymmetry, dispositional mood and personality. *Personality and Individual Differences*, 27, 541–568.

Hall, E.E., Ekkekakis, P., & Petruzzello, S.J. (2002). The affective beneficence of vigorous exercise revisited. *British Journal of Health Psychology*, 7, 47–66.

(2010). Predicting affective responses to exercise using resting EEG frontal asymmetry: Does intensity matter? *Biological Psychology*, 83, 201–206.

Hansen, C.J., Stevens, L.C., & Coast, J. R. (2001). Exercise duration and mood state: How much is enough to feel better? *Health Psychology*, 20, 267–275.

Hardy, C.J., & Rejeski, W.J. (1989). Not what but how one feels: The measurement of affect during exercise. *Journal of Sport and Exercise Psychology*, 11, 304–317.

Harmon-Jones, E. (2004). Contributions from research on anger and cognitive dissonance to understanding the motivational functions of asymmetrical frontal brain activity. *Biological Psychology*, 67, 51–76.

(2007a). Trait anger predicts relative left frontal cortical activation to anger-inducing stimuli. *International Journal of Psychophysiology*, 66, 154–160.

(2007b). Asymmetrical frontal cortical activity, affective valence, and motivational direction. In E. Harmon-Jones & P. Winkielman (Eds.), *Social neuroscience: Integrating biological and psychological explanations of social behavior* (pp. 137–156). New York: Guilford.

Harmon-Jones, E., & Allen, J.J.B. (1998). Anger and frontal brain activity: EEG asymmetry consistent with approach motivation despite negative affective valence. *Journal of Personality and Social Psychology*, 74, 1310–1316.

Harmon-Jones, E., & Sigelman, J. (2001). State anger and prefrontal brain activity: Evidence that insult-related relative left-prefrontal activation is associated with experienced anger and aggression. *Journal of Personality and Social Psychology*, 80, 797–803.

Haslam, N. (1995). The discreteness of emotion concepts: Categorical structure in the affective circumplex. *Personality and Social Psychology Bulletin*, 21, 1012–1019.

Hemenover, S.H., & Schimmack, U. (2007). That's disgusting! ..., but very amusing: Mixed feelings of amusement and disgust. *Cognition and Emotion*, 21, 1102–1113.

Herbert, M., Johns, M.W., & Doré, C. (1976). Factor analysis of analogue scales measuring subjective feelings before and after sleep. *British Journal of Medical Psychology*, 49, 373–379.

Herring, M.P., O'Connor, P.J., & Dishman, R.K. (2010). The effect of exercise training on anxiety symptoms among patients: A systematic review. *Archives of Internal Medicine*, 170, 321–331.

Hillerås, P.K., Jorm, A.F., Herlitz, A., & Winblad, B. (1998). Negative and positive affect among the very old: A survey on a sample age 90 years or older. *Research on Aging*, 20, 593–610.

Hodes, R.L., Cook, E.W. III, & Lang, P.J. (1985). Individual differences in autonomic response: A conditioned association or conditioned fear? *Psychophysiology*, 22, 545–560.

Hoffman, M.D., & Hoffman, D.R. (2008). Exercisers achieve greater acute exercise-induced mood enhancement than nonexercisers. *Archives of Physical Medicine and Rehabilitation*, 89, 358–363.

Huelsman, T.J., Furr, R.M., & Nemanick, R.C. Jr. (2003). Measurement of dispositional affect: Construct validity and convergence with a circumplex model of affect. *Educational and Psychological Measurement*, 63, 655–673.

Huelsman, T.J., Nemanick, R.C. Jr., & Munz, D.C. (1998). Scales to measure four dimensions of dispositional mood: Positive energy, tiredness, negative activation, and relaxation. *Educational and Psychological Measurement*, 58, 804–819.

Hulley, A., Bentley, N., Clough, C., Fishlock, A., Morrell, F., O'Brien, J., & Radmore, J. (2008). Active and passive commuting to school: Influences on affect in primary school children. *Research Quarterly for Exercise and Sport*, 79, 525–534.

Hunsley, J. (1990). Dimensionality of the Multiple Affect Adjective Check List – Revised: A comparison of factor analytic procedures. *Journal of Psychopathology and Behavioral Assessment*, 12, 81–91.

Hutchison, K.E., Trombley, R.P., Collins, F.L. Jr., McNeil, D.W., Turk, C.L., Carter, L.E., … Leftwich, M.J.T. (1996). A comparison of two models of emotion: Can measurement of emotion based on one model be used to make inferences about the other? *Personality and Individual Differences*, 21, 785–789.

Ito, T.A., Cacioppo, J.T., & Lang, P.J. (1998). Eliciting affect using the international affective picture system: Trajectories through evaluative space. *Personality and Social Psychology Bulletin*, 24, 855–879.

Izard, C.E. (1993). Organizational and motivational functions of discrete emotions. In M. Lewis & J.M. Haviland (Eds.), *Handbook of emotions* (pp. 631–641). New York: Guilford.

Jacob, R.G., Simons, A.D., Manuck, S.B., Rohay, J.M., Waldstein, S., & Gatsonis, C. (1989). The circular mood scale: A new technique of measuring ambulatory mood. *Journal of Psychopathology and Behavioral Assessment*, 11, 153–173.

Jacob, R.G., Thayer, J.F., Manuck, S.B., Muldoon, M.F., Tamres, L.K., Williams, D.M., … Gatsonis, C. (1999). Ambulatory blood pressure responses and the circumplex model of mood: A 4-day study. *Psychosomatic Medicine*, 61, 319–333.

Jerome, G.J., Marquez, D.X., McAuley, E., Canaklisova, S., Snook, E., & Vickers, M. (2002). Self-efficacy effects on feeling states in women. *International Journal of Behavioral Medicine*, 9, 139–154.

Johansson, M., Hassmén, P., & Jouper, J. (2008). Acute effects of qigong exercise on mood and anxiety. *International Journal of Stress Management*, 15, 199–207.

John, O.P. & Benet-Martínez, V. (2000). Measurement: Reliability, construct validation, and scale construction. In H.T. Reis and C.M. Judd (Eds.),

Handbook of research methods in social and personality psychology (pp. 339–369). New York: Cambridge University Press.

Kahneman, D. (1999). Objective happiness. In D. Kahneman, E. Diener, & N. Schwarz (Eds.), *Well-being: The foundations of hedonic psychology* (pp. 3–25). New York: Russell Sage Foundation.

(2003). A perspective on judgment and choice: Mapping bounded rationality. *American Psychologist*, 58, 697–720.

Karageorghis, C.I., Vlachopoulos, S.P., & Terry, P.C. (2000). Latent variable modelling of the relationship between flow and exercise-induced feelings: An intuitive appraisal perspective. *European Physical Education Review*, 6, 230–248.

Katula, J.A., Blissmer, B.J., & McAuley, E. (1999). Exercise intensity and self-efficacy effects on anxiety reduction in healthy, older adults. *Journal of Behavioral Medicine*, 22, 233–247.

Keltner, D., & Gross, J.J. (1999). Functional accounts of emotions. *Cognition and Emotion*, 13, 467–480.

Kerlinger, F.N. (1979). *Behavioral research: A conceptual approach*. New York: Holt, Rinehart and Winston.

King, A.C., de Wit, H., McNamara, P.J., & Cao, D. (2011). Rewarding, stimulant, and sedative alcohol responses and relationship to future binge drinking. *Archives of General Psychiatry*, 68, 389–399.

King, M.G., Burrows, G.D., & Stanley, G.V. (1983). Measurement of stress and arousal: Validation of the stress/arousal adjective checklist. *British Journal of Psychology*, 74, 473–479.

Kishi, T., & Elmquist, J.K. (2005). Body weight is regulated by the brain: A link between feeding and emotion. *Molecular Psychiatry*, 10, 132–146.

Kleinginna, P.R. Jr., Kleinginna, A.M. (1981). A categorized list of emotion definitions, with suggestions for a consensual definition. *Motivation and Emotion*, 5, 345–379.

Knapen, J., Sommerijns, E., Vancampfort, D., Sienaert, P., Pieters, G., Haake, P., ... Peuskens, J. (2009). State anxiety and subjective well-being responses to acute bouts of aerobic exercise in patients with depressive and anxiety disorders. *British Journal of Sports Medicine*, 43, 756–759.

Koball, A.M., Meers, M.R., Storfer-Isser, A., Domoff, S.E., & Musher-Eizenman, D.R. (2012). Eating when bored: Revision of the Emotional Eating Scale with a focus on boredom. *Health Psychology*, 31, 521–524.

Koksal, F., & Power, K.G. (1990). Four Systems Anxiety Questionnaire (FSAQ): A self-report measure of somatic, cognitive, behavioral, and feeling components. *Journal of Personality Assessment*, 54, 534–545.

Koob, G.F. (2008). Hedonic homeostatic dysregulation as a driver of drug-seeking behavior. *Drug Discovery Today: Disease Models*, 5, 207–215.

Kuhn, T.S. (1996). *The structure of scientific revolutions* (3rd edn.). University of Chicago Press. (Original work published 1962).

Kunst-Wilson, W.R., & Zajonc, R.B. (1980). Affective discrimination of stimuli that cannot be recognized. *Science*, 207, 557–558.

Kuppens, P., Oravecz, Z., & Tuerlinckx, F. (2010). Feelings change: Accounting for individual differences in the temporal dynamics of affect. *Journal of Personality and Social Psychology*, 99, 1042–1060.

Kwan, B.M., & Bryan, A.D. (2010a). In-task and post-task affective response to exercise: Translating exercise intentions into behaviour. *British Journal of Health Psychology*, 15, 115–131.

(2010b). Affective response to exercise as a component of exercise motivation: Attitudes, norms, self-efficacy, and temporal stability of intentions. *Psychology of Sport and Exercise*, 11, 71–79.

LaCaille, R.A., Masters, K.S., & Heath, E.M. (2004). Effects of cognitive strategy and exercise setting on running performance, perceived exertion, affect, and satisfaction. *Psychology of Sport and Exercise*, 5, 461–476.

Lang, P.J. (1980). Behavioral treatment and bio-behavioral assessment: Computer applications. In J.B. Sodowski, J.H. Johnson, & T.A. Williams (Eds.), *Technology in mental health care delivery systems* (pp. 119–137). Norwood, NJ: Ablex.

Larsen, J.T., & McGraw, A.P. (2011). Further evidence for mixed emotions. *Journal of Personality and Social Psychology*, 100, 1095–1110.

Larsen, J.T., McGraw, A.P., & Cacioppo, J.T. (2001). Can people feel happy and sad at the same time? *Journal of Personality and Social Psychology*, 81, 684–696.

Larsen, J.T., McGraw, A.P., Mellers, B.A., & Cacioppo, J.T. (2004). The agony of victory and thrill of defeat: Mixed emotional reactions to disappointing wins and relieving losses. *Psychological Science*, 15, 325–330.

Larsen, J.T., Norris, C.J., McGraw, A.P., Hawkley, L.C., & Cacioppo, J.T. (2009). The evaluative space grid: A single-item measure of positivity and negativity. *Cognition and Emotion*, 23, 453–480.

Larsen, R.J., & Diener, E. (1992). Promises and problems with the circumplex model of emotion. In M.S. Clark (Ed.), *Emotion* (pp. 25–59). Newbury Park, CA: Sage.

Larsen, R.J., & Fredrickson, B.L. (1999). Measurement issues in emotion research. In D. Kahneman, E. Diener, & N. Schwarz (Eds.), *Well-being: The foundations of hedonic psychology* (pp. 40–60). New York: Russell Sage Foundation.

Lazarus, R.S. (1982). Thoughts on the relations between emotion and cognition. *American Psychologist*, 37, 1019–1024.

(1991a). *Emotion and adaptation*. New York: Oxford University Press.

(1991b). Cognition and motivation in emotion. *American Psychologist*, 46, 352–367.

(1994). The stable and the unstable in emotion. In P. Ekman & R.J. Davidson (Eds.), *The nature of emotion: Fundamental questions* (pp. 79–85). New York: Oxford University Press.

Leathwood, P.D., & Pollet, P. (1982/1983). Diet-induced mood changes in normal populations. *Journal of Psychiatric Research*, 17, 147–154.

Lehrer, P.M., & Woolfolk, R.L. (1982). Self-report assessment of anxiety: Somatic, cognitive, and behavioral modalities. *Behavioral Assessment*, 4, 167–177.

LePage, M.L., & Crowther, J.H. (2010). The effects of exercise on body satisfaction and affect. *Body Image*, 7, 124–130.

Lerner, J.S., & Keltner, D. (2000). Beyond valence: Toward a model of emotion-specific influences on judgement and choice. *Cognition and Emotion*, 14, 473–493.

Levenson, R.W. (2003). Blood, sweat, and fears: The autonomic architecture of emotion. *Annals of the New York Academy of Sciences*, 1000, 348–366.

Leventhal, H., & Scherer, K. (1987). The relationship of emotion to cognition: A functional approach to a semantic controversy. *Cognition and Emotion*, 1, 3–28.

Liebert, R.M., & Morris, L.W. (1967). Cognitive and emotional components of test anxiety: A distinction and some initial data. *Psychological Reports*, 20, 975–978.

Lishner, D.A., Cooter, A.B., & Zald, D.H. (2008). Addressing measurement limitations in affective rating scales: Development of an empirical valence scale. *Cognition and Emotion*, 22, 180–192.

Lochbaum, M.R. (2006). Viability of resting electroencephalograph asymmetry as a predictor of exercise-induced affect: A lack of consistent support. *Journal of Sport Behavior*, 29, 315–336.

Lochbaum, M.R., Karoly, P., & Landers, D.M. (2004). Affect responses to acute bouts of aerobic exercise: A test of opponent-process theory. *Journal of Sport Behavior*, 27, 330–348.

Lonigan, C.J., Hooe, E.S., David, C.F., & Kistner, J.A. (1999). Positive and negative affectivity in children: Confirmatory factor analysis of a two-factor model and its relation to symptoms of anxiety and depression. *Journal of Consulting and Clinical Psychology*, 67, 374–386.

Lorr, M. (1989). Models and methods for measurement of mood. In R. Plutchik & H. Kellerman (Series Eds.), *Emotion: Theory, research, and experience* (Vol. 4, pp. 37–53). San Diego, CA: Academic Press.

(1997). The circumplex model applied to interpersonal behavior, affect, and psychotic syndromes. In R. Plutchik & H.R. Conte (Eds.), *Circumplex models of personality and emotions* (pp. 47–56). Washington, DC: American Psychological Association.

Lorr, M., Daston, P., & Smith, I.R. (1967). An analysis of mood states. *Educational and Psychological Measurement*, 27, 89–96.

Lorr, M., McNair, D.M., & Fisher, S. (1982). Evidence for bipolar mood states. *Journal of Personality Assessment*, 46, 432–436.

Lorr, M., McNair, D.M., & Heuchert, J.W.P., (2003). *Profile of Mood States: Bi-polar manual supplement*. Cheektowaga, NY: Multi-Health Systems.

Lorr, M., McNair, D.M., & Weinstein, G.J. (1963). Early effects of chlordiaz-epoxide (librium) used with psychotherapy. *Journal of Psychiatric Research*, 1, 257–270.

Lorr, M., McNair, D.M., Weinstein, G.J., Michaux, W.W., & Raskin, A. (1961). Meprobamate and chlorpromazine in psychotherapy: Some effects on anxiety and hostility of outpatients. *Archives of General Psychiatry*, 4, 381–389.

Lorr, M., & Shea, T.M. (1979). Are mood states bipolar? *Journal of Personality Assessment*, 43, 468–472.

Lorr, M., Shi, A.Q., & Youniss, R.P. (1989). A bipolar multifactor conception of mood states. *Personality and Individual Differences*, 10, 155–159.

Lorr, M., & Wunderlich, R.A. (1988). A semantic differential mood scale. *Journal of Clinical Psychology*, 44, 33–36.

Loughead, T.M., Patterson, M.M., & Carron, A.V. (2008). The impact of fitness leader behavior and cohesion on an exerciser's affective state. *International Journal of Sport and Exercise Psychology*, 6, 53–68.

Lox, C.L., Jackson, S., Tuholski, S.W., Wasley, D., & Treasure, D.C. (2000). Revisiting the measurement of exercise-induced feeling states: The Physical Activity Affect Scale (PAAS). *Measurement in Physical Education and Exercise Science*, 4, 79–95.

Lox, C.L., & Rudolph, D.L. (1994). The Subjective Exercise Experiences Scale (SEES): Factorial validity and effects of acute exercise. *Journal of Social Behavior and Personality*, 9, 837–844.

Lox, C.L., & Treasure, D.C. (2000). Changes in feeling states following aquatic exercise during pregnancy. *Journal of Applied Social Psychology*, 30, 518–527.

Lubin, B., Zuckerman, M., Hanson, P.G., Armstrong, T., Rinck, C.M., & Seever, M. (1986). Reliability and validity of the Multiple Affect Adjective Check List – Revised. *Journal of Psychopathology and Behavioral Assessment*, 8, 103–117.

Lutter, M., & Nestler, E.J. (2009). Homeostatic and hedonic signals interact in the regulation of food intake. *Journal of Nutrition*, 139, 629–632.

Macht, M. (1999). Characteristics of eating in anger, fear, sadness and joy. *Appetite*, 33, 129–139.

(2008). How emotions affect eating: A five-way model. *Appetite*, 50, 1–11.

Mackay, C., Cox, T., Burrows, G., & Lazzerini, T. (1978). An inventory for the measurement of self-reported stress and arousal. *British Journal of Social and Clinical Psychology*, 17, 283–284.

Mackay, G.J., & Neill, J.T. (2010). The effect of "green exercise" on state anxiety and the role of exercise duration, intensity, and greenness: A quasi-experimental study. *Psychology of Sport and Exercise*, 11, 238–245.

MacKinnon, N.J., & Keating, L.J. (1989). The structure of emotions: Canada–United States comparisons. *Social Psychology Quarterly*, 52, 70–83.

Magid, V., Colder, C.R., Stroud, L.R., Nichter, M., & Nichter, M. (2009). Negative affect, stress, and smoking in college students: Unique associations independent of alcohol and marijuana use. *Addictive Behaviors*, 34, 973–975.

Markland, D., Emberton, M., & Tallon, R. (1997). Confirmatory factor analysis of the Subjective Exercise Experiences Scale among children. *Journal of Sport and Exercise Psychology*, 19, 418–433.

Marquez, D.X., Jerome, G.J., McAuley, E., Snook, E.M., & Canaklisova, S. (2002). Self-efficacy manipulation and state anxiety responses to exercise in low active women. *Psychology and Health*, 17, 783–791.

Marshall, G.D., & Zimbardo, P.G. (1979). Affective consequences of inadequately explained physiological arousal. *Journal of Personality and Social Psychology*, 37, 970–988.

Martin, C.S., Earleywine, M., Musty, R.E., Perrine, M.W., & Swift, R.M. (1993). Development and validation of the Biphasic Alcohol Effects Scale. *Alcoholism: Clinical and Experimental Research*, 17, 140–146.

Martin Ginis, K.A., Burke, S.M., & Gauvin, L. (2007). Exercising with others exacerbates the negative effects of mirrored environments on sedentary women's feeling states. *Psychology and Health*, 22, 945–962.

Martin Ginis, K.A., Jung, M.E., & Gauvin, L. (2003). To see or not to see: Effects of exercising in mirrored environments on sedentary women's feeling states and self-efficacy. *Health Psychology*, 22, 354–361.

Martinsen, E.W., & Morgan, W.P. (1997). Antidepressant effects of physical activity. In W.P. Morgan (Ed.), *Physical activity and mental health* (pp. 93–106). Washington, DC: Taylor and Francis.

Masheb, R.M., & Grilo, C.M. (2006). Emotional overeating and its associations with eating disorder psychopathology among overweight patients with binge eating disorder. *International Journal of Eating Disorders*, 39, 141–146.

Maslach, C. (1979). Negative emotional biasing of unexplained arousal. *Journal of Personality and Social Psychology*, 37, 953–969.

Matthews, G., Jones, D.M., & Chamberlain, A.G. (1990). Refining the measurement of mood: The UWIST Mood Adjective Checklist. *British Journal of Psychology*, 81, 17–42.

McAuley, E., Blissmer, B., Katula, J., & Duncan, T.E. (2000). Exercise environment, self-efficacy, and affective responses to acute exercise in older adults. *Psychology and Health*, 15, 341–355.

McAuley, E., & Courneya, K.S. (1994). The Subjective Exercise Experiences Scale (SEES): Development and preliminary validation. *Journal of Sport and Exercise Psychology*, 16, 163–177.

McAuley, E., Mihalko, S.L., & Bane, S.M. (1996). Acute exercise and anxiety reduction: Does the environment matter? *Journal of Sport and Exercise Psychology*, 18, 408–419.

McAuley, E., & Rudolph, D.L. (1995). Physical activity, aging, and psychological well-being. *Journal of Aging and Physical Activity*, 3, 67–96.

McCormick, I.A., Walkey, F.H., & Taylor, A.J.W. (1985). The stress arousal checklist: An independent analysis. *Educational and Psychological Measurement*, 45, 143–146.

McCrae, C.S., McNamara, J.P.H., Rowe, M.A., Dzierzewski, J.M., Dirk, J., Marsiske, M., & Craggs, J.G. (2008). Sleep and affect in older adults: Using multilevel modeling to examine daily associations. *Journal of Sleep Research*, 17, 42–53.

McGrath, P.A., de Veber, L.L., & Hearn, M.T. (1985). Multidimensional pain assessment in children. In H.L. Fields, R. Dubner, & F. Cervero (Eds.), *Advances in pain research and therapy* (Vol. 9, pp. 387–393). New York: Raven.

McKinney, A. (2010). A review of the next day effects of alcohol on subjective mood ratings. *Current Drug Abuse Reviews*, 3, 88–91

McKinney, A., & Coyle, K. (2006). Alcohol hangover effects on measures of affect the morning after a normal night's drinking. *Alcohol and Alcoholism*, 41, 54–60.

McNair, D.M., & Lorr, M. (1964). An analysis of mood in neurotics. *Journal of Abnormal and Social Psychology*, 69, 620–627.

McNair, D.M., Lorr, M., & Droppleman, L.F. (1971). *Profile of Mood States (POMS) manual*. San Diego, CA: Educational and Industrial Testing Service.

(1992). *Profile of Mood States (POMS) manual*. San Diego, CA: Educational and Industrial Testing Service.

Meddis, R. (1972). Bipolar factors in mood adjective check lists. *British Journal of Social and Clinical Psychology*, 11, 178–184.

Meehl, P.E. (1999). Clarifications about taxometric method. *Applied and Preventive Psychology*, 8, 165–174.

Mehrabian, A. (1995). Framework for a comprehensive description and measurement of emotional states. *Genetic, Social, and General Psychology Monographs*, 121, 339–361.

(1997). Comparison of the PAD and PANAS as models for describing emotions and for differentiating anxiety from depression. *Journal of Psychopathology and Behavioral Assessment*, 19, 331–357.

Mehrabian, A., & Russell, J.A. (1974). *An approach to environmental psychology*. Cambridge, MA: MIT Press.

Mermelstein, R., Hedeker, D., & Weinstein, S. (2010). Ecological momentary assessment of mood-smoking relationships in adolescent smokers. In J.D. Kassel (Ed.), *Substance abuse and emotion* (pp. 217–236). Washington, DC: American Psychological Association.

Miller, B.M., Bartholomew, J.B., & Springer, B.A. (2005). Post-exercise affect: The effect of mode preference. *Journal of Applied Sport Psychology*, 17, 263–272.

Mineka, S., Watson, D., & Clark, L.A. (1998). Comorbidity of anxiety and unipolar mood disorders. *Annual Review of Psychology*, 49, 377–412.

Mohr, C.D., Brannan, D., Mohr, J., Armeli, S., & Tennen, H. (2008). Evidence for positive mood buffering among college student drinkers. *Personality and Social Psychology Bulletin*, 34, 1249–1259.

Mook, J., Kleijn, W.C., & van der Ploeg, H.M. (1991). Symptom-positively and -negatively worded items in two popular self-report inventories of anxiety and depression. *Psychological Reports*, 69, 551–560.

Mook, J., van der Ploeg, H.M., & Kleijn, W.C. (1992). Symptom-positive and symptom-negative items in the State-Trait Anxiety Inventory: A comparison and replication. *Anxiety, Stress, and Coping*, 5, 113–123.

Moon, J. & Lee, J.-H. (2011). Predicting cigarette-seeking behavior: How reward sensitivity and positive emotions influence nicotine cravings. *Social Behavior and Personality*, 39, 737–746.

Moore, B.A. & O'Donohue, W.T. (2008) Hedonic approach to pediatric and adolescent weight management. In W.T. O'Donohue, B.A. Moore, & B.J. Scott, (Eds.) *Handbook of pediatric and adolescent obesity treatment* (pp. 143–151). New York: Routledge.

Morgan, R.L. & Heise, D. (1988). Structure of emotions. *Social Psychology Quarterly*, 51, 19–31.

Morgan, W.P. (1984). Exercise and mental health. In H.M. Eckert & H.J. Montoye (Eds.), *Exercise and health* (pp. 132–145). Champaign, IL: Human Kinetics.

Morris, J.D. (1995). SAM: The Self-Assessment Manikin, an efficient cross-cultural measurement of emotional response. *Journal of Advertising Research*, 35, 63–68.

Morris, W.N. (1992). A functional analysis of the role of mood in affective systems. In M.S. Clark (Ed.), *Review of personality and social psychology* (Vol. 13, pp. 256–293). Newbury Park, CA: Sage.

(1999). The mood system. In D. Kahneman, E. Diener, & N. Schwarz (Eds.), *Well-being: The foundations of hedonic psychology* (pp. 169–189). New York: Russell Sage Foundation.

Morris, L.W., Davis, M.A., & Hutchings, C.H. (1981). Cognitive and emotional components of anxiety: Literature review and a revised worry-emotionality scale. *Journal of Educational Psychology*, 73, 541–555.

Mossholder, K.W., Kemery, E.R., Harris, S.G., Armenakis, A.A., & McGrath, R. (1994). Confounding constructs and levels of constructs in affectivity measurement: An empirical investigation. *Educational and Psychological Measurement*, 54, 336–349.

Motl, R.W., O'Connor, P.J., & Dishman, R.K. (2004). Effects of cycling exercise on the soleus H-reflex and state anxiety among men with low or high trait anxiety. *Psychophysiology*, 41, 96–105.

Nemanick, R.R. Jr., & Munz, D.C. (1994). Measuring the poles of negative and positive mood using the Positive Affect Negative Affect Schedule and Activation Deactivation Adjective Check List. *Psychological Reports*, 74, 195–199.

Nesse, R.M. (2004). Natural selection and the elusiveness of happiness. *Philosophical Transactions of the Royal Society of London (Series B)*, 359, 1333–1347.

Norcross, J.C., Guadagnoli, E., & Prochaska, J.O. (1984). Factor structure of the Profile of Mood States (POMS): Two partial replications. *Journal of Clinical Psychology*, 40, 1270–1277.

Norris, C.J., Gollan, J., Berntson, G.G., & Cacioppo, J.T. (2010). The current status of research on the structure of evaluative space. *Biological Psychology*, 84, 422–436.

Nowlis, V. (1965). Research with the mood adjective checklist. In S.S. Tomkins & C.E. Izard (Eds.), *Affect, cognition, and personality* (pp. 352–389). New York: Springer.

(1970). Mood: Behavior and experience. In M.B. Arnold (Ed.), *Feelings and emotions: The Loyola symposium* (pp. 261–277). New York: Academic Press.

Nowlis, V., & Nowlis, H.H. (1956). The description and analysis of mood. *Annals of the New York Academy of Sciences*, 65, 345–355.

Nunnally, J.C., & Bernstein, I.H. (1994). *Psychometric theory* (3rd edn.). New York: McGraw-Hill.

O'Connor, P.J., Bryant, C.X., Veltri, J.P., & Gebhardt, S.M. (1993). State anxiety and ambulatory blood pressure following resistance exercise in females. *Medicine and Science in Sports and Exercise*, 25, 516–521.

O'Connor, P.J., Raglin, J.S., & Martinsen, E.W. (2000). Physical activity, anxiety, and anxiety disorders. *International Journal of Sport Psychology*, 31, 136–155.

O'Connor, P.J., Petruzzello, S.J., Kubitz, K.A., & Robinson, T.L. (1995). Anxiety responses to maximal exercise testing. *British Journal of Sports Medicine*, 29, 97–102.

Oatley, K., Keltner, D., & Jenkins, J.M. (2006). *Understanding emotions* (2nd edn.). Malden, MA: Blackwell.

Ong, J.C., Cardé, N.B., Gross, J.J., & Manber, R. (2011). A two-dimensional approach to assessing affective states in good and poor sleepers. *Journal of Sleep Research*, 20, 606–610.

Ortony, A., & Turner, T.J. (1990). What's basic about basic emotions? *Psychological Review*, 97, 315–331.

Osburn, H.G. (2000). Coefficient alpha and related internal consistency reliability coefficients. *Psychological Methods*, 5, 343–355.

Osgood, C.E. (1962). Studies on the generality of affective meaning systems. *American Psychologist*, 17, 10–28.

Osgood, C.E., & Suci, G.J. (1955). Factor analysis of meaning. *Journal of Experimental Psychology*, 50, 325–338.

Osgood, C.E., Suci, G.J., & Tannenbaum, P.H. (1957). *The measurement of meaning*. Urbana, IL: University of Illinois Press.

Ostafin, B.D., Marlatt, G.A., & Greenwald, A.G. (2008). Drinking without thinking: An implicit measure of alcohol motivation predicts failure to control alcohol use. *Behaviour Research and Therapy*, 46, 1210–1219.

Panksepp, J. (1998). The periconscious substrates of consciousness: Affective states and the evolutionary origins of the self. *Journal of Consciousness Studies*, 5, 566–582.

    (2005). On the embodied neural nature of core emotional affects. *Journal of Consciousness Studies*, 12, 158–184.

Parfitt, G., Rose, E.A., & Burgess, W.M. (2006). The psychological and physiological responses of sedentary individuals to prescribed and preferred intensity exercise. *British Journal of Health Psychology*, 11, 39–53.

Parrott, A.C., Gibbs, A., Scholey, A.B., King, R., Owens, K., Swann, P., ... Stough, C. (2011). MDMA and methamphetamine: Some paradoxical negative and positive mood changes in an acute dose laboratory study. *Psychopharmacology*, 215, 527–536.

Pedhazur, E.J., & Pedhazur Schmelkin, L. (1991). *Measurement, design, and analysis: An integrated approach*. Hillsdale, NJ: Lawrence Erlbaum.

Peeling, P., & Dawson, B. (2007). Influence of caffeine ingestion on perceived mood states, concentration, and arousal levels during a 75-min university lecture. *Advances in Physiology Education*, 31, 332–335.

Perkins, K.A., Karelitz, J.L., Conklin, C.A., Sayette, M.A., & Giedgowd, G.E. (2010). Acute negative affect relief from smoking depends on the affect situation and measure but not on nicotine. *Biological Psychiatry*, 67, 707–714.

Perrinjaquet, A., Furrer, O., Usunier, J.C., Cestre, G., & Valette-Florence, P. (2007). A test of the quasi-circumplex structure of human values. *Journal of Research in Personality*, 41, 820–840.

Petruzzello, S.J., Jones, A.C., & Tate, A.K. (1997). Affective responses to acute exercise: A test of opponent-process theory. *Journal of Sports Medicine and Physical Fitness*, 37, 205–212.

Potter, P.T., Zautra, A.J., & Reich, J.W. (2000). Stressful events and information processing dispositions moderate the relationship between positive and negative affect: Implications for pain patients. *Annals of Behavioral Medicine*, 22, 191–198.

Power, M., & Dalgleish, T. (2008). *Cognition and emotion: From order to disorder* (2nd edn.). New York: Psychology Press.

Pronk, N.P., Crouse, S.F., & Rohack, J.J. (1995). Maximal exercise and acute mood response in women. *Physiology and Behavior*, 57, 1–4.

Puente, R., & Anshel, M.H. (2010). Exercisers' perceptions of their fitness instructor's interacting style, perceived competence, and autonomy as a function of self-determined regulation to exercise, enjoyment, affect, and exercise frequency. *Scandinavian Journal of Psychology*, 51, 38–45.

Purcell, A.T. (1982). The structure of activation and emotion. *Multivariate Behavioral Research*, 17, 221–251.

Rafaeli. E., & Revelle, W. (2006). A premature consensus: Are happiness and sadness truly opposite affects? *Motivation and Emotion*, 30, 1–12.

Rafaeli, E., Rogers, G.M., & Revelle, W. (2007). Affective synchrony: Individual differences in mixed emotions. *Personality and Social Psychology Bulletin*, 33, 915–932.

Raglin, J.S. (1997). Anxiolytic effects of physical activity. In W.P. Morgan (Ed.), *Physical activity and mental health* (pp. 107–126). Washington, DC: Taylor and Francis.

Raglin, J.S., Turner, P.E., & Eksten, F. (1993). State anxiety and blood pressure following 30 min of leg ergometry or weight training. *Medicine and Science in Sports and Exercise*, 25, 1044–1048.

Raglin, J.S., & Wilson, M. (1996). State anxiety following 20 minutes of bicycle ergometer exercise at selected intensities. *International Journal of Sports Medicine*, 17, 467–471.

Ralevski, E., Perry, E.B. Jr., D'Souza, D.C., Bufis, V., Elander, J., Limoncelli, D., … Petrakis I. (2012). Preliminary findings on the interactive effects of IV ethanol and IV nicotine on human behavior and cognition: A laboratory study. *Nicotine and Tobacco Research*, 14, 596–606.

Räikkönen, K., Matthews, K.A., Kondwani, K.A., Bunker, C.H., Melhem, N.M., Ukoli, F.A.M., … Jacob, R.G. (2004). Does nondipping of blood pressure at night reflect a trait of blunted cardiovascular responses to daily activities? *Annals of Behavioral Medicine*, 27, 131–137.

Reddon, J.R., Marceau, R., & Holden, R.R. (1985). A confirmatory evaluation of the Profile of Mood States: Convergent and discriminant item validity. *Journal of Psychopathology and Behavioral Assessment*, 7, 243–259.

Ree, M.J., French, D., MacLeod, C., & Locke, V. (2008). Distinguishing cognitive and somatic dimensions of state and trait anxiety: Development and validation of the State-Trait Inventory for Cognitive and Somatic Anxiety (STICSA). *Behavioural and Cognitive Psychotherapy*, 36, 313–332.

Reich, J.W., & Zautra, A.J. (2002). Arousal and the relationship between positive and negative affect: An analysis of the data of Ito, Cacioppo, and Lang (1998). *Motivation and Emotion*, 26, 209–222.

Reich, J.W., Zautra, A.J., & Davis, M. (2003). Dimensions of affect relationships: Models and their integrative implications. *Review of General Psychology*, 7, 66–83.

Reisenzein, R. (1994). Pleasure-arousal theory and the intensity of emotions. *Journal of Personality and Social Psychology*, 67, 525–539.

Rejeski, W.J., Hardy, C.J., & Shaw, J. (1991). Psychometric confounds of assessing state anxiety in conjunction with acute bouts of vigorous exercise. *Journal of Sport and Exercise Psychology*, 13, 65–74.

Rejeski, W.J., Reboussin, B.A., Dunn, A.L., King, A.C., & Sallis, J.F. (1999). A modified Exercise-induced Feeling Inventory for chronic training and baseline profiles of participants in the Activity Counseling Trial. *Journal of Health Psychology*, 4, 97–108.

Remington, N.A., Fabrigar, L.R., & Visser, P.S. (2000). Reexamining the circumplex model of affect. *Journal of Personality and Social Psychology*, 79, 286–300.

Rhodes, R.E., Fiala, B., & Conner, M. (2009). A review and meta-analysis of affective judgments and physical activity in adult populations. *Annals of Behavioral Medicine*, 38, 180–204.

Robinson, J.D., Lam, C.Y., Carter, B.L., Wetter, D.W., & Cinciripini, P.M. (2012). Negative reinforcement smoking outcome expectancies are associated with affective response to acute nicotine administration and abstinence. *Drug and Alcohol Dependence*, 120, 196–201.

Robinson, T.E., & Berridge, K.C. (2008). The incentive sensitization theory of addiction: Some current issues. *Philosophical Transactions of the Royal Society of London. Series B: Biological Sciences*, 363, 3137–3146.

Rolls, E.T. (2007). Understanding the mechanisms of food intake and obesity. *Obesity Reviews*, 8 *(Suppl 1)*, 67–72.

Roseman, I.J., Wiest, C., & Swartz, T.S. (1994). Phenomenology, behaviors, and goals differentiate discrete emotions. *Journal of Personality and Social Psychology*, 67, 206–221.

Rousseau, G.S., Irons, J.G., & Correia, C.J. (2011). The reinforcing value of alcohol in a drinking to cope paradigm. *Drug and Alcohol Dependence*, 118, 1–4.

Rueger, S.Y., McNamara, P.J., & King, A.C. (2009). Expanding the utility of the Biphasic Alcohol Effects Scale (BAES) and initial psychometric support for the Brief–BAES (B–BAES). *Alcohol: Clinical and Experimental Research*, 33, 916–924.

Russell, J.A. (1978). Evidence of convergent validity on the dimensions of affect. *Journal of Personality and Social Psychology*, 36, 1152–1168.

(1979). Affective space is bipolar. *Journal of Personality and Social Psychology*, 37, 345–356.

(1980). A circumplex model of affect. *Journal of Personality and Social Psychology*, 39, 1161–1178.

(1989). Measures of emotion. In R. Plutchik, & H. Kellerman (Series Eds.), *Emotion: Theory, research, and experience* (Vol. 4, pp. 83–111). San Diego, CA: Academic Press.

(1991). In defense of a prototype approach to emotion concepts. *Journal of Personality and Social Psychology*, 60, 37–47.

(1997). How shall an emotion be called? In R. Plutchik & H.R. Conte (Eds.), *Circumplex models of personality and emotions* (pp. 205–220). Washington, DC: American Psychological Association.

(2003). Core affect and the psychological construction of emotion. *Psychological Review*, 110, 145–172.

(2005). Emotion in human consciousness is built on core affect. *Journal of Consciousness Studies*, 12, 26–42.

Russell, J.A., & Bullock, M. (1985). Multidimensional scaling of emotional facial expressions: Similarity from preschoolers to adults. *Journal of Personality and Social Psychology*, 48, 1290–1298.

(1986). On the dimensions preschoolers use to interpret facial expressions of emotion. *Developmental Psychology*, 22, 97–102.

Russell, J.A., & Carroll, J.M. (1999a). On the bipolarity of positive and negative affect. *Psychological Bulletin*, 125, 3–30.

(1999b). The phoenix of bipolarity: Reply to Watson and Tellegen (1999). *Psychological Bulletin*, 125, 611–617.

Russell, J.A., & Feldman Barrett, L. (1999). Core affect, prototypical emotional episodes, and other things called emotion: Dissecting the elephant. *Journal of Personality and Social Psychology*, 76, 805–819.

(2009). Core affect. In D. Sander & K.R. Scherer (Eds.), *The Oxford companion to emotion and the affective sciences* (p. 104). New York: Oxford University Press.

Russell, J.A., & Mehrabian, A. (1974). Distinguishing anger and anxiety in terms of emotional response factors. *Journal of Consulting and Clinical Psychology*, 42, 79–83.

(1977). Evidence for a three-factor theory of emotions. *Journal of Research in Personality*, 11, 273–294.

Russell, J.A., & Steiger, J.H. (1982). The structure in persons' implicit taxonomy of emotions. *Journal of Research in Personality*, 16, 447–469.

Russell, J.A., Ward, L.M., & Pratt, G. (1981). Affective quality attributed to environments: A factor analytic study. *Environment and Behavior*, 13, 259–288.

Russell, J.A., Weiss, A., & Mendelsohn, G.A. (1989). Affect Grid: A single-item scale of pleasure and arousal. *Journal of Personality and Social Psychology*, 57, 493–502.

Ryan-Harshman, M., Leiter, L.A., & Anderson, G.H. (1987). Phenylalanine and aspartame fail to alter feeding behavior, mood and arousal in men. *Physiology and Behavior*, 39, 247–253.

Salmon, P. (2001). Effects of physical exercise on anxiety, depression, and sensitivity to stress: A unifying theory. *Clinical Psychology Review*, 21, 33–61.

Saxon, L., Skagerberg, S., Borg, S., & Hiltunen, A.J. (2010). Should mood during intravenous alcohol administration be studied as a bi- or unipolar phenomenon? A pilot study. *Alcohol*, 44, 393–400.

Schachter, S., & Singer, J.E. (1962). Cognitive, social, and physiological determinants of emotional state. *Psychological Review*, 69, 379–399.

(1979). Comments on the Maslach and Marshall-Zimbardo experiments. *Journal of Personality and Social Psychology*, 37, 989–995.

Scherer, K.R. (1984). On the nature and function of emotion: A component process approach. In K.R. Scherer & P.E. Ekman (Eds.), *Approaches to emotion* (pp. 293–317). Hillsdale, NJ: Erlbaum.

(2005). What are emotions? And how can they be measured? *Social Science Information*, 44, 695–729.

Schimmack, U. (2001). Pleasure, displeasure, and mixed feelings: Are semantic opposites mutually exclusive? *Cognition and Emotion*, 15, 81–97.

(2005). Response latencies of pleasure and displeasure ratings: Further evidence for mixed feelings. *Cognition and Emotion*, 19, 671–691.

Schimmack, U., & Crites, S.L. Jr. (2005). The structure of affect. In D. Albarracín, B.T. Johnson, & M.P. Zanna (Eds.), *The handbook of attitudes* (pp. 397–435). Mahwah, NJ: Lawrence Erlbaum.

Schimmack, U., & Grob, A. (2000). Dimensional models of core affect: A quantitative comparison by means of structural equation modeling. *European Journal of Personality*, 14, 325–345.

Schimmack, U., & Reisenzein, R. (2002). Experiencing activation: Energetic arousal and tense arousal are not mixtures of valence and activation. *Emotion*, 2, 412–417.

Schleicher, H.E., Harris, K.J., Catley, D., & Nazir, N. (2009). The role of depression and negative affect regulation expectancies in tobacco smoking among college students. *Journal of American College Health*, 57, 507–512.

Schlosberg, H. (1952). The description of facial expressions in terms of two dimensions. *Journal of Experimental Psychology*, 44, 229–237.

(1954). Three dimensions of emotions. *Psychological Review*, 61, 81–88.

Schmitt, N. (1996). Uses and abuses of coefficient alpha. *Psychological Assessment*, 8, 350–353.

Schmukle, S.C., & Egloff, B. (2009). Exploring bipolarity of affect ratings by using polychoric correlations. *Cognition and Emotion*, 23, 272–295.

Schmukle, S.C., Egloff, B., & Burns, L.R. (2002). The relationship between positive and negative affect in the Positive and Negative Affect Schedule. *Journal of Research in Personality*, 36, 463–475.

Schutz, R.W. (1993). Methodological issues and measurement problems in sport psychology. In S. Serpa, J. Alves, V. Ferreira, & A. Paulo-Brito (Eds.), *Proceedings of the VIII World Congress of Sport Psychology* (pp. 119–131). Lisbon, Portugal: International Society of Sport Psychology.

Schwartz, G.E., Davidson, R.J., & Goleman, D.J. (1978). Patterning of cognitive and somatic processes in the self-regulation of anxiety: Effects of meditation versus exercise. *Psychosomatic Medicine*, 40, 321–328.

Schwartz, S.H., & Boehnke, K. (2004). Evaluating the structure of human values with confirmatory factor analysis. *Journal of Research in Personality*, 38, 230–255.

Scollon, C.N., Diener, E., Oishi, S., & Biswas-Diener, R. (2005). An experience sampling and cross-cultural investigation of the relation between pleasant and unpleasant affect. *Cognition and Emotion*, 19, 27–52.

Shaver, P., Schwartz, J., Kirson, D., & O'Connor, C. (1987). Emotion knowledge: Further exploration of a prototype approach. *Journal of Personality and Social Psychology*, 52, 1061–1086.

Sherwood, R.D., & Westerback, M.E. (1983). A factor analytic study of the State Trait Anxiety Inventory utilized with preservice elementary teachers. *Journal of Research in Science Teaching*, 20, 225–229.

Shevlin, M., Miles, J.N.V., Davies, M.N.O., & Walker, S. (2000). Coefficient alpha: A useful indicator of reliability? *Personality and Individual Differences*, 28, 229–237.

Shiffman, S., & Gwaltney, C.J. (2008). Does heightened affect make smoking cues more salient? *Journal of Abnormal Psychology*, 117, 618–624.

Shiffman, S., West, R.J., & Gilbert, D.G. (2004). Recommendations for the assessment of tobacco craving and withdrawal in smoking cessation trials. *Nicotine and Tobacco Research*, 6, 599–614.

Sijtsma, K. (2009). On the use, the misuse, and the very limited usefulness of Cronbach's alpha. *Psychometrika*, 74, 107–120.

Simons, J.S., Dvorak, R.D., Batien, B.D., & Wray, T.B. (2010). Event-level associations between affect, alcohol intoxication, and acute dependence symptoms: Effects of urgency, self-control, and drinking experience. *Addictive Behaviors*, 35, 1045–1053.

Sjöberg, L., Svensson, E., & Persson, L.-O. (1979). The measurement of mood. *Scandinavian Journal of Psychology*, 20, 1–18.

Skinner, B.F. (1953). *Science and human behavior.* New York: Free Press.

Smith, C.A., & Ellsworth, P.C. (1985). Patterns of cognitive appraisal in emotion. *Journal of Personality and Social Psychology*, 48, 813–838.

Smith, J.C., O'Connor, P.J., Crabbe, J.B., & Dishman, R.K. (2002). Emotional responsiveness after low- and moderate-intensity exercise and seated rest. *Medicine and Science in Sports and Exercise*, 34, 1158–1167.

Solomon, R.L. (1980). The opponent-process theory of acquired motivation: The costs of pleasure and the benefits of pain. *American Psychologist*, 35, 691–712.

(1991). Acquired motivation and affective opponent processes. In J. Madden IV (Ed.), *Neurobiology of learning, emotion, and affect* (pp. 307–347). New York: Raven.

Sonnentag, S., Binnewies, C., & Mojza, E.J. (2008). "Did you have a nice evening?" A day-level study on recovery experiences, sleep, and affect. *Journal of Applied Psychology*, 93, 674–684.

Spielberger, C.D. (1966). Theory and research on anxiety. In C.D. Spielberger (Ed.), *Anxiety and behavior* (pp. 3–20). New York: Academic Press.

(1972a). Anxiety as an emotional state. In C.D. Spielberger (Ed.), *Anxiety: Current trends in theory and research* (Vol. 1, pp. 23–49). New York: Academic Press.

(1972b). Review of the Profile of Mood States. *Professional Psychology*, 3, 387–388.

(1983). *Manual for the State-Trait Anxiety Inventory (Form Y).* Palo Alto, CA: Consulting Psychologists.

(1985). Assessment of state and trait anxiety: Conceptual and methodological issues. *Southern Psychologist*, 2, 6–16.

Spielberger, C.D., Golzalez, H.P., Taylor, C.J., Algaze, B., & Anton, W.D. (1978). Examination stress and test anxiety. In C.D. Spielberger & I.G. Sarason (Eds.), *Stress and anxiety* (Vol. 5, pp. 167–191). Washington, DC: Hemisphere.

Spielberger, C.D., Gorsuch, R.L., & Lushene, R.E. (1970). *Manual for the State-Trait Anxiety Inventory.* Palo Alto, CA: Consulting Psychologists Press.

Spielberger, C.D., Lushene, R.E., & McAdoo, W.G. (1977). Theory and measurement of anxiety states. In R.B. Cattell & R.M. Dreger (Eds.), *Handbook of modern personality theory* (pp. 239–253). New York: Wiley.

Spielberger, C.D., & Reheiser, E.C (2004). Measuring anxiety, anger, depression, and curiosity as emotional states and personality traits with the STAI, STAXI, and STPI. In M.J. Hilsenroth & D.L. Segal (Eds.), *Comprehensive handbook of psychological assessment* (Vol. 2, pp. 70–86). Hoboken, NJ: Wiley.

Steiger, J.H. (1979). Multicorr: A computer program for fast, accurate, small-sample testing of correlational pattern hypotheses. *Educational and Psychological Measurement*, 39, 677–680.

(1980). Testing pattern hypotheses on correlation matrices: Alternative statistics and some empirical results. *Multivariate Behavioral Research*, 15, 335–352.

Stone, A.A. (1997). Measurement of affective response. In S. Cohen, R.C. Kessler, & L. Underwood Gordon (Eds.), *Measuring stress: A guide for health and social scientists* (pp. 148–171). New York: Oxford University Press.

Stritzke, W.G.K., Lang, A.R., & Patrick, C.J. (1996). Beyond stress and arousal: A reconceptualization of alcohol-emotion relations with reference to psychophysiological methods. *Psychological Bulletin*, 120, 376–395.

Stroebe, W., Papies, E.K., & Aarts, H. (2008). From homeostatic to hedonic theories of eating: Self-regulatory failure in food-rich environments. *Applied Psychology: An International Review*, 57, 172–193.

Stroth, S., Hille, K., Spitzer, M., & Reinhardt, R. (2009). Aerobic endurance exercise benefits memory and affect in young adults. *Neuropsychological Rehabilitation*, 19, 223–243.

Svebak, S., & Murgatroyd, S. (1985). Metamotivational dominance: A multimethod validation of reversal theory constructs. *Journal of Personality and Social Psychology*, 48, 107–116.

Svensson, E. (1977). Response format and factor structure in mood adjective check lists. *Scandinavian Journal of Psychology*, 18, 71–78.

Taylor, A., Katomeri, M., & Ussher, M. (2006). Effects of walking on cigarette cravings and affect in the context of Nesbitt's paradox and the circumplex model. *Journal of Sport and Exercise Psychology*, 28, 18–31.

Taylor, A.H., & Oliver, A.J. (2009). Acute effects of brisk walking on urges to eat chocolate, affect, and responses to a stressor and chocolate cue: An experimental study. *Appetite*, 52, 155–160.

Tellegen, A. (1985). Structures of mood and personality and their relevance to assessing anxiety, with an emphasis on self-report. In A.H. Tuma & J.D. Maser (Eds.), *Anxiety and the anxiety disorders* (pp. 681–706). Hillsdale, NJ: Lawrence Erlbaum.

Tellegen, A., Watson, D., & Clark, L.A. (1999a). On the dimensional and hierarchical structure of affect. *Psychological Science*, 10, 297–303.

(1999b). Further support for a hierarchical model of affect: Reply to Green and Salovey. *Psychological Science*, 10, 307–309.

Tenenbaum, G., Furst, D., & Weingarten, G. (1985). A statistical reevaluation of the STAI anxiety questionnaire. *Journal of Clinical Psychology*, 41, 239–244.

Terracciano, A., McCrae, R.R., & Costa, P.T. Jr. (2003). Factorial and construct validity of the Italian Positive and Negative Affect Schedule (PANAS). *European Journal of Psychological Assessment*, 19, 131–141.

Terry, P. (1995). The efficacy of mood state profiling with elite performers: A review and synthesis. *Sport Psychologist*, 9, 309–324.

Terry, P.C., & Lane, A.M. (2000). Normative values for the Profile of Mood States for use with athletic samples. *Journal of Applied Sport Psychology*, 12, 93–109.

Terry, P.C., Lane, A.M., Lane, H.J., & Keohane, L. (1999). Development and validation of a mood measure for adolescents. *Journal of Sports Sciences*, 17, 861–872.

Thayer, R.E. (1967). Measurement of activation through self-report. *Psychological Reports*, 20, 663–678.

(1978a). Factor analytic and reliability studies on the Activation-Deactivation Adjective Check List. *Psychological Reports*, 42, 747–756.

(1978b). Toward a psychological theory of multidimensional activation (arousal). *Motivation and Emotion*, 2, 1–34.

(1986). Activation-Deactivation Adjective Check List: Current overview and structural analysis. *Psychological Reports*, 58, 607–614.

(1987a). Energy, tiredness, and tension effects of a sugar snack versus moderate exercise. *Journal of Personality and Social Psychology*, 52, 119–125.

(1987b). Problem perception, optimism, and related states as a function of time of day (diurnal rhythm) and moderate exercise: Two arousal systems in interaction. *Motivation and Emotion*, 11, 19–36.

(1989). *The biopsychology of mood and arousal*. New York: Oxford University Press.

Thompson, B., & Vacha-Haase, T. (2000). Psychometrics is datametrics: The test is not reliable. *Educational and Psychological Measurement*, 60, 174–195.

Tomarken, A.J., Davidson, R.J., Wheeler, R.E., & Doss, R.C. (1992). Individual differences in anterior brain asymmetry and fundamental dimensions of emotion. *Journal of Personality and Social Psychology*, 62, 676–687.

Tomkins, S. (1962). *Affect, imagery, consciousness* (Vol. 1). New York: Springer.

Tracey, T.J.G. (2000). Analysis of circumplex models. In H.E.A. Tinsley & S.D. Brown (Eds.), *Handbook of applied multivariate statistics and mathematical modeling* (pp. 641–664). San Diego, CA: Academic.

Treasure, D.C., & Newbery, D.M. (1998). Relationship between self-efficacy, exercise intensity, and feeling states in a sedentary population during and following an acute bout of exercise. *Journal of Sport and Exercise Psychology*, 20, 1–11.

Tuccitto, D.E., Giacobbi, P.R. Jr., & Leite, W.L. (2010). The internal structure of positive and negative affect: A confirmatory factor analysis of the PANAS. *Educational and Psychological Measurement*, 70, 125–141.

Vagg, P.R., Spielberger, C.D., & O'Hearn, T.P. Jr. (1980). Is the State-Trait Anxiety Inventory multidimensional? *Personality and Individual Differences*, 1, 207–214.

Vandekerckhove, M., Weiss, R., Schotte, C., Exadaktylos, V., Haex, B., Verbraecken, J., & Cluydts, R. (2011). The role of presleep negative emotion in sleep physiology. *Psychophysiology*, 48, 1738–1744.

Van Schuur, W.H., & Kiers, H.A.L. (1994). Why factor analysis often is the incorrect model for analyzing bipolar concepts, and what model to use instead. *Applied Psychological Measurement*, 18, 97–110.

Van Schuur, W. H., & Kruijtbosch, M. (1995). Measuring subjective well-being: Unfolding the Bradburn Affect Balance Scale. *Social Indicators Research*, 36, 49–74.

Västfjäll, D., Friman, M., Gärling, T., Kleiner, M. (2002). The measurement of core affect: A Swedish self-report measure derived from the affect circumplex. *Scandinavian Journal of Psychology*, 43, 19–31.

Västfjäll, D., & Gärling, T. (2007). Validation of a Swedish short self-report measure of core affect. *Scandinavian Journal of Psychology*, 48, 233–238.

Vautier, S., & Raufaste, E. (2003). Measuring dynamic bipolarity in positive and negative activation. *Assessment*, 10, 49–55.

Vlachopoulos, S., Biddle, S., & Fox, K. (1996). A social-cognitive investigation into the mechanisms of affect generation in children's physical activity. *Journal of Sport and Exercise Psychology*, 18, 174–193.

Vocks, S., Hechler, T., Rohrig, S., & Legenbauer, T. (2009). Effects of a physical exercise session on state body image: The influence of pre-experimental body dissatisfaction and concerns about weight and shape. *Psychology and Health*, 24, 713–728.

Walker, M.P. (2009). The role of sleep in cognition and emotion. *Annals of the New York Academy of Sciences*, 1156, 168–197.

Wardell, J.D., Read, J.P., Curtin, J.J., & Merrill, J.E. (2012). Mood and implicit alcohol expectancy processes: Predicting alcohol consumption in the laboratory. *Alcoholism: Clinical and Experimental Research*, 36, 119–129.

Warr, P., Barter, J., & Brownbridge, G. (1983). On the independence of positive and negative affect. *Journal of Personality and Social Psychology*, 44, 644–651.

Watson, D. (1988). The vicissitudes of mood measurement: Effects of varying descriptors, time frames, and response formats on measures of positive and negative affect. *Journal of Personality and Social Psychology*, 55, 128–141.

(2002). Positive affectivity: The disposition to experience positive emotional states. In C.R. Snyder & S.J. Lopez (Eds.), *Handbook of positive psychology* (pp. 106–119). New York: Oxford University Press.

(2009). Locating anger in the hierarchical structure of affect: Comment on Carver and Harmon-Jones (2009). *Psychological Bulletin*, 135, 205–208.

Watson, D., & Clark, L.A. (1984). Negative affectivity: The disposition to experience aversive emotional states. *Psychological Bulletin*, 96, 465–490.

(1992). Affects separable and inseparable: On the hierarchical arrangement of the negative affects. *Journal of Personality and Social Psychology*, 62, 489–505.

(1994a). Emotions, moods, traits, and temperaments: Conceptual distinctions and empirical findings. In P. Ekman & R.J. Davidson (Eds.), *The nature of emotion: Fundamental questions* (pp. 89–93). New York: Oxford University Press.

(1994b). *The PANAS-X: Manual for the Positive and Negative Affect Schedule (Expanded Form)*. Unpublished manuscript, University of Iowa, Iowa City.

(1997). Measurement and mismeasurement of mood: Recurrent and emergent issues. *Journal of Personality Assessment*, 68, 267–296.

Watson, D., Clark, L.A., & Carey, G. (1988). Positive and negative affectivity and their relation to anxiety and depressive disorders. *Journal of Abnormal Psychology*, 97, 346–353.

Watson, D., Clark, L.A., & Tellegen, A. (1988). Development and validation of brief measures of positive and negative affect: The PANAS scales. *Journal of Personality and Social Psychology*, 54, 1063–1070.

Watson, D., & Kendall, P.C. (1989). Understanding anxiety and depression: Their relation to negative and positive affective states. In P.C. Kendall & D. Watson (Eds.), *Anxiety and depression: Distinctive and overlapping features* (pp. 3–26). San Diego, CA: Academic Press.

Watson, D., & Tellegen, A. (1985). Toward a consensual structure of mood. *Psychological Bulletin*, 98, 219–235.

(1999). Issues in the dimensional structure of affect – effects of descriptors, measurement error, and response formats: Comment on Russell and Carroll (1999). *Psychological Bulletin*, 125, 601–610.

Watson, D., & Vaidya, J. (2003). Mood measurement: Current status and future directions. In J.A. Schinka & W.F. Velicer (Eds.), *Handbook of psychology: Research methods in psychology* (Vol. 2, pp. 351–375). Hoboken, NJ: John Wiley & Sons.

Watson, D., Wiese, D., Vaidya, J., & Tellegen, A. (1999). The two general activation systems of affect: Structural findings, evolutionary considerations, and psychobiological evidence. *Journal of Personality and Social Psychology*, 76, 820–838.

Weiner, B. (1985). An attributional theory of achievement motivation and emotion. *Psychological Review*, 92, 548–573.

Whalen, C.K., Jamner, L.D., Henker, B., & Delfino, R.J. (2001). Smoking and moods in adolescents with depressive and aggressive dispositions: Evidence from surveys and electronic diaries. *Health Psychology*, 20, 99–111.

Whalen, C.K., Jamner, L.D., Henker, B., Delfino, R.J., & Lozano, J.M. (2002). The ADHD spectrum and everyday life: Experience sampling of adolescent moods, activities, smoking, and drinking. *Child Development*, 73, 209–227.

Wiers, R.W. (2008). Alcohol and drug expectancies as anticipated changes in affect: Negative reinforcement is not sedation. *Substance Use and Misuse*, 43, 429–444.

Wiggins, J.S., Steiger, J.H., & Gaelick, L. (1981). Evaluating circumplexity in models of personality. *Multivariate Behavioral Research*, 16, 263–289.

Wilkinson, L. (1999). Statistical methods in psychology journals: Guidelines and explanations. *American Psychologist*, 54, 594–604.

Williams, D.M. (2008). Exercise, affect, and adherence: An integrated model and a case for self–paced exercise. *Journal of Sport and Exercise Psychology*, 30, 471–496.

World Health Organization (2008). *International statistical classification of diseases and related health problems* (10th Rev., Vol. 1). Geneva: Switzerland: Author.

Wundt, W. (1912). *An introduction to psychology* (R. Pintner, Trans.). London: George Allen. (Original work published 1911)

Yik, M.S.M., & Russell, J.A. (2003). Chinese affect circumplex: I. Structure of recalled momentary affect. *Asian Journal of Social Psychology*, 6, 185–200.

Yik, M.S.M., Russell, J.A., & Feldman Barrett, L. (1999). Structure of self-reported current affect: Integration and beyond. *Journal of Personality and Social Psychology*, 77, 600–619.

Yik, M., & Russell, J.A., & Steiger, J.H. (2011). A 12-point circumplex structure of core affect. *Emotion*, 11, 705–731.

Young, P.T. (1959). The role of affective processes in learning and motivation. *Psychological Review*, 66, 104–125.

Youngstedt, S.D. (2010). Comparison of anxiolytic effects of acute exercise in older versus younger adults. *Journal of Applied Gerontology*, 29, 251–260.

Youngstedt, S.D., O'Connor, P.J., Crabbe, J.B., & Dishman, R.K. (1998). Acute exercise reduces caffeine-induced anxiogenesis. *Medicine and Science in Sports and Exercise*, 30, 740–745.

Zajonc, R.B. (1980). Feeling and thinking: Preferences need no inferences. *American Psychologist*, 35, 151–175.

Zautra, A.J., Berkhof, J., & Nicolson, N.A. (2002). Changes in affect interrelations as a function of stressful events. *Cognition and Emotion*, 16, 309–318.

Zautra, A.J., Potter, P.T., & Reich, J.W. (1998). The independence of affects is context-dependent: An integrative model of the relationship between positive and negative affect. In M.P. Lawton (Series Ed.), *Annual review of gerontology and geriatrics* (Vol. 17, pp. 75–103). New York: Springer.

Zautra, A.J., Reich, J.W., Davis, M.C., Potter, P.T., & Nicolson, N.A. (2000). The role of stressful events in the relationship between positive and negative affects: Evidence from field and experimental studies. *Journal of Personality*, 68, 927–951.

Zevon, M.A., & Tellegen, A. (1982). The structure of mood change: An idiographic/nomothetic analysis. *Journal of Personality and Social Psychology*, 43, 111–122.

Zuckerman, M. (1960). The development of an affect adjective check list for the measurement of anxiety. *Journal of Consulting Psychology*, 24, 457–462.

Zuckerman, M. & Lubin, B. (1965a). *Manual for the Multiple Affect Adjective Check List*. San Diego, CA: Educational and Industrial Testing Service.

(1965b). Normative data for the Multiple Affect Adjective Check List. *Psychological Reports*, 16, 438.

Zuckerman, M., Lubin, B., & Rinck, C.M. (1983). Construction of new scales for the Multiple Affect Adjective Check List. *Journal of Behavioral Assessment*, 5, 119–129.

Zuckerman, M., Lubin, B., Vogel, L., & Valerius, E. (1964). Measurement of experimentally induced affects. *Journal of Consulting Psychology*, 28, 418–425.

Index

activation
  difficulty in explaining meaning to
    respondents, 127
  not just a physiological construct, 124
Activation Deactivation Adjective Check
  List, 62, 76, 78, 129, 133, 151
  and circumplex structure, 25, 134, 136
  criticism, 134
  floor effects, 135
  response scale, 134
Affect Grid, 124, 127, 129
affective contrast (in Solomon's
  opponent-process theory), 85
American Psychological Association Task
  Force on Statistical Inference, 16, 18
amygdala, 87, 88
anger
  as a category, 56
anxiety
  and appraisal of threat, 50
  comorbidity with depression, 34
  as a distinct state, 55
  is an emotion, 14, 34
  as a mood, 14, 15, 34
  and raising autonomic activity, 50
arousal. *See* activation

basic emotions, 55
Biphasic Alcohol Effects Scale, 140, 145,
  146, 147

categorical approach, 56, 156
Circular Mood Scale, 125, 127
circumplex, 23, 25, 26, 28, 57, 64, 152
  circular stochastic process model, 25
  description of, 57
  and emotions, 68
  modeling, 25
  pattern of correlations, 22, 26
cognitive appraisal
  dimensional models, 74
  and emotion, 42

combinations of measures, 10, 11
confirmatory factor analysis, 18, 32, 97
  constraining factor correlation, 22
  goodness-of-fit, 18, 19, 27, 31, 97
constraining factor correlation, 20, 22,
  23, 25
construct underrepresentation.
  See domain underrepresentation
construct-irrelevant variance, 147, 150,
  151
core affect
  approach-avoidance, 40
  as component of emotion and mood,
    39, 51
  definition of, 38
  evolutionary perspective, 39
  function, 40

definitions
  as conventions, 36
Diagnostic and Statistical Manual of
  Mental Disorders, 3, 34
dimensional approach, 56, 156
dimensional models
  criticisms, 68
discriminant validity, 20, 21
distinct-states approach, 55, 102
domain specificity, 9, 27, 144, 149, 155
domain underrepresentation, 19, 28, 30,
  142, 147, 154, 155, 156
dopamine, 87

emotion
  appraisal dimensions, 43
  cognitive appraisal as defining element,
    42, 49
  cognitive appraisal themes, 43
  comprising multiple components, 41
  definition of, 40
  duration, 42
  Ekman's criteria for distinguishing
    emotions from moods, 44